THE EXPLICIT ANIMAL

The Explicit Animal

A Defence of Human Consciousness

Raymond Tallis

Published in Great Britain by
MACMILLAN PRESS LTD
Houndmills, Basingstoke, Hampshire RG21 6XS and London
Companies and representatives throughout the world

A catalogue record for this book is available from the British Library.

ISBN 0–333–76319–X

Published in the United States of America by
ST. MARTIN'S PRESS, INC.,
Scholarly and Reference Division,
175 Fifth Avenue, New York, N.Y. 10010

ISBN 0–312–22418–4

Library of Congress Cataloging-in-Publication Data
Tallis, Raymond.
The explicit animal : a defence of human consciousness / Raymond
Tallis.
  p. cm.
Originally published: Basingstoke [England] : Macmillan Academic
and Professional, 1991.
Includes bibliographical references and index.
ISBN 0–312–22418–4 (cloth)
1. Philosophy of mind. 2. Consciousness. I. Title.
BD418.3.T35 1999
128'.2—dc21   99–18536
                                                                        CIP

This book is printed on paper suitable for recycling and made from fully managed and
sustained forest sources.

10   9   8   7   6   5   4   3   2   1
08   07   06   05   04   03   02   01   00   99

Printed and bound in Great Britain by
Antony Rowe Ltd, Chippenham, Wiltshire

This book is dedicated with love to those very special human consciousnesses Ben and Lawrence Tallis – for many happy hours

Contents

Acknowledgements

I could not have written this book without the privilege of attending the meetings of what for the want of a name I call the Liverpool Mind Group. Members of the group – Jim Russell, Richard Latto, Mark Sacks, John Williams, Rick Hanley, Richard Benthall and, most recently, Barry Daintrey – have all contributed to making this a considerably better book than it might otherwise have been. I am especially grateful to Howard Robinson who has inspired and led the group through the fifty or sixty meetings we have had since 1982. His debating style – rigorous without being pedantic, scrupulous and at the same time imaginative – and his ability to intuit, elucidate and improve the point one is trying to make (even where it is counter to his own position) has made the group an ideal forum for philosophical debate and for thinking better and harder about the manifold and endlessly fascinating problems of mind.

The whole character of a species, its generic character, is contained in its manner of vital activity, and free conscious activity is the species-characteristic of man.

Karl Marx

Man looks about the universe in awe at its wonders and forgets that he himself is the greatest wonder of all.

St Augustine

Preface to the 1999 Reprint

It is somewhat depressing to reflect that, in the eight years since *The Explicit Animal* was published, the approaches to the philosophy of mind which it criticised, far from being discredited, have become better established in both professional and public consciousness. Computational and biological (evolutionary and neurological) accounts of the human mind have received more widespread attention and appear to be attracting increasing support.

How the Mind Works,[1] Stephen Pinker's engagingly written and compendious popular account of contemporary neurophilosophy – justly described as 'a grand synthesis of the most satisfying explanations of mental life that have been proposed in cognitive science and evolutionary biology' – is only the latest example of a growing bibliography of works which contentedly and confidently build on the fallacies that are exposed in *The Explicit Animal*. When Pinker asserts that 'the mind is a system of organs of computation designed by natural selection to solve the problems faced by our evolutionary ancestors in their foraging way of life' (p. x), and defines the goal of his massive book as being to weave ideas in cognitive neuroscience into a cohesive picture using the computational theory of mind and theory of the natural selection of replicators, I suppose I should at least take comfort that *The Explicit Animal* was not attacking straw men.

The three ideas that constitute the theoretical framework of neurophilosophy – and which I believe are satisfactorily disposed of in the following pages – are, it therefore appears, still alive and kicking:

a) the notion that consciousness can be explained by neural impulses;
b) the belief that consciousness or mind stands to brain as software to hardware;
c) the assumption that the nature and origin of mind or consciousness can be explained in evolutionary terms.

The intractability of these erroneous ideas should occasion no surprise: they are built into the very language of neurophilosophical discourse. In subsequent discussions of 'neuromythology', I have on more than one occasion cited this passage from Wittgenstein:

> A *picture* held us captive. And we could not get outside of it for it
> lay in our language and language seemed to repeat it to us
> inexorably.[2]

There is another reason for the continuing prosperity of
neurophilosophy: very few errors can have been so fortunate in
their proponents. Materialist, computational, Darwinian accounts
of mind seem to attract the most gifted and witty expositors,
resourceful in their use of metaphor and extremely skilled at
assuming the appropriate linguistic register to communicate their
ideas in a user-friendly and non-patronising manner. It is always a
pleasure to read Daniel Dennett; and, even when he is in the throes
of conceptual confusion concealed by the most cunning use of
transferred epithets, the impression is always one of lucidity. And
the same is true of Pinker, the Churchlands and many other
expositors of what has (to expropriate the term used by Gilbert Ryle
of Cartesian dualism) become The Official Doctrine. They write
well, these neurophilosophers; but they also cheat. And the
important thing is to look past the seductive style to the underlying
deceptions and self-deceptions.

In the case of Stephen Pinker, it is a question of 'the bit where you
say it and the bit where you take it back'. I referred earlier to his
book titled *How the Mind Works*. But he admits in the Preface that
'we don't know how the mind works' (p. ix). This admission is
immediately qualified by the claim that, while we may not know
how the mind works, 'we have insights, increasing knowledge, and
an inkling of what we are looking for'. We haven't yet arrived, but
we are at least finally underway; we are pointing in the right
direction and making progress towards understanding the nature
and mechanisms of mind. This generous assessment of current
cognitive neuroscience is, however, further modified about 150
pages later when he admits that, while the computational theory of
mind may explain what he calls 'consciousness in the sense of
access', it cannot make any contribution to 'consciousness in the
sense of sentience'. Now for most people, sentience is no small part
of consciousness: it is not entirely eccentric to consider it as the
ground floor of mind and the basis of intelligent behaviour.
(Indeed, I have argued[3] that it is not possible, without a prior
explanation of sentience, to begin to account for intelligent,
purposeful behaviour such as humans typically exhibit in daily life;

that without 'knowing what one is doing', based upon sentience, it is not possible to behave in the way that human beings ordinarily do behave.) Pinker, however, claims that 'our incomprehension of sentience does not impede our understanding of how the mind works in the very least' (p. 147)!

Dennett's cheating is rather more brazen. In his wonderfully rich and witty *Consciousness Explained*,[4] he avoids the embarrassment of not being able to explain consciousness by arguing that what he – and his version of neurophilosophy – cannot explain does not exist. For most people, subjective experience lies at the heart of consciousness. But this is what neuroscience, as inevitably follows from its third-person viewpoint, cannot explain. So Dennett simply discounts – or, to use his word, 'disqualifies' – qualia, the phenomenal qualities of our experiences, the entities that lie at the heart of the experience of being a subject and, indeed, form its fabric. Ontologically, they are, according to Dennett, half-way between nothingness and something he calls 'dispositional properties of brains' (p. 460). His ducking and weaving with respect to sentience, sensations, qualia, subjective experience and the rest is, however, extremely complex and he is quite difficult to pin down. Even so, he does not succeed in dispelling the impression of dodging the really difficult, interesting and central questions about consciousness. The unbewitched reader will be inclined to agree with Galen Strawson's remark, in his review of *Consciousness Explained* in the *Times Literary Supplement*,[5] that Dennett should be arraigned under the Trades Description Act for failing to deliver on his title.

One way of reconciling the wild promises implicit in the titles used by best-selling neurophilosophers with the modest delivery that follows is hinted at by Pinker:

> The qualia-debunkers do have a point. At least for now, we have no scientific purchase on the special extra ingredient that gives rise to sentience. As far as scientific explanation goes, it might as well not exist. It's not just that claims about sentience are perversely untestable; it's that testing them would make no difference to anything anyway. Our incomprehension of sentience does not impede our understanding of how the mind works in the least. (p. 147)

There could be no better example of the deep confusion and inveterate *shiftiness* in the arguments of neurophilosophers than this. It would be possible to unpack from it the essence of the MIT-nik intellectual culture. Suffice it to note, for the present, how Pinker seems to be arguing that things that cannot be explained by science and have no reasonable prospect of scientific explanation may as well not exist from the point of view of scientific explanation and that this means that they may as well not exist at all! And if 'they may as well not exist at all', not explaining them will not impede understanding!

At the end of his very generous review of *The Explicit Animal* for the *Times Literary Supplement*,[6] Professor Stephen Clarke expressed the hope that I would find time to continue the explorations in this book. I have continued those explorations and the fruit of this further work is to be found in *On the Edge of Certainty*, a collection of essays published in 1999. *On the Edge of Certainty*, however, does not render *the Explicit Animal* redundant – not only because the arguments of the latter do not seem yet to have diminished the ascendancy of the neuromythologists, but also because *On the Edge of Certainty* builds on *The Explicit Animal*. It is in *The Explicit Animal* that the detailed arguments for the outlook that informs much of *On the Edge of Certainty* are set out.

I would go further: *The Explicit Animal* holds the philosophical key to pretty well everything else I have published. It comes closest to expressing the vision that motivates much of what is to be found in my other publications, as well as what I have, for nearly thirty years, been trying to capture (largely unsuccessfully so far) in a new kind of writing which combines fiction and philosophy. Michael Grant first made me aware of this when he pointed out the connection between my hostility to post-Saussurean and much postmodern thought and my defence of human consciousness unreduced by scientistic thinking.[7] And this connection is spelt out explicitly in the more recent *Enemies of Hope*,[8] where the 'marginalisers of consciousness' – post-Saussureans and cognitive scientists and others – are grouped together and seen collectively to undermine the role of the conscious human agent upon whom our hope of a better future must rest.

My (scarcely revolutionary) vision of the human creature as an *essentially* explicit animal whose explicit consciousness cannot be explained in terms of biological science or, indeed, captured by any science working within a third-person, materialist framework, is a challenge to rethink many current questions: the relationship between mind and matter, mind and body, mind and brain, of course; but also the nature of truth and factual knowledge; the inexplicable miracle of human language shot through at every level with metalanguage; and, most teasingly, the respective roles of agency and mechanism in human life. That human activity cannot be understood except in terms of explicitness, of deliberately and knowingly doing what we do, so that action cannot be reduced to reaction, opens up larger problems. If, as biological science reminds us again and again, the possibility of action depends upon complex mechanisms largely hidden from us, how do we explicit animals carve agency out of the causal net – without which, of course, no agency is possible?

The fundamental thesis of *The Explicit Animal* leaves everything largely unexplained. Its aim, however, is to redefine the questions or to reinstate the mystery and so help ensure that the right questions are asked. These questions will not be asked so long as the idea of mental mechanisms, rooted in neural activity and serving an evolutionary agenda, holds sway as our model of human consciousness. The lack of explanatory power of the central idea of *The Explicit Animal* causes me particular concern, not the least because it may be inferred that I do not believe that progress in our understanding of the brain is possible and that I am hostile to neuroscience. This would be an unusual position for an individual such as myself whose primary professional interest is in the neurological problems of older people – in particular stroke and epilepsy – and who is motivated by the wish to improve our management of such problems by ever greater advances in clinical neuroscience. I have reconciled my weekday and weekend selves through an argument, presented towards the end of 'The Poverty of Neurophilosophy' (op. cit.), to the effect that neuroscience helps us to define the necessary conditions of ordinary human consciousness and behaviour, but it takes us no further towards understanding the sufficient conditions. This, as I have pointed out, is not an entirely satisfactory account of the matter, but it is the best I can do at present. We will not do any better so long as we stay with daft ideas supported by ingenious arguments and energetic sales talk.

I am extremely grateful to Chairman Hearne and Tim Farmiloe for agreeing to the reissue of this book. It is but the latest step in a history of generous support that now extends back over a decade.

Notes and references

1. Stephen Pinker, *How the Mind Works* (Harmondsworth: Penguin Books, 1997).
2. Ludwig Wittgenstein, *Philosophical Investigations*, translated by Elizabeth Anscombe (Oxford: Blackwell, 1953), p. 115.
3. Raymond Tallis, 'The Poverty of Neurophilosophy', in *On the Edge of Certainty* (London: Macmillan, 1999).
4. Daniel C. Dennett, *Consciousness Explained* (Harmondsworth: Penguin Books, 1991).
5. Galen Strawson, Review of Daniel Dennett, in *Times Literary Supplement*, 4664:56, 21 August 1992.
6. Stephen R.L. Clarke, 'Aware if Alive', *Times Literary Supplement*, 6 August 1993, p. 28.
7. Michael Grant 'Realism and the Defence of Consciousness: On the Work of Raymond Tallis', *PN Review* 94, Vol. 20, No. 2 (November/December 1993), pp. 37–9.
8. Raymond Tallis, *Enemies of Hope: a Critique of Contemporary Pessimism* (Macmillan: London, 1998).

Overture

In the introduction to the first part of his great treatise on Frege,[1] Michael Dummett remarks that reading a book without a preface 'is like arriving at someone's house for dinner, and being conducted straight into the dining room'. I share this view: a book without a preface seems somehow unoccasioned. That is why, even though a personal vestibule to a book on the somewhat impersonal theme of the philosophy of mind may seem an authorial self-indulgence, I offer these introductory remarks. There is a further reason: the arguments of *The Explicit Animal* are rooted in and driven by a personal vision, an intuition about our nature. These opening pages seem to me an opportunity to state as clearly and as early as possible what that intuition is and to hint at the vision from which the book has grown; in short, to sound straight away the themes that will be elaborated in the body of the text. For this reason, these pages amount to a bit more than a Preface. An Overture, perhaps.

The period of any life in which it is possible to philosophise innocently is brief. Truly metaphysical moments tend to be the privilege of early youth when the tragi-comedies of sexual love, the promise of freedom and the threat of responsibility are all new, so that the world confronting a mind discovering its own powers for the first time is a strange and estranging place, as well as an exciting and frightening one. Soon, for a variety of reasons, astonishment fades, to be revived, if at all, with ever-decreasing frequency and diminishing intensity. For the small minority who continue to think about philosophical problems, philosophy evolves into a *discipline* that, like any other, has its ongoing debates and its rules of procedure. Perplexity expresses itself obliquely in critical arguments whose agenda is to some extent determined by a more or less scholarly knowledge of what others have thought on the matters in hand.

To pass from the state of innocent wonder to active engagement in philosophy as it is defined by others sometimes seems like a fall from grace. The thinker countering others' counter-arguments with counter-counter-arguments of his own may look back on the adolescence in which he was directly *troubled* by the underlying problems as a kind of golden age, despite its frequent periods of despair; as a lost paradise (or authentic hell) of unity between the thinking mind and the living person. Nevertheless, it should be enough that philosophy continues to be motivated by a first-order perplexity, rather than solely by a second-order irritation with the views of those with whom one disagrees – even if the memory of adolescent wonder lives on to haunt fluency as its bad conscience.

There are gains as well as losses. Naive wonder is insufficient. There is little to commend agenda-less philosophising that is ignorant of what the sharpest minds have already thought. For its results are less often original than simply incompetent and muddled; or, worse, a kind of rhymeless, rhythmless ejaculatory poetry that the author had best kept to himself. Philosophy is, inescapably, a dialogic activity and good dialogue implies an informed and sympathetic understanding of what the other person, or the philosophical community at large, thinks. At its best, it is the result of a precarious compromise between, on the one hand, the experience of the solitary, innocently wondering individual, isolated by a true appreciation of the ultimate unintelligibility of the world and of his own existence, and, on the other, that of the inescapably social being consumed by the demands of biological and social survival and moved by the forces, within and around him, of practical necessity and common sense. Published work is a mongrel child whose mother (or father) is speechless wonder and whose father (or mother) is a sometimes all-too-fluent dialogue.

The Explicit Animal goes back a long way, at least to my early teens. It is a delayed response to, perhaps even an epitaph upon, a recurrent experience, a fleeting dizziness, whose precise object is difficult to pin down; a sense of wonder that seems not so much inexpressible as expressible only in banal statements of the self-evident. I am inclined to characterise it as an astonishment at having been given this self to live and this world to live in, at being *this* thing under these very particular circumstances, and at the fact that I am *knowingly* this thing and that to a greater or lesser degree I enact my self deliberately. This astonishment informs most of the positions taken up in the pages that follow, though it is often deeply buried and surfaces only in the last two chapters. It is captured in part in the title: The Explicit Animal. It may perhaps be better expressed diagrammatically.

Diagram 0.1 is not meant to depict an evolving process, a chronological sequence of emergence, but rather to mark out a distance, or series of distances, between what we are and the

Increasing explicitness   *Diagram 0.1*

?	
X	Existents
that X [is the case]	Awareness of existents
'X'	Explicit awareness of existents
'Someone said/believed that "X" '	Explicit explicitness, etc.

scientific and metaphysical *notions* of (unconscious) matter. For a central purpose of this book is to refute physicalism and any other materialist account of what it is to be a human being. I want to draw attention to the obvious fact (though not so obvious that philosophers and others can't overlook it) that *explicitness* is the central fact of our humanity, of our being there. Such explicitness – which is capable of limitless unfolding through ever more complex layers of self-reflexiveness – is *underivable*, least of all from matter, however the latter is conceived. This intuition could also be expressed as Diagram 0.2.

Increasing explicitness   *Diagram 0.2*

?	
Discrete existents	Whatever there is in the absence of consciousness
Explicit existents	Objects of perception
Explicit awareness of existents	Explicit objects of perception
Explicit explicitness	Discourse about perception
Explicit explicit explicitness	Meta-language; discourse about discourse

Again, I must emphasise that Diagram 0.2 is not meant to depict ontogenetic relations between different kinds of entities. I do not, for example, believe that unconscious matter preceded consciousness and that explicitness arose out of it; that explicitness 'emerged' or 'supervened' when matter happened to fall into certain arrangements. Quite the reverse: the overthrow of this kind of thinking is a major purpose of this book.

Since the intuitions driving this book first occurred to me, my initial astonishment at the fact of the consciousness and self-consciousness of man, 'the explicit animal', has been to some degree supplanted by amazement at theories of consciousness (and of what it is to be a human being) that overlook it. These theories occupy most of this book: *The Explicit Animal* has been written with the intention of clearing them away, and so creating a space in which the true nature of consciousness can be shown forth; and in the hope of restoring my original astonishment and perhaps of communicating it also. For although there is a huge distance between the arguments laid out here and the adolescent intuitions, the former are, however remotely, mobilised in the service of the latter.

Because *The Explicit Animal* is rooted, if precariously, in wonder, it is a hopeful book. This may be obscured by its negative stance towards most of the theories that populate its pages. Admittedly, the positive doctrines occupy only a small part of the book and are less clearly defined than my objections to others' views of consciousness. Like many others before me, I have found it easier to say what consciousness is not than what it is. On account of this negativity, the underlying tendency of *The Explicit Animal* may be vulnerable to another sort of misunderstanding to which it is worth devoting a few words.

Since it is hostile to much modern thinking about mental phenomena, particularly thinking inspired by computer technology, the book might be misconstrued as an attack on secular world pictures and upon technology itself. I should regret this. I would not wish to be numbered among those who point to the dangers of technology while taking its immeasurable benefits (and its mystery) for granted – typing out their polemics against 'modern gadgetry' on the most advanced word processors.[2] Nor would I wish to deny that contemporary neurobiology represents one of the most exciting intellectual, and spiritual, adventures undertaken by man. I applaud its efforts to understand the working of the brain, though I do not know what metaphysical place to grant its apparent successes. Nor am I in favour of a boring, incurious mysticism – *Ignoramas et ignorabimus*. Nor, finally, do I underestimate the collective genius expressed in computer science and embodied to some degree in the humblest pocket calculator.

This essay, then, is not written in a spirit of disapproval directed against modern technology and neurobiology. It is certainly not intended as a plea to re-spiritualise consciousness along traditional pre-secular lines. The true mystery of the world lies outwith the old-established spiritual institutions, with their professional functionaries who would enclose the greatness of the world within local moral systems and penny numbers of the soul and their gods who seem curious chimeras – half Big Bang and half petulant schoolchild. No, *The Explicit Animal* is an act of restitution made to the mystery of things, in particular the mystery – too deep for any ready-made discourses, religious or otherwise, to plumb – of the senseless fact that the human world makes explicit sense.

In other words, I have no partisan spiritual axe to grind. I do not, for example, share the naive idea that twentieth-century atrocities are connected with contemporary materialist philosophies. (Indeed, much of what is asserted routinely about the present age seems to me to be based upon a lack of knowledge of, or a failure to remember, what life was like for most people in previous ages.)[3] It would be a comforting delusion to believe that in defending consciousness I am fighting for the world's soul but, unlike many academics, I do not feel in the need of such a delusion. I want only to tease out and to preserve (or at least prolong) the joy that I have felt from time to time when I have caught sight of the extraordinary and mysterious entities we are obliged and privileged to be.

One final point. In the pages that follow, several books are subjected to repeated criticism. They include *The Computer and the Mind* by P. N. Johnson-Laird,[4] *Mindwaves* edited by Colin Blakemore and Susan Greenfield,[5] and Paul Churchland's *Matter and Consciousness*.[6] They have been singled out for their merits, not their deficiencies: they seem to me to provide the clearest, the most lucid, the most comprehensive and the most honest accounts of the current state of play in the philosophy of mind and cognitive neurobiology presently available. I have found them immensely helpful and am grateful to their progenitors. My enormous debt to these books is in no wise diminished by my disagreement with pretty well everything of theoretical substance that is contained in them.

1

Losing Consciousness

There has, in recent years, been a remarkable convergence of interest and even of opinion between philosophers of mind and neurobiologists and, more particularly, philosophers and psychologists.

For many years, philosophers and psychologists held each other in something like mutual contempt. Psychology, hungry for status as an empirical science (and presumably for the funding that goes with it) kept its distance from the armchair musings of the philosophers. And philosophers were unimpressed with the activities of psychologists: data there were aplenty but they seemed to cast little light on the object of study – the mind. (This was in part due to the ascendancy of schools of thought in which the first article of faith was that the mind did not really exist.) The attitude of many philosophers to psychology was typified by Wittgenstein's dismissive remarks in *Philosophical Investigations*:[1]

> The confusion and barrenness of psychology is not to be explained by calling it a 'young science'; its state is not comparable with that of physics, for instance, in its beginnings . . . For in psychology there are experimental methods and *conceptual confusion*.
>
> The existence of the experimental method makes us think we have the means of solving the problems which trouble us; though problem and method pass one another by.

And philosophers and neurophysiologists, with a few exceptions, saw little need to take detailed notice of each other. They were far enough apart for mutual ignorance of each other's work to cause no embarrassment. The widespread assumption by brain scientists that philosophising 'led nowhere', that it was a hangover from pre-science, and the tendency of philosophers to believe that empirical observations of the nervous system, or indeed of anything, had no bearing on the essentially conceptual or linguistic problems of the philosophy of mind, ensured that mutual curiosity did not get out of hand. If the business of the philosopher were linguistic or conceptual analysis, the facts discovered within the framework of incompletely analysed concepts could have no bearing on the arguments and conclusions of philosophers.

The situation has now changed dramatically. Since U. T. Place's seminal paper[2] showed how the relationship between mind and brain could be discussed without inviting the Rylean charge of 'category error', philosophers have taken an increasing interest in the brain and in the findings of brain scientists. For if, as Place and those who were influenced by his arguments believed, the mind is identical with some brain processes, it is not unreasonable for a philosopher with a passing interest in the mind to concern himself with what neurophysiologists and psychologists have discovered, and think about, brain processes. And this interest is reciprocated: neurophysiologists such as Eccles, Sperry, Llinas and Blakemore write about problems that are explicitly philosophical. Cognitive psychologists seem equally at home in psychology and philosophy and have much to say in both areas. This trend of converging interest is symptomatised in recent books such as Patricia Churchland's *Neurophilosophy* and the excellent *Mindwaves* edited by Susan Greenfield and Colin Blakemore,[3] which incorporate a good deal of physiological information, along with detailed philosophical argument, and try to relate the one to the other.

This change in the relations between the disciplines has been matched by equally dramatic changes inside them. Within neurophysiology there has been an increasing emphasis on the intrinsic organisation of the central nervous system (CNS) and on the way that its structure influences the kinds of events that are detected and how event detection is built up into a picture of the world. Psychology has seen the rise of cognitive psychology, with a shift of emphasis from overt behaviour to the role of mediating mental processes. Out of this has grown cognitive science, in which the concepts of computer technology, and in particular, of the application of this technology to the development of artificial intelligence, are in turn applied to the workings of the mind; and, a variant of this, cognitive neurobiology, in which the findings of brain scientists are taken account of in computational modelling of mental function. In philosophy, we have seen a major shift of interest towards philosophical psychology. As Simon Blackburn has put it, there has been a displacement of the philosophy of language by the philosophy of mind with the latter being installed as the 'Queen of the philosophical sciences'.[4]

No discipline is an island and the cross-fertilisation between disciplines, the swapping and sharing of facts, ideas, models and metaphors, has created an unparalleled excitement among philosophers, cognitive scientists and brain physiologists researching the nature and basis of minds. With philosophers better informed and psychologists more conceptually sophisticated one could be forgiven for sharing the general optimism regarding the possibility of some kind of breakthrough in understanding mind in the near future. And it is certainly true that new approaches are being developed and many interesting discoveries have been made about what is usually referred to as 'information processing' in the mind-brain. This, along with recent rapid advances in computer technology and the development of artefacts with increasingly mind-like activities, seems to justify the expectation that it will not be long before we understand the mind and are able to create minds ourselves.

The claims made nowadays are less wild than those made in the early days of artificial intelligence when the kingdom of the unattainable seemed just round the corner and machines that could think, translate, and find their way round the chaos of contingencies called the world, were expected any minute. Thinking machines are still a long way off; computerised translation and natural language programming are in their infancy because computers seem to be required to have a certain amount of worldly wisdom in order to make non-ludicrous sense of ordinary talk; and robots that can stroll aimlessly but safely about the world, parsing a universe of things served up without prior preparation, seem as remote as they did in H. G. Wells's day. But the expectation of breakthrough is still there; indeed, it has recently been fuelled by the excitement surrounding neural networks and parallel distributed processing. Moreover, there is the feeling that, even if the answers are going to take an unspecified long time to turn up, those who are thinking about real minds or trying to create artificial ones are at last on the right track; that *this time* the conceptual framework at least is right.

It is the burden of this book that the increasingly close relations between philosophy, psychology and physiology may have been beneficial for the latter two but they have not been very good for philosophy. The philosophy of mind is now marked by a degree of conceptual confusion it would not have permitted had it not been so impressed by its scientific partners and so eager to contribute to the scientific conversation. I submit that, as a result of the advocacy of physicalist philosophers, for whom the final truth about all things is con-terminous with the physico-chemical laws uncovered by science, consciousness, far from being brought closer to explanation, has rather been obliterated, squeezed out between inappropriate descriptive and explanatory paradigms.

Much recent philosophy and psychology has been characterised by attempts to deny the peculiar and distinctive nature of consciousness or of its role in human behaviour or, more commonly, both. There is a move to explain away or, indeed, to eliminate consciousness. Things that human beings do consciously and deliberately are redescribed or interpreted as if they were things that merely happen in them; while consciousness itself is either overlooked, or marginalised, or eliminated by various ploys. These include seeing it as an embarrassing leftover from 'folk psychology', a construct that will eventually be regarded much as we regard 'phlogiston' now, and not therefore requiring explanation.[5] Or, alternatively, as a concept illegitimately introduced into our stock of ideas by Descartes; a seventeenth-century invention, unknown, for example, to the Greeks, and due for retirement.[6]

In short, there is a move to eliminate or somehow lose consciousness – either by redescribing it in terms that bring conscious behaviour closer to unconscious mechanism or by dismissing it as a conceptual leftover from a pre-scientific age. Consistent with this attempt to abolish consciousness, or at least greatly to diminish its role in human behaviour, there has been a widespread tendency to 'biologise' consciousness and to assimilate the activities of conscious human beings to the behaviour of non-human, or even non-conscious, organisms. This tendency of course antedates recent developments in philosophy. It goes back at least to the Enlightenment; and the avoidance of reference to consciousness in the explanation of behaviour was exemplified in the cruder forms of behaviourism that dominated psychology in the first half of the twentieth century.

For behaviourists, behaviour can be analysed into stereotyped elements ('responses') triggered by the environment, itself understood as a source of 'stimuli'. The connections between stimuli and responses are shaped by classical or operant conditioning and energised by drives or instincts. In the context of these and other biologistic interpretations of behaviour, conscious intentions, and indeed the conscious perceptions upon which they are based, become awkward lay-bys out of the causal net that encompasses the organism and its environment. If consciousness is acknowledged to exist, its role becomes difficult to determine; for an organism would seem to be able to function just as well – or better – if it were an unconscious automaton.

Behaviourism fell into disrepute amongst psychologists because the belief that behaviour was a set of conditioned or unconditioned responses to external events failed to explain many aspects of complex behaviour, for example the serial ordering of its components. In a famous paper,[7] the erstwhile behaviourist Karl Lashley pointed out that the force or meaning of an element of behaviour was often determined less by its intrinsic properties than by its relation to other, future elements. This was particularly evident in the case of linguistic behaviour; and Lashley instanced the sentence 'Rapidly righting with his uninjured hand, the canoeist managed to negotiate the rapids'. The similar-sounding opening 'Rapidly writing with his uninjured hand. . .' would have an entirely different force. It is only when the end of the sentence is reached that the meaning of the first half is revealed. The problem of serial order, and the importance of the relations of behavioural elements to future (i.e. currently non-existent) elements, implied that stimulus-response behaviourism, however sophisticated, was bound to prove inadequate. Such considerations, emphasised by psychologists working in the field of language and influenced by Chomsky, prompted the drift away from behaviourism to cognitive psychology, where there was an increasing emphasis on meaning and internal organisation.

Some philosophers sympathetic to behaviourism tried to refine its underlying concepts. Logical or dispositional behaviourism came to the fore in the 1950s after the publication of Ryle's *The Concept of Mind*[8] – at a time when behaviourism was starting to lose ground in psychology. These refinements did not fully answer the criticism that behaviourism could not take account of subjective experience and mental contents such as sensations and specific, occurrent memories, whose existence, however scientifically awkward, could not be denied. Attempts to translate mental contents – thoughts, memories, mental images, feelings, sensations, perceptions, etc. – into dispositions to behave in a certain way were unconvincing. There are many mental contents that do not get expressed in, or are equivalent to, behaviour, let alone dissolve without remainder into behaviour or the statistical probability of a certain sort of behaviour. Whereas it may seem possible (if one does not think too hard about it) that certain mental states – such as believing or waiting – are dispositions to do one sort of thing rather than another, this does not seem even plausible in the case of sensations such as feeling pain or seeing the colour red.

Nevertheless, behaviourism of a sort still continues to exert an attraction on both philosophers and psychologists, because it seems to demystify mind. Functionalism, which could fairly be described as the dominant theory of mind among not only philosophers but also cognitive scientists and psychologists, and which brings to their logical conclusion many strands of thought in modern philosophical psychology, is a form of behaviourism, as will be discussed in Chapter 5. It is an absolutely characteristic contemporary theory because it effectively empties consciousness of contents, or replaces the contents by relations, introspectible qualia by external causal or functional connections.

Such consciousness as remains after modern reductions is explained in terms of its survival value. If consciousness is not empty, or a mere embarrassment that a mature psychology will eliminate as mature chemistry eliminated phlogiston, then it is to be explained, and in a sense explained away, in terms of the advantage it confers upon the creatures possessing it. The biologisation of consciousness – another important aspect of modern philosophy of mind – has two facets: explaining the origin of consciousness in evolutionary terms; and explaining the value of its contents by ensuring that they are true. What ensures the truth – and hence the adaptive value – of the contents of consciousness is their being caused by that which they are conscious of. The causal theory of perception guarantees that perception will be about things that are 'really out there'.

An alternative, non-biological, approach to the denial of the distinctive nature, and the centrality of, consciousness in human life is to place consciousness on a par with the processes that may be observed in various artefacts. Consciousness is either a machine-like property or a property whose nature can be understood in terms of the human body, in particular the brain, itself regarded as an incredibly complex machine or collection of machines. The choice of artefacts with which to compare the brain-machine depends upon the currently most successful technology. Electrical images replaced hydraulic ones and these were in turn replaced by electronic images. The brain is a computer; in the more recent literature, it is a parallel distributed processor rather than a serial logic processor. Consciousness is seen as 'a flow of information' through a computer-like organism. For the purpose of this metaphor, 'information' is intermittently uncoupled from its anthropomorphic origins and used in a sense that enables it to flow through machines even when they are not in the presence of human beings informed by them.[9] The computational 'information-processing' view of consciousness typically sees mind as standing to brain as software to hardware, and the structure of its programs relates to actual experience as syntax to semantics.

What both biologistic and computational interpretations of consciousness have in common is a desire to *mechanise* it, and/or to displace deliberate behaviour by mechanisms.[10] In the computational model of consciousness, behaviour and mental events are reduced to the mechanical properties of protoplasmic machines, or the mechanical operation of algorithms. In ordinary talk, we contrast that which was done deliberately with that which was executed by a mechanism: we distinguish actions from mere events. 'I did this' is opposed to 'This happened' or 'This came about'. Of course we recognise that there are elements of automaticity in all forms of behaviour – even in, for example, the very act of writing about automaticity. Most of what is done in the carrying out of a skilled action is not even available to introspection, never mind the result of deliberate execution. Nevertheless, there is a clear distinction between something that was done 'in full consciousness', deliberately, explicitly, and an event, which as a twitch, that merely happened. The former seem to be opposite to merely mechanical events. There are trends in recent thought that would like to deny this difference and, indeed, would like to overlook or delete a whole family of oppositions:

Conscious	Mechanical
Deliberate	Automatic
Willed	Involuntary
Freely chosen	Reflex

Tailor-made	Stereotyped
Action	Event
Explicit	Implicit

It is a central purpose of this book to reassert the fundamental importance of these distinctions between opposing categories.

The unprejudiced reader may already be puzzled by the denial of the obvious: why should anyone wish to dispute the reality of consciousness? And, if he did, how should he be believed? I shall deal with the first question presently. As for the second, I have to admit, I have no clear answer. However, it seems to me that over the last century or so there have been trends in thinking that have marginalised the role of human consciousness in human life.

I shall discuss these trends in a separate work but it is worth noting here how many apparently disparate thinkers, who have had an enormous influence on twentieth-century thought, share a common propensity to deny the role of individual consciousness in human life. Although none of them goes so far as to deny the reality of consciousness, they have contributed to a climate of opinion in which it is possible to hold, with the functionalists, that mental states are to be understood in terms of their functional roles and relations rather than their contents; that consciousness is, effectively, empty. Such thinkers include:

1. Political theorists, in particular Marxists, for whom consciousness, and conscious understanding of the world as expressed in political opinions and ideologies, is shaped by unconscious attitudes determined by the individual's class or historical situation.
2. Social theorists, as exemplified by Durkheim, for whom voluntary behaviour, religious sentiments, the sense of self and even basic general concepts are the result of unconscious internalisation of social forces and collective representations.
3. Freud, for whom a large part of the mind was unconscious and much apparently rational behaviour was determined by the operation of unacknowledged and often irrational instincts.
4. Post-Saussurean thinkers for whom even verbal expression, apparently the most deliberate and self-aware form of behaviour, is determined by the structures of the system, so that it seems as if 'language speaks us' rather than that we speak

language. For such thinkers, the linguistic decentring of the speaking subject opens the way to a more radical displacement of the self.[11]

5. Helmholtz and his descendents among cognitive psychologists who place great emphasis on unconscious inference and other unconscious processing in perception and other mental activities.

And why should anyone wish to marginalise or empty consciousness? Behind the denial of consciousness, deliberateness, etc. and the attempted reduction of human acts to mechanism is the further purpose of gathering all phenomena, including conceptually untidy ones like human beings, and their subjectivities, under a single set of laws and logics originating from the physical sciences. This has been famously criticised by Thomas Nagel in his poignantly-titled *The View from Nowhere*.[12] Nevertheless, many philosophers prefer to ignore or to deny the potency of Nagel's case. Dennett, for example, tells us that he begins 'with a tactical choice':

> I declare my starting point to be the objective, materialistic, third-person world of the physical sciences. This is the orthodox choice today in the English speaking world.[13]

What is wrong with this? A unified world picture has, after all, always been the goal of philosophy and it is both a respectable and an exciting regulative idea. Without it, and more specifically the belief that all phenomena may be explained in terms of laws derived from 'the objective, materialistic, third-person world of the physical sciences', Dennett argues, various promising avenues of scientific research are closed. In response to this, I would emphasise that it is not the effort at unification that is at fault but the choice of framework within which the unification is attempted. Although it is methodologically easier to work within the 'materialistic third-person world of the physical sciences', and to ignore or to diminish the role of conscious experience and of deliberate intention in human life, it is neither good science nor good philosophy to turn these methodological decisions into ontological facts. I submit that the present attempts at unification lead to disastrous distortions which in turn cause us to overlook what is most peculiar about us human beings and to deny what we essentially are; in short, to repress the distinctive mystery of our being here.

For if we are animals, we are, uniquely, explicit animals; and, if we are machines, we are conscious machines. And these qualifications make us ultimately, finally and most importantly, neither animals nor machines.

The various trends of thought alluded to in this chapter are related to one another in Figure 1.1 which, essentially, lays out the agenda for the next four chapters. Chapter 2 deals with the evolutionary explanations of the origin of consciousness. Chapter 3 looks at the metaphysical framework of physiological explanations of consciousness – in particular perception. These are both aspects of the trend towards 'biologising' consciousness. Chapter 4 examines computational theories of consciousness. These converge with biological theories in those neurobiological accounts that conceive of consciousness as the neural activity of the cerebral computer. Chapter 5 looks at functionalism, the reduction to absurdity of biological and computational theories, which empties consciousness. The diagram also refers to certain thinkers – Marx, Freud, Durkheim, Saussure and Helmholtz – whose writings have emphasised the importance of the unconscious in human life and behaviour at the expense of consciousness; who, in short, have marginalised consciousness.

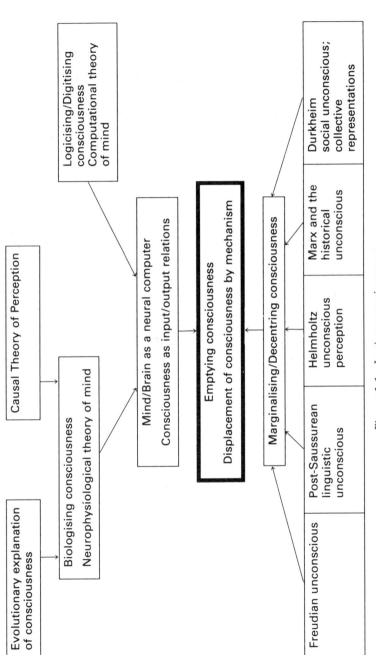

Figure 1.1 Losing consciousness

2

Biologising Consciousness
I. Evolutionary Theories

In this chapter and the next, I want to examine the belief that
consciousness is, in Paul Churchland's words 'a wholly natural
phenomenon'[1] and that 'conscious intelligence is the activity of
suitably organised matter'. These beliefs seem to relate to two
others. The first is that consciousness can be explained within the
framework of evolutionary theory: as Churchland puts it, 'the
sophisticated organisation responsible for [conscious] intelligence
is, on this planet at least, the outcome of billions of years of
chemical, biological, and neurophysiological evolution'. The
second is that consciousness is explained by, or even identical
with, processes occurring in a particular biological structure – the
brain – and that these processes are the result of a causal chain of
events originating in the perceived object. Both beliefs assume, or
are imbued with the assumption, that consciousness can be understood in terms of the *purposes* it serves. The idea that consciousness
exists because it serves a purpose is explicit in the evolutionary
account of it (which I shall examine in this chapter); but it is also
implicitly present in impingement or causal theories of consciousness (which I shall examine in the next).

Throughout this chapter, and often elsewhere in this book,
'consciousness' is referred to as if it were a unitary phenomenon.
Of course it is not: consciousness is a term that encompasses a
wide variety of types, modes and degrees of awareness. One could
mention crude sensations, formed perceptions, propositional attitudes such as desires and beliefs, explicit intentions and conscious
occurrent thoughts which may be more or less general, more or
less abstract and more or less self-reflexive. I have lumped them
together, in part because discussions of the purpose of consciousness tends to do just this; and in part because I believe that, despite
the variousness and modularity of consciousness, there is something that all of its manifestations have in common: a greater or
lesser degree of explicitness. All the manifestations of conscious-

ness are aspects of making explicit, a fact which is often missed and which is, as I have already indicated, the real theme of this book, though it does not emerge fully until the last two chapters.

For some, this tendency to talk about 'consciousness' without further specification may make my arguments seem unfocused. The points I make, however, apply equally to all manifestations of consciousness. Nevertheless, the reader may, if he or she wishes, think of the argument as being applicable to any or all of the following:

1. the explicit possession of sensations or perceptions; subjective experience of what is there;
2. the explicit formulation of plans, on the basis of beliefs and purposes, which inform deliberate actions as opposed to mechanically-determined responses to external stimuli;
3. the trend leading from sensations to perceptions; from sensations and perceptions to desires and beliefs and explicit purposes based on them; and from explicit purposes to conscious occurrent thoughts and thoughts about thoughts.

Most of the arguments I present here are as much about the lower storeys of consciousness (where non-propositional pains are suffered and sensations of light and warmth are experienced, etc.) as about the upper storeys (where plans get formulated and philosophical problems discussed), though some are specifically about the latter.

The Evolutionary Theory of Consciousness

At the heart of this theory of (or, perhaps, attitude towards) consciousness, is the belief that the very existence of consciousness can be explained on the basis of the superior capacity for survival it confers upon organisms endowed with it: the notion that some creatures are endowed with consciousness because consciousness is a good thing to have since it enhances the chances of survival and hence of reproduction. Nervous systems are the *sine qua non* of consciousness; and the advantages of having a nervous system (and hence consciousness) are described succinctly by Patricia Churchland:

From the very beginning, mobile creatures whose excitable cells were capable of conveying information about conditions outside the body had a survival advantage over those whose movements were independent of what was going on outside. Obviously, the organism that flees in the absence of predators and feeds willy-nilly is going to be doomed to be prey for those more lucky organisms fitted out with cells coordinating representations of the world with movement in the world. With increased complexity of behavioural repertoire comes increased capacity for representing the environment.[2]

In short, Patricia Churchland tells us, 'neurons are evolution's solution to the problem of adaptive movement' (p. 14). Complex nervous systems and their simpler antecedents were selected because of the advantages enjoyed by creatures whose behaviour was controlled by them. As Paul Churchland says (p. 76):

> brains were selected for because brains conferred a reproductive advantage . . . because they allowed individuals to anticipate their environment, to distinguish food from non-food, predators from non-predators, safety from peril, and mates from non-mates; in sum, a brain gave them knowledge and control of the *external world*.

It all seems inescapable common sense. If, in a hostile world, you want to make smart, life-preserving moves rather than foolish, or random, life-threatening ones, you'd better know what you're doing and that means getting yourself a brain and being conscious.[3] If you wanna get ahead, getta brain.

Anyone who takes issue against evolutionary explanations of any aspect of life, and in particular of a fundamental feature of human beings such as consciousness, needs to take account of the recent closely and brilliantly argued defence of neo-Darwinism by Richard Dawkins in *The Blind Watchmaker*.[4] I don't want to summarise Dawkins's arguments here. A bald summary would denature the neo-Darwinist vision he advances in his book. Suffice it to say that he mounts a powerful argument in support of his belief that the emergence of those incredibly complex objects we call living organisms – things whose constituent parts are arranged in a way that is unlikely to have arisen by chance alone – could in principle be accounted for by the cumulative effect of natural selection operating over immensities of time. Although the complexity of living organisms makes it seem as if they were unlikely to have arisen by chance alone, Dawkins points out that the emergence of complex species seems less improbable once we recognise that, while mutation is random, natural selection is the very opposite of random:

> We have seen that living things are too improbable and too beautifully 'designed' to have come into existence by chance. How, then, did they come into existence? The answer, Darwin's answer, is by gradual step-by-step transformations from simple beginnings, from primordial entities sufficiently simple to have come into existence by chance. Each successive change in the gradual evolutionary process was simple enough, *relative to its predecessor*, to have arisen by chance. But the whole sequence of cumulative steps constitutes anything but a chance process, when you consider the complexity of the final end-product relative to the original starting point. The cumulative process is directed by nonrandom survival. (p. 43)

Dawkins demonstrates how non-random survival imposes a directionality upon change, despite the randomness of the mutations that underlie it: 'The progeny in any one generation are different from their parents in random directions. But which of those progeny is selected to go forward into the next generation is not random'. By this means the great journeys through genetic space represented by the transition from primitive organisms to complex ones can be accomplished.

Having rendered complex organisms rather less improbable, Dawkins even goes on to explain why their emergence should seem improbable to our brains, themselves the product of evolution:

> Evolution has equipped our brains with a subjective consciousness of risk and improbability suitable for creatures with a lifetime of less than one century . . . we are beings whose brains are equipped with a spotlight of comprehensible risk that is a pencil-thin beam illuminating the far left-hand end of the mathematical continuum of calculable risks. Our subjective judgement of what seems like a good bet is irrelevant to what is actually a good bet . . . Our own subjective judgement about the plausibility of a theory of the origin of the life is likely to be wrong by a factor of a hundred million. (pp. 162–3)

What makes Dawkins's neo-Darwinism particularly impressive is that it deliberately addresses itself to the really hard cases for the theory of evolution – those which seem to demand that we invoke a Great Designer to explain – such as the echo-location mechanisms of a bat. He argues convincingly that, even though our knowledge of the details is still incomplete, we can be confident that the magnificently designed creatures that populate this planet do not require us to postulate the existence of a Great Designer.

One of the greatest problems for Darwinism is the evolution of organ systems. For these seem to have to be quite well-developed before they confer advantage in the struggle for survival. Consider, for example, the eye. The transition from an eyeless creature to one which has something like a recognisable eye represents a long journey across genetic space. Many thousands of mutations are required. Biologists such as Goldschmidt have pointed out that, since the first few thousand mutations would confer no advantage, the organisms affected by them would not enjoy preferential survival. And this would seem to suggest that the long journey from sightlessness to vision would not be likely even to begin unless all the necessary mutations took place at once – an event that has a negligible probability. Dawkins solves this problem by arguing that even the smallest steps towards an eye might confer advantage: for example, a single photo-sensitive spot on an organism's surface would give it some kind of edge over the competition.

His arguments are richer and much more subtle than I have presented them. However, he leaves one very large problem outstanding: that of the emergence of consciousness. It is significant that the index to Dawkins's book has no entries under 'consciousness' or 'mind'.

Consciousness has always been an awkward customer for biology – and evolutionary theorists – to deal with. Samuel Butler complained that Darwinism 'banished mind from the universe'. What he meant was that it removed not only the need for a purposeful Creator to explain the origin of the species but also intention and purpose from the entire evolutionary process. This hasn't worried many biologists, for whom it is a positive virtue of the theory. But it does make it rather difficult to find a place for mind, or consciousness, in the scheme of things. Let us now, therefore, subject to critical examination the notion that consciousness emerged as a property of certain organisms *because* it conferred survival value upon them.

It is possible to identify three separate assumptions behind the evolutionary theory of consciousness. They are as follows:

1. Consciousness has survival value.
2. Certain animals (including human beings) have consciousness *because* of its survival value.
3. Consciousness evolved *gradually*, in a manner similar to that of other features of successful organisms, by the operation of natural selection.

I shall deal with each of these assumptions in turn.

1. Consciousness Has Survival Value

At first sight, this would seem obvious. An animal that has conscious goals can plan ahead, anticipating problems before they emerge, and so on. But in practice the advantage of consciousness is less self-evident. Does consciousness help species – or, more generally (to avoid what we might call 'biomorphism'), types of entities – to survive?

A reasonable starting point is to look at the evidence that conscious species survive longer. If survival is understood in terms of the longevity of individuals, rather than of the species as a whole, then the sceptic can point out that there are many unconscious forms of matter that live longer than man, the form of matter blessed (or cursed) with the most highly developed consciousness. Rocks, for example, seem better at staving off death, in the sense of transformation to the point of no longer being recognisable, than men. And, if one confines oneself to living matter, there are non-conscious organisms that seem to do very well indeed – from the point of view of the longevity of individuals. They seem to do equally well if one looks at the longevity of the species as a whole – the time for which the species has been around the planet relatively unchanged. Indeed, survivorship curves for genera of lowly bivalves show them to be more long-lived than the considerably higher carnivores. A number of genera of bivalves have existed for over 300 million years.[5] As for the amoeba, it has (as Mary Midgley points out[6]) 'not only long been unchanged as a tribe, but since it reproduces by division, its first members are in a sense still here in person'. Man, indubitably the most conscious, is, after all, by no means the most enduring of the species.

Now it might be objected – against the longevity-of-the-species-as-a-whole argument – that because Man came on the scene late, he hasn't had time yet to compete with the longevity of more ancient species. Fair enough; but this means that the hypothesis that consciousness enables a species to survive longer has not yet been tested and will not be testable for many hundreds of millions of years to come. Moreover, if one looks at carnivores that have become extinct and compares their species longevity with those of the bivalves that have become extinct, it emerges that the mean species survival of the latter is less than a tenth of that of the former. And in bivalves, but not in carnivores, there are far more surviving genera with a very long survival than would be expected from the survival times of extinct genera.[7] As Midgley points out, not all non-survivors have been evidently 'low; and "the supreme survivors can be very 'low' indeed"' (p. 153). Midgley uses this, and related observations, to criticise the whole idea of evolutionary progress and the reduction of all measures of the 'height' or 'lowliness' of a species 'to the basic one of efficiency in surviving' (pp. 152–3) and the idea of an evolutionary ladder which a species either climbs or falls off:

> Ruthless marches, relentless pressure, brutal cutthroat competition and all the rest of it sound like a mode of ensuring that whatever does not climb the ladder is bound to perish. It isn't. It can just stay at the bottom. (p. 153)

From the point of view of the survival of individual members of the species, it is by no means the case that there is a correlation between the apparent level or complexity of consciousness and life expectancy. Quite the reverse, as a comparison between the long-lived rather dim cartilaginous fish and the short-lived, bright shrew will show. As Midgley puts it, 'If the "aim", the steady, impartially determined advantage, were just surviving, amoebas would be just the thing to be' (p. 150). As for geographical range, and the ability to adapt to or survive in a wide variety of environments, certain worms and certain bacteria have a greater range than all conscious creatures with the possible exception of man.

It may be objected that arguments that depend on inter-species comparisons are misconceived and indicate a fundamental mis-understanding of the kinds of pressures that drive the evolutionary process. The point that many animals do well without conscious-ness could be equally well used against the adaptive or survival value of feet or wings. To determine the adaptive value of any feature one should consider the advantage conferred upon a particular organism compared with the competition, in other words with other organisms of the same species or other species in the same ecological niche. The comparison of bacteria and man, or of shrews and cartilaginous fish, made above is therefore arguably inappropriate. We should not try to test the survival value of consciousness in an abstract and global way, assessing its value independently of specific contexts; rather we should think of its having adaptive value in a particular context, conferring a relative advantage in a certain setting against other specific types of individuals not possessed of it.

To concede this, however, is to undermine the empirical status of the evolutionary explanation of consciousness. It is to concede that the assertion that behaviour guided by consciousness has a greater adaptive value than, say, increasingly finely tuned mechanisms is untestable. For we cannot set up an experiment in which we compare the survival of types of organisms that are identical in every respect except the possession of consciousness.

The typical longevity of individuals within a species and of species as a whole remains the only conceivable proof of the adaptive value of consciousness. And yet it would appear that this test is impossible. In the absence of such a test, however, the advantage conferred upon species by the possession of conscious-ness remains empirically unproven. The only way in which the greater survival value of the possession of consciousness over (say) increasingly efficient unconscious mechanisms could be proved would be to observe and compare the changing survival, range and numerousness of the descendents of a species which took both of these two evolutionary paths. This is, of course, impossible. Set against this lack of evidence for the evolutionary advantage of consciousness is the strong evidence that near-automatons – spiders, termites, earthworms, slugs, bivalves, etc. – have proved extremely durable. If consciousness is advantageous, most of the advantage has been reaped in man only over the last few hundred thousand years, millions of years after consciousness of a sort had emerged. Prior to that, automata had done very nicely, thank you.

Indeed, it could be argued that consciousness is of advantage only to forms of matter that have a certain vulnerability or, to put it less tendentiously, a certain sort of instability. In many cases this instability is linked with the object's being so structured that it is able to be conscious, inasmuch as a certain kind of instability, non-inertness, is the *sine qua non* of the responsiveness of an entity to that which is outside of it. This responsiveness, irrespective of whether it has any specific cognitive component, seems to be the very essence of that in which consciousness is rooted. So we can see that even if consciousness can be intelligibly described as 'useful', its utility tends to be especially apparent in those organisms that are burdened with consciousness. We seem to have a kind of circularity here: conscious is necessary only if you want to be conscious.

This circularity is mirrored in one version (man's version) of what counts as survival: namely, being conscious or having the potentiality to become, or recover, consciousness. Human survival is regarded as synonymous with conscious survival, if only because prior possession of, and hence dependency upon, consciousness makes one a very bad automaton: conscious beings have to remain conscious to resist rapid change and loss of form; to enjoy free and independent life. They have to do deliberately what takes place automatically in more primitive, unconscious organisms; what might be solved by tropisms in the latter requires careful planning in the former. The automated drift of a primitive organism towards water may be contrasted with the highly skilled behaviour – dependent on memory and elaborate acquired motor skills – required for me to draw a glass of water from a tap and to ensure that I have paid my water rates so that the supply from the tap is maintained. For creatures with advanced consciousness, consciousness is not a mere luxury or even merely an important something giving the organism an edge over the competition: it is essential for survival itself. (I am leaving aside the rather special case of the patient in coma who is able to survive because other conscious organisms ensure his continuing survival).

In assessing the survival value of consciousness, we tend to be guided by intuitions that are properly applied only to a comparison between the viability of a conscious organism when it is conscious versus the viability of the same organism when it is unconscious (e.g. in coma). These intuitions are inappropriate when it comes to thinking about the potential value of consciousness *per se* for a species that does not possess it; or its potential value in a world (the Earth hundreds of millions of years ago) where there were no conscious organisms. If we do not adopt a viewpoint that assumes the prior existence of conscious organisms but consider merely what is required for adaptive movement, the value of consciousness becomes less evident.

Consider, for example, the extraordinary feats of 'adaptive movement' achieved by naturally occurring automata. Johnson-Laird reports[8] how Reichardt and his colleagues have demonstrated that a housefly's flight pattern is controlled by rapid and automatic mechanisms. Although vision in the sense that higher organisms such as humans enjoy – conscious vision – appears to be unavailable to the fly, it manages, none the less, to find its way round the world. This and other examples (see note 9) confirm that so much can be achieved by mindless automatons that it is difficult to see what advantage consciousness offers the organism in search of 'adaptive movement' over progressively more sophisticated automatons. Consciousness does not seem necessary for a long life. Most of us would, of course, regard it as the *sine qua non* of a rich and full one; the evolutionary process, however, at least as understood by biologists, is concerned with survival – of individuals and so of species – rather than spiritual satisfaction.[10]

There is no necessary relationship between having an advanced nervous system, of the kind designed to ensure adaptive movement, and being conscious. As Eccles has pointed out, the functioning of the brain, understood as a means of connecting (sensory) inputs with (motor) outputs, can be described without reference to consciousness:

> We can, in principle, explain all input-output performance in terms of activity of neuronal circuits; and consequently, consciousness seems to be absolutely unnecessary! . . . as neurophysiologists we simply have no use for consciousness in our attempts to show how the nervous system works.[11]

In other words, consciousness is superfluous when it comes to the evolutionarily important task of connecting the right input to the right output, of ensuring that movement is adaptive with respect to the surroundings. Its apparent interventions are not only a scientific embarrassment, they are also seemingly *de trop*. A sophisticated nervous system may be necessary to ensure complex adaptive movements but it need not be conscious.

The arguments that evolutionists such as Dawkins deploy to show how extremely complex creatures can emerge and be viable without needing to invoke a designer emphasise this point about automatons: for, if consciousness is not required to bring such creatures into being, it can hardly be regarded as essential for the less demanding task of assisting their survival. Both the emergence of the brain during evolution and the growth of the brain in embryo appear to take place without the intervention of consciousness. The assumption that evolution, including the evolution of organs such as the brain, is an unconscious process, ungoverned by deliberate purpose, is a cornerstone of evolutionary theory. And, of course, we could hardly expect the growth of the brain in an individual to be directed by the very consciousness the possession of a brain is supposed to make possible. Now it seems to me that the building of a brain – ontogenetically or embryologically – is a much more complex and difficult process than ensuring that responses to the environment are adaptive rather than random or maladaptive. Building a brain, in other words, seems to be a greater achievement than using one for the purposes defined by evolutionary theory. The 'cleverness' apparently required to ensure that all the many millions of cells grow and come together in the way that they do seems much greater than that required to avoid a predator. (And this is supported by the fact that most organisms can manage the latter deliberately whereas none comes anywhere near to doing the former.) If brain-building can be accomplished without the involvement of a purposive intelligence, then surely organisms can survive without conscious intelligence. Consciousness, therefore, would seem to be superfluous from the evolutionary point of view. If it *is* superfluous, its emergence cannot be explained as a response to evolutionary imperatives.

It might be objected that (standardised) brain development can be programmed, while ordinary behaviour – which cannot be standardised because it involves reactions to unforeseen contingencies – cannot, and that this is why consciousness is necessary for the survival of the organism while it is not required for the species' evolution to an advanced state or the individual's growth to maturity. The implication of this is that one needs consciousness only to deal with singulars, while one does not need it to build a standardised brain in standardised internal conditions.

This argument does not hold up. No two developing organs are precisely alike. However closely controlled the genetic material guiding growth, there will always be variations in phenotypical expression, itself in part due to the slightly different environments developing organs encounter. As an organ grows, the dividing cells will have to adhere to, or recover, the blueprint in unique and changing circumstances. Now, one might claim that the brain learns unconsciously to deal with new situations; it is shaped by the environment as well as by programmed growth. But this would take away the point of the supposed contrast between programmed growth and adaptive responses to the unforeseen contingencies of everyday life and so leave consciousness still superfluous from the evolutionary point of view.

2. Consciousness Has Emerged in Certain Organisms *Because* of its Survival Value

Is survival value a sufficient condition for a new property of matter to emerge? Standard evolutionary theory, which begins with matter, proceeds to living matter and then to conscious living matter, assumes that matter obeys its own laws throughout and that the emergence of species is merely the emergence of differrently arranged forms of matter. Now this must mean one of three things:

(a) Consciousness was a possibility in matter from the beginning, even before living forms appeared.

This is a form of panpsychism, a vision of mind among things. Such magic thinking leads to a slippery slope, at the bottom of which is the belief that, say, the consciousness of a philosopher thinking about the nature of matter was present in some embryonic form in the most ancient rock formations.

(b) Consciousness emerged by accident at a certain point and matter was able to carry it.

This would 'de-evolutionise' the emergence of consciousness, making the leap of matter towards consciousness an event that occurred independently of the needs of living organisms and of the pressures of natural selection.

(c) Consciousness was not a possibility in matter from the beginning but came into being only when certain organisms found it to be convenient, from the point of view of survival, to plan ahead, to think, to imagine possibilities, in short to be conscious.

Of these, (c) warrants more detailed consideration. If consciousness *was* a genuinely new property of matter, one not foreseen in the physico-chemical universe, one that lay outside the constraints of physico-chemical laws, then its emergence couldn't really be explained in terms of the 'needs' of non-conscious living organisms. For nobody, I take it, would wish to suggest that evolutionary pressures (whatever they are – see Midgley, note 6 on this) can summon up *any* property, including properties not implicit in, or foreseeable from, the material of which organisms are made. It would be very useful, for example, for an animal faced with a predator to be able to dematerialise in one place and rematerialise in another; but the obvious survival value of this has not resulted in the emergence of animals possessing this capability. Nobody, moreover, is surprised that this very useful skill has not emerged; from which it must follow that the acquisition of consciousness – which *is* considered by evolutionists to have been summoned up in response to evolutionary pressures – is not thought of as an entirely novel property or phenomenon in the way that protective dematerialisation would appear to be. Consciousness, it would seem to be tacitly assumed by evolutionary theorists, is one of the options available to the evolutionary process from the beginning. It is, in short, a property implicit in the 'lowest forms' of matter. We would have to go further than Samuel Butler, who, not entirely seriously, suggested that 'even a potato in a dark cellar has a certain low cunning which serves him in excellent stead' and assert, entirely seriously, that 'even a rock on a not-yet inhabited planet has a certain dim consciousness – or the potential for it – which will serve his evolutionary descendents in excellent stead'. We are back with panpsychism.

3. That Consciousness Emerged *Gradually*

All forms of Darwinism require that organs and other large scale systems, or complex faculties, should emerge gradually as a cumulative effect of selection acting on random mutations. Only in this way can evolution be directional on a large scale without the guiding hand of a Designer. Recall Dawkins's succinct formulation: 'The progeny in any one generation are different from their parents in random directions. But which of those progeny is selected to go forward into the next generation is not random'. By emphasising the distinction between random mutations and non-random selection, it is possible to counteract such arguments as these:

> The eye either functions as a whole, or not at all. So how did it come to evolve by slow, steady, infinitesimally small Darwinian improvements? Is it really so plausible that thousands upon thousands of lucky chance mutations happened coincidentally so that the lens and retina, which cannot work without each other, evolved in synchrony? What survival value can there be in an eye that doesn't see?[12]

Dawkins claims that even the most primitive progenitor of an eye – a single photosensitive spot, for example – would confer sufficient advantage on its possessor to ensure preferential survival. A gradual evolutionary journey towards eye-hood is therefore possible.

Can the same argument be deployed in relation to the emergence of consciousness? Are we entitled to envisage consciousness emerging in the same gradual fashion as a result of the operation of natural selection on random change? At first sight it would seem so. One could imagine a long evolutionary journey, a Great Trek across genetic space, from the 'low cunning' of the potato in the dark cellar (or *E. coli* in some even darker place) to the much higher cunning of the fully conscious human being. But *is* consciousness a property, a feature of organisms that can emerge gradually in this way? Can consciousness come into being in the piecemeal fashion of organ systems or plumage? It seems that there is a clear difference between consciousness (or mind) in this respect and life, which *can*, it seems, come into being by degrees. This has been expressed by Colin McGinn:

> In the case of life there is a gradual transition from the plainly inanimate to the indisputably living; but in the case of consciousness we cannot take such a gradualist view . . .The emergence of consciousness must be compared to a sudden switching on of a light . . . and we conceive the minds of lowly creatures as consisting in . . . a small speck of consciousness quite definitely possessed, not in the partial possession of something admitting of degrees.[13]

Consciousness is either there or not: you can't be a little bit conscious any more than you can be a teeny-weeny bit pregnant.

The single photo-sensitive spot, from which the long evolutionary journey of the eye may have begun, is not 'a little spot of consciousness'. This is implicit in Dennett's question: 'Does *any* action-guiding benefit derived from photosensitivity count as seeing?'[14]

It is easy to overlook this difference between life and consciousness when we think about the evolution of sensory systems such as the eye and confuse the mechanisms apparently underlying vision with vision itself, identifying chemical sensitivity to light with vision. Photosensitive cells not possess visual consciousness – or even ur-consciousness or proto-consciousness – any more than the photoelectric cells in light meters do. Photosensitivity is not vision – or ur-vision or proto-vision. The tendency to confuse the two encourages a false analogy between, on the one hand, lights of different degrees, of different intensities, the imperceptible passage from darkness to light and, on the other, the transition from light (as a physical phenomenon) to vision, from light to consciousness of light. The false analogy is between

Dark ⟶ (Gradual, continuous change) --- ➤ Light

and

Light ⟶ (Non-gradual, discontinuous change) --- ➤ Sight

There is something suspect, therefore, in the idea that consciousness itself (as opposed to its content or form) could evolve gradually over many generations through the process of selective survival acting on the species as a whole. And there is a consequent difficulty in accepting the idea that conscious intelligence (not just behaviour, or adaptive movement, simulating intelligence) has slowly emerged as a result of a protracted selection process. If consciousness does *not* emerge gradually, however, we have to envisage points in the evolutionary process where it would descend, fully formed, like Grace, upon individuals.

One would expect that the mutations upon which the emergence of consciousness would depend might be expected to run into many thousands; none of these would be of any survival value until all of them were in place. There would therefore be no selection pressures to protect the first mutation until the second came along, the first and second until the third came along, and so on until the thousand or so that were required had arrived. The chances of all the mutations being co-present in a single organism, which would then become conscious, are therefore negligible, even allowing for the great stretches of time evolution has at its disposal. Francis Hitching's argument quoted above, which questions the additional survival value conferred by an eye that does not yet see, an argument Dawkins treats with scorn, would seem to have a valid application to consciousness even if it cannot be applied to unconscious organ systems. (There is another possibility: that the necessary mutations were preserved because they were useful in some other respect than contributing to consciousness. They could therefore be accrued by the species before consciousness emerged. This, however, seems to depend upon a horde of remarkable coincidences and so bring us back into the realm of astronomical improbability that neo-Darwinism tries to avoid.)

Other Problems with the Evolutionary Account of Consciousness

Fundamental Concepts of Evolutionary Theory
The fundamental concepts of evolutionary theory – 'organism', 'environment', 'adaptation', 'purpose' – may not be applicable in a world prior to the emergence of consciousness or a world conceived of in the absence of consciousness.

Evolution takes as given the distinct existence of the organism and 'its' environment. Its account of the history of the biological universe revolves around the interaction between these two protagonists, the organism and its environment; and the viewpoint it adopts is that of the organism trying to survive in a world from which it has been differentiated and into which (on death) it will be re-assimilated. Although the interaction is seen as being both cooperative and adversarial, with the environment providing both the necessary means to survival and the source of most threats to survival, it is almost invariably described from the viewpoint of the organism. Evolutionary theory is, in a word, partisan. And yet the world it depicts is one without conscious purpose and, for the most part, without consciousness at all. The question that needs to be considered – and one that has largely passed unnoticed – is whether it is admissible to adopt the viewpoint of the organism, or whether even we can assume the validity of the distinction between organism and environment in the context of a mindless evolutionary process, especially when we consider evolution prior to the emergence of nervous systems.

Is it permissible to look at the living world at the level of DNA chemistry and still think about organisms and 'their' environments? Does a molecule of DNA have an environment? Or is it rather itself part of an environment? The answer, of course, is that it can be viewed as both the possessor of an environment and as part of one, depending which point of view is taken. But the molecule itself is intrinsically – in the absence of a higher consciousness able to take a view on the matter – neither. And this must apply to the whole unconscious organism as much as it applies to DNA. In a world observed solely from a physico-chemical standpoint, there are no viewpoints, no organisms, and no environments. The physical world, in itself, has no points of view. It has no privileged sites.

Radical neo-Darwinian evolutionary theory, which purports to discard, and at least disinfects, teleological explanation, appeals to the rhetoric of physico-chemical laws but rarely looks at the world from as far back as them. It abolishes conscious purposes without following the consequences of this to their logical conclusion. It retains, in a mindless world of atoms and energy exchanges, concepts that belong to a world of conscious beings, beings who have viewpoints; and it is to these that it owes much of its explanatory force. And this is how, also, it manages to simulate a physico-chemical standpoint while its discourse still manages to remain recognisably biological. A purely physical world, or a biological world construed in purely physical terms, does not have points of view; and a truly consistent physicalism cannot retain the distinction between organism and environment.[15] Evolutionary theory without the concepts of organism, environment and survival is pretty well devoid of specifically biological content. Evolutionary theory that retains them must part company from physicalism because there can be no physicalist account of how matter differentiates into environment and organism; of how some matter emerges as 'privileged' material whose survival is at issue.

There is therefore a deep insincerity in neo-Darwinism, which does not take its physicalism as seriously as it pretends to do. Darwinian evolutionary theory 'banishes mind from the universe' not only by denying that the emergence of the species is the result of the conscious activity of a Great Designer but also by denying mind a role in determining the course of evolution. Neo-Darwinian physicalist evolutionary theory should go further and refuse to appeal to mind (implicit in purpose) to account for the behaviour of organisms. Dennett,[16] argues that physicalism should ignore function and purpose and make purely Laplacean predictions. At the very least it should avoid attributing purpose to the physical events that it observes; for this, under its own terms, is anthropomorphism. To admit that certain bits of matter have purpose or exhibit changes that are amenable to teleological explanation while others do not, is to allow a distinction that cannot be retained within physicalism; for it cannot be accommodated without an appeal to consciousness.

Consciousness Seems Rather to Exceed its Evolutionary Brief
A good deal of conscious behaviour – hobbies, loving people as well as lusting after them, creating and enjoying art – and many of the uses to which consciousness is put (such as speculating about the origin of consciousness) seem to have little to do with survival in any but the most tenuous or metaphorical sense. Indeed, much of conscious human behaviour even in the undeveloped world, and certainly in the developed world, is concerned less with survival than with happiness or satisfaction. The pursuit of knowledge far exceeds the seeking out of information necessary to satisfy physiological need. It is as though consciousness, if it had originally developed to help us to avoid tigers and catch cows, has gone out of control so that it now allows (or drives) us to enjoy reading philosophy and talking about music, and to try to make a more complete sense of our origins and destinations by, for example, constructing theories of evolution.

It is difficult to believe that such an 'exceeding of its brief' is purely accidental, or even that it is merely secondary; on the contrary, it seems closely related to the essential nature of consciousness. Conversely, the evolutionary view of consciousness as a mere servant of adaptive behaviour, a mere instrument of survival, something that serves a particular, defined purpose, seems to be untrue to the facts of everyday experience: we are conscious of much more than is expressed in our behaviour and there are many forms of consciousness for which there is no behavioural expression relevant to survival.

According to the evolutionary theory, consciousness exists because it has a purpose – that of, in some way, aiding survival. But does there not appear to be something profoundly misconceived about the idea that consciousness can be explained in terms of a purpose, even if that purpose is as fundamental and as broadly conceived as 'survival'? For purposes are surely posterior to the emergence of consciousness; one cannot think of there being such things as purposes until consciousness appears on the scene. It is consciousness that brings purposes in its train rather than purposes evoking consciousness. The events in (unconscious) matter may conform to laws (that themselves have explicit existence only in the consciousness of human beings) but they do not express purposes. Of course, conscious beings such as teleologising biologists may discern purpose in the behaviour of unconscious organisms; but such purposes are imported from without and belong to the biologist's interpretative system. (This may be one of the few places where Dennettian intentionality – the intentionality of an entity as the product of the intentional stance of some outside agency attributing intentionality for interpretive purposes – seems to correspond to something real!)[17]

It is bad enough when consciousness is explained as some kind of general purpose 'facility'. When it is tied to a specific or narrow purpose, as when consciousness is understood as something that has a very particular job to do, then one moves from the dubious to the ludicrous. The prize for the most absurd teleological explanation of consciousness must go to the psychologist Nick Humphrey, who has argued[18] that consciousness serves to help us cope with the most tricky problem of all – that of social interaction with other people. Pressures from social complexity, he tells us, made it useful for consciousness to evolve: we developed consciousness in order to be able to understand each other better:

> The fact that we are complex social creatures produces this . . . strong need for us to attribute consciousness to other creatures so that we can predict their behaviour by role-playing and other forms of thought.

Humphrey sees consciousness as 'an inner eye' whose field of view is not the outside world but the brain itself. This inner eye (as crude a homuncular organ as is currently on offer in contemporary 'thought') has been designed by natural selection to give a useful picture that tells the animal as much as it needs to know. The main purpose of the inner eye is to make it possible for the animal to 'do natural psychology':

> By showing each and every one of us how our own mind/brain works, consciousness provides us with an extraordinarily effective tool for understanding – by analogy – the minds of others like ourselves.

Humphrey's argument towards this absurd idea – which includes the customary naive idea of consciousness as an inner scanning device – seems to have the following general form:

(a) Consciousness must be of some use because evolutionary theory does not permit anything to exist that does not contribute to an organism's biological success.

(b) Consciousness appears useless because most of what we do could be carried out just as well, or better, automatically.

(c) However, there is one thing that couldn't be carried out without consciousness, namely detecting the consciousness of others. For without the inner eye on to our own brain, we should not even have the intuition that others are conscious and would have no information to enable us to imagine what their consciousness might contain. Consciousness helps us to imagine what others might be thinking since it provides us with direct access to what we ourselves are thinking.

(d) Consciousness evolved because it is the only device by which we could reliably detect consciousness.

Even if one overlooks the absurdity of an account of consciousness that narrows it from an all-encompassing state to a tool with a very specific function, Humphrey's notion of the purpose of consciousness still seems ludicruous; for its role seems to be circular: consciousness is a device whose function is to detect consciousness (cf. a hammer is a device whose rationale is that it enables us to detect hammers). So *that's* why we're conscious: if we weren't, we should have considerable difficulty knowing what we are all thinking! It seems hardly necessary to make the obvious objection that if we *weren't* conscious there wouldn't be any thoughts to know or to miss out on; that without consciousness it wouldn't be merely *more difficult* to get access to our own thoughts – there wouldn't be any thoughts to get access to.

The teleological account of consciousness need not necessarily lead to the kind of ludicrous views that Humphrey puts forward. Nevertheless, absurdity always lies near at hand when the *level* at which the function of consciousness is sought is such as is implicit in this kind of narrow teleological explanation. It is rather reminiscent of the suggestion that we are endowed with consciousness so that we can fill in the football pools accurately or get good marks at school and so not upset our teachers. Humphrey's ideas do not deserve consideration on their own account but rather for the illustrative purpose they serve. They show the kind of nonsense that may result when consciousness is explained in terms of some specific function it may have.[19]

The Power of Generalisation of the Human Mind

One feature of consciousness often cited by evolutionists is the way it confers the power of generalisation, of induction, on organisms. It is difficult, however, to see how induction can be automated, how an algorithm for valid generalisation could be implanted in a species by pressures of selection. The robin that treats every red mark against a brown background as a rival robin to be attacked is a model not of human powers of generalisation but evidence of how automated generalisation goes wrong. It seems to underline the differences between the properties of human consciousness and those behavioural responses which have plausibly evolved in response to selective pressures. One would not expect the latter to produce scientists able to discover and refine upon laws of immense generality, or philosophers able to criticise those laws.

I am tempted to say that it is hardly surprising that the theory of evolution does not explain the power of conscious organisms to generalise as it is itself an enormous generalisation. Nor is it surprising that it fails to explain the origin of consciousness because it has itself originated from within consciousness. This, however, seems to me an at best glib and at worst a dubious line of argument.

Further Thoughts on Mechanism

Darwinians would agree that there would be no evolutionary pressures to produce (ever more highly developed) consciousness, if the need for 'adaptive movements' could be met by mechanisms. Even the suggestion that nascent consciousness emerged by accident as a result of changes in organisms interacting with their environment would fail to account for the continuing existence and development of consciousness, unless consciousness were superior, from the evolutionary point of view, to any conceivable mechanism. Just suppose that the evolutionary process took the form of the emergence of more and more complex (but unconscious) systems with increasingly efficient mechanisms to support survival. Suppose also that nervous systems emerged simply as the unconscious basis for the mechanism of adaptive behaviour. Suppose, finally, that there emerged, epiphenomenally, from some – but only some – of these increasingly complex nervous systems something increasingly like the consciousness of human beings. Would natural selection favour those nervous systems that were epiphenomenally endowed with consciousness? Are we entitled to assume that this trend

Advanced mechanism ⟶ Advanced mechanisms + Consciousness

would inevitably be favoured by natural selection over this one

Advanced mechanism ⟶ Very advanced mechanism?

Is there, in short, any a priori reason for assuming the intrinsic adaptive superiority of actions mediated by consciousness over mechanisms highly tuned to the environment? Are we entitled to presuppose that a trend to increasing consciousness confers a greater benefit than a trend towards increasingly slick mechanisms more precisely attuned towards the requirement for adaptive movement? The assumption that consciousness *must* have the edge over mechanism is, I believe, rooted in three sorts of error: (a) underrating the adaptive possibilities of mechanism; (b) overrating the adaptive advantage of consciousness; and (c) anthropomorphising the question from the outset.

Underrating Mechanism   There seems to be no limit to what can be achieved by unconscious mechanisms. I have already discussed the remarkable properties of the unicellular *E. coli* and of the housefly. And I have pointed out that, according to evolutionary theory, all organisms were produced without the aid of conscious process and that the growing human embryo produces the world's most complex object, its own brain, without the assistance of consciousness. Let me now develop the point about the remarkable efficacy of mechanism by discussing the work of Weiskrantz and others (summarised in note 20) who have shown that many so-called 'higher' functions can be retained in the absence of consciousness.

Patients with bilateral damage to the temporal lobes suffer from the amnesic syndrome: despite retaining normal intelligence and perceptual and cognitive skills they appear to remember nothing from minute to minute. They exhibit perceptual and motor-skill learning but, unlike the observers, they do not recognise this and remember nothing of the learning process. There is, in other words, a sharp dissociation between the capacity to learn and retain and the capacity to know that one has learned something. It is as if the behavioural response mechanisms can be tuned to the particular environment without the mediation of the kind of memory that is central to everyday awareness: namely, occurrent memory for a particular event one recalls experiencing *in propria persona*. Even more interesting are patients who exhibit so-called 'blindsight'. They have suffered lesions in the striate cortex and have large scotomata or apparently blind areas in their visual fields. Such patients will demonstrate a very good capacity to discriminate, to detect 'visual' events in the 'blind' area, to locate them in space, to make judgements about the orientation of lines or gratings, to detect the onset and termination of movement, and even to do simple pattern discriminations. The patients themselves, however, are quite unaware of any visual stimuli as such and say when questioned that they are just guessing and playing the experimenter's game.

In both the amnesic syndrome and blindsight patients demonstrate striking capacities in the absence of their own conscious knowledge. There is a separation of discrimination, learning, of adaptive behaviour from conscious awareness. It would appear from these observations, in which patients are disconnected from any awareness of the stimuli they are successfully discriminating, that much more than was hitherto thought can be achieved by unconscious mechanisms, without consciousness, especially without the self-conscious awareness that characterises so much of human everyday consciousness. The capabilities of mechanism seem limitless.

Overrating the Adaptive Advantage of Consciousness   It is a common observation that many procedures that can be carried out automatically may be performed less efficiently, or indeed break down altogether, if the subject tries to enact them deliberately, consciously executing each step. Consciousness has to be kept in check if the many activities of daily life are to be accomplished with the requisite expedition and fluency. It is an equally common observation that, as a skill is acquired, mechanism increasingly dominates over conscious and deliberate action. A learner driver at first specifically addresses himself to the tasks of changing gear, keeping the car in place by moving the steering wheel, braking when instructed, etc. The experienced driver no longer does these actions separately and deliberately but simply drives himself from A to B. It is possible to find that one has driven 50 or 100 miles along a motorway without being able to recall 'doing driving' at all – the so-called 'time-gap experience'. This emphasises the way in which skilled behaviour is hierarchically organised, so that its components become automatised. Consciousness-driven activity emerges out of background driving only when the unexpected happens – for example, a sudden obstacle has to be avoided – although even in such cases appropriate responses have often been initiated before conscious decisions have been taken. Conscious intervention in acquired skills may be a necessary preliminary to further improvement; apart from this, however, it is the road to paralysis, to the inhibition that results from a dysfunctional self-consciousness.

The value of consciousness in the performance of adaptive movements may therefore be overrated. It may not be necessary even in the acquisition of new skills, as opposed to the execution of acquired ones. The remarkable achievements of artificial neural networks, trained by repeated exposure to examples and correction of their responses to make complex discriminations that were thought to be beyond man-made devices, (see Chapter 4) can only deepen doubt about the function of consciousness in ensuring adaptive movements. The social value of consciousness – suggested by writers such as Humphrey (see above) – may also be overrated. Weiskrantz points out that the ability to detect the consciousness of others, far from improving social cohesiveness, may be counterproductive.[20]

Man is the only creature that perversely gets into social difficulties of any really serious kind, and one reason for this is that he is conscious and can think about all the social complications he might confront or deviously try to exploit for gain or for protection. (p. 311)

Consciousness – and consciousness of others' consciousness – is the necessary precondition of paranoia and other abnormal and maladaptive psychological states.[21]

Anthropomorphising the Question from the Outset What is the basis for our thinking that consciousness would make processes go better than mechanisms would? I think it is rooted in our beginning from the standpoint of organisms that are conscious. Clearly, organisms such as man that are typically conscious function better when awake than when in coma. Just as winged animals function better when they have those wings than when they have been removed; indeed, wingless, they will probably die. But this does not mean that wings are a necessary condition of life. To start from the fact that conscious man functions better than comatose man is to start from the end-point, from one solution to a problem that has, anyway, emerged only near the end-point, *after* the evolution of conscious organisms. If we begin where we should – from the beginning, from a viewpoint uncontaminated by prolepsis – then we may be less likely to conclude that consciousness is superior to mechanism in ensuring that things happen in one way rather than another.

Consider the extraordinarily complex ordering process that is associated with crystallisation. Would a solution of copper sulphate produce better crystals if the individual molecules knew what they were about, if they got together and defined their aims and objectives? Of course not. It might be objected that the analogy is not fair, because the crystallisation of copper sulphate is not a conscious objective whose realisation is to be carved out of natural process. But since, according to Darwinist theory, the universe from which consciousness emerged was that of unconscious and purposeless matter, in which there were no conscious processes, the analogy seems perfectly fair. So we cannot explain the emergence of consciousness on the basis of the needs created by the adoption of conscious purposes.

Reducing the Difference Consciousness Makes to the Use(s) It Has
The fundamental assumption of – and the fundamental flaw in – evolutionary theories of consciousness is that consciousness can be understood in terms of its *use* to the organism that possesses it. In the essay discussed earlier (see note 18), Humphrey offers the following general answer to Diderot's question 'what difference does consciousness make?': 'it helps in some way to keep the animal alive'. The difference made by consciousness is narrowed by Humphrey to some particular purpose that it serves, which in turn helps to keep the conscious organism alive. In order to

address the question of what difference consciousness makes, we must therefore, Humphrey goes on to say, 'escape from a definition of consciousness that renders it self-evidently useless and irrelevant, for example, private states of mind of which the subject alone is aware'.

This only goes to show that if we reduce the difference made by consciousness to the use consciousness serves, then we shall have to eject every aspect of consciousness that cannot be assimilated to, or subordinated to, use. But private states of mind, for all that they are evolutionarily awkward, indubitably exist. And *they* are precisely the difference that consciousness makes. Pain, pleasure, anguish, delight, the continuum of subjective experience, are the very essence of one's life as a conscious human being and cannot be excluded from the definition of consciousness. And when this is appreciated, the difference made by consciousness is seen to be *all the difference in the world* and not some narrow use. It is the difference of being *worlded*: to be without consciousness is to be without a world, at any rate for oneself; for under such circumstances, being worlded is a set of relations perceived by another consciousness. Without this second consciousness, there is no worldedness. Put more bluntly, one cannot reduce consciousness to a particular function since without consciousness matter does not matter; there simply is no mattering.

In the next chapter, I shall discuss the causal theory of perception and its relation to the biologisation of consciousness. But one theme belonging to that chapter also belongs here as well. One of the reasons for the attractiveness of the causal theory of perception – the theory that our perceptions are ultimately caused by the things they are perceptions of, that the contents of perception owe their causal ancestry at least in part to the objects of perception – is that the theory appears to constrain perception to be of things that are, for the most part, *really there*. The causal theory seems to build some kind of guarantee of truth into ordinary or normal perception. From the evolutionary point of view, this is linked with the role of perception, and more particularly consciousness, in enhancing chances of survival. The causal theory seems to explain how perceiving organisms usually 'get it right' and the evolutionary theory of consciousness seems to explain how organisms that 'got it right' would be the ones to emerge. What both theories – or both aspects of the biologisation of consciousness – fail to confront is the emergence of getting it right (or wrong) at all.[22] Why there is an explicit sense of what is there. Why, in short – to reiterate the question that evolutionary theory leaves conspicuously un-answered – there is consciousness.

3

Biologising Consciousness II. The Causal Theory of Perception

INTRODUCTION

So much for the biological origin, or 'justification', of consciousness. How, in biological terms, does consciousness work? How is it that there is such a thing as consciousness and how does it come to have the right content? How does it manage successfully to be 'of' the real world? Most answers to these questions start out from the assumption that we are conscious in virtue of the energy impinging on our bodies. We get to know the world, are worlded, because our bodies and the world bump into one another and there is an exchange of energy between them.

This is so widely accepted that it seems less like a theory, or even a theoretical framework, than a piece of common sense; and in one form or another it encompasses the views of the majority of Anglo-American philosophers about the basis of consciousness or, at the very least, of perception. Although some philosophers and psychologists would emphasise the role of action in controlling perception and some talk of 'top down' constraints on the interpretation of the perceived, the causal role of incident energy remains fundamental and the Causal Theory of Perception (CTP) essentially unchallenged. For most English-speaking philosophers and cognitive psychologists, perception is, implicitly or explicitly, 'the terminus of a causal sequence involving at an earlier stage some event or process in the history of the perceived object'.[1] Though some, including Grice whom I have just quoted, would question whether this was in itself enough, there is a sense that the causal relation somehow explains the perception. According to the CTP, then, *I am aware of this object in front of me because events in the object are part of*

45

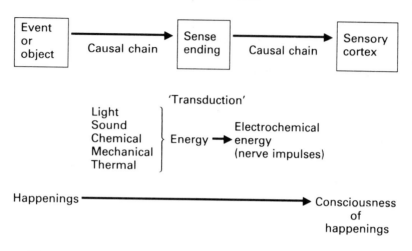

Figure 3.1   The neurophysiological version of the causal theory of
perception

a causal chain that impinges on my body. This causal chain terminates in a
part of my brain and the events with which it terminates are my perception
of the object. For example, I see this flower in front of me now
because events in the flower (in particular its interaction with light)
initiate a causal chain of events that in some sense terminates in my
brain.

Most philosophers who espouse the CTP subscribe explicitly to
the neurophysiological version (see Figure 3.1), which holds that
perception is the result of the constant interaction between the
material world and the nervous system, the details of which are
being elucidated by physiologists and others. In particular, perceptual awareness, and so consciousness itself, is identified with
certain events taking place in the higher reaches of the central
nervous system where a chain of events, collectively described as
sensory processing, and originating from the object that is perceived, reaches a terminus. I perceive this flower because light
which has been reflected from it impinges on my retina and causes
trains of nerve impulses to travel along the visual pathways to
the visual cortex. The events in the visual cortex correspond to
perception of the flower. Out of such events the visual field,
indeed the visual world, is composed. And these, along with other
cortical events relating to other sensory pathways, are the basis

of consciousness and of our state of being 'worlded'. Sensation, perception, experience, consciousness, boil down to large numbers of trains or patterns of nerve impulses.

It would appear, then, that common sense, philosophy and scientific physiology are agreed that we perceive objects and events because they impinge upon our bodies. More specifically, we perceive what is 'out there' or what is 'around us' as a result of the transfer of energy from objects or events to specialised parts of the body known collectively as 'the sensory system'. Most of those who currently have an opinion on the matter believe, like Thomas Hobbes, that:

> The cause of sense is the external body, or object, which presseth the organ proper to each sense, either immediately, as in taste or touch; or mediately, as in seeing, hearing or smelling.[2]

The external object

> worketh on the eyes, ears and other parts of a man's body; and by diversity of working, produceth diversity of experience.

We experience the world, indeed are worlded, because the contents of the world *impinge* on us, impingement being understood as involving, essentially, the transfer of energy from the external world into the nervous system of the individual for whom it is external.

HOW THE DIVERSITY OF WORKING PRODUCETH DIVERSITY OF EXPERIENCE

All of this is taken for granted in modern physiology and the main theme of sensory neurophysiology has been to establish in more precise detail how 'the diversity of working produceth diversity of experience' – the modern term for which is 'coding of sensory information'.

The framework of contemporary sensory neurophysiology was laid down in the nineteenth and early twentieth centuries when the business of explaining the material basis of perception was transformed into the more specific project of correlating the physical properties of perceived objects and events with the pattern of activity in the nervous system and the latter with the subjective properties of the experience:

Physical properties : Pattern of neural : Subjective properties
of stimulus   activity   of experience

This is the theoretical framework of sensory physiology – and of the science of psychophysics, whose first researches revolved round the attempt to relate the subjective brightness of a light stimulus to its objective physical luminance.

It was early appreciated that, apart from, say, minor variations in the speed of conduction, the impulses in all nerve fibres have essentially identical characteristics. This was explicitly recognised by the early twentieth-century physiologists, who saw their fundamental task as that of discovering how the infinite variety of the perceived world could be reflected in, or reconstructed in, the rather monotonous nervous system. With the advent of digital computers and the development of information theory in the 1940s and 1950s, this job was interpreted as being that of finding out how the nervous system 'encoded' reality in a digital form. The task of the nervous system was seen, as we shall discuss in the next chapter, to be a computational one.

We can think of experience as being differentiated both quantitatively and qualitatively. Let us look at how neurophysiologists and neuropsychologists have tried to relate these dimensions of experience to the intrinsic properties of the experienced object or event (usually regarded as the 'stimulus') and to the patterns of discharges in the sensory system.

Qualitative Aspects of Experience

The *quality* – or *modality* – of the experience depends on which parts of the sensory system are activated: stimulation of the retinal receptors causes an experience of light; stimulation of the receptors in the inner ear gives rise to the experience of sound; and so on. Müller's nineteenth-century 'doctrine of specific energies'[3] formalised the ordinary observation that different sense organs are sensitive to different properties of the world and that when they are stimulated sensations specific to those organs are experienced. It was proposed that there are endings (or receptors) within the nervous system which are attuned to specific types of energy.

For example, retinal receptors respond to light energy, cochlear endings to vibrations in the air, and so on. Of course, high energy stimulation even of the wrong kind may stimulate a sensory ending; for example, excessive pressure on the eyeball will produce a sensation of light. Contrariwise, over-intense stimulation of the appropriate kind will evoke pain. These are, however, abnormal situations; for ordinary perception, the doctrine of specific energies holds.

This early framework for sensory physiology – of a piece with the Hobbesian/common sense idea of 'the organ proper to each sense' – has undergone a good deal of refinement. Within the cochlea, for example, it has been shown that there are end organs that respond preferentially to sounds of high rather than low pitch. More centrally, in the cerebral cortex, the afferent fibres from groups of receptors are 'wired together' so that more complex stimuli – such as edges or lines of a certain inclination – may preferentially elicit neural activity and the corresponding subjective experience. Hubel and Wiesel's work, in particular,[4] put the idea of neurones as 'feature detectors' on the map, supporting the idea that for each cell in the striate cortex there was a specific pattern of excitation that would reliably excite it. Each cell had its own stimulus requirements and when it became active this said something about the nature of the event or object in its own part of the visual field. One main theme of twentieth-century sensory physiology has been inward movement of the doctrine of specific energies from the sensory ending towards and into the cortex.

There is a further aspect of Müller's doctrine, at least as it is now interpreted. The kind of sensation evoked by nerve impulses ultimately depends upon the particular part of the cerebral cortex that is finally activated. Activation of the occipital cortex evokes visual sensations, activation of the post-central gyrus tactile sensations, and so on. These modality-specific sensations will be experienced irrespective of the point at which the relevant pathway is stimulated: it doesn't matter, from the point of view of the cortex, and so of the experiencing subject, whether the train of impulses terminating in the cortex is initiated in the conventional way in the periphery or more centrally. The pathways, moreover, retain their distinctness all the way from the sensory ending (e.g. retinal receptor in the eye or Pacinian corpuscle in the skin) to the cortex (occipital lobe or precentral gyrus).

Quantitative Aspects of Experience

There are three fundamental dimensions of *quantity* in experience: (a) intensity; (b) (spatial) extensity; and (c) duration. At a neurophysiological level, the intensity of an experience is typically reflected in the number of neurones activated (the phenomenon of 'recruitment' observed as the intensity of the stimulus increases) and, more specifically, in the firing frequency of the relevant neurones. Extensity (e.g. the size of a patch of light) usually correlates with the number and spatial distribution of receptors activated. Finally, duration is correlated with the period of time for which the relevant neurones are active. (The relationships are complicated by phenomena such as accommodation whereby a constant stimulus when sustained may activate the nervous system progressively less intensively, with a corresponding reduction in the perceived intensity of the stimulus. These, and other phenomena of adaptation, do not invalidate the underlying conceptual framework.)

The earliest psychophysical observations demonstrated a correlation between the intensity of the physical stimulus and subjective reports of the intensity of the resultant experience. These were eventually summarised in the Weber–Fechner law which reported a log-linear relationship between stimulus intensity and subjective experience, the sensation increasing in proportion to the logarithm of the physical stimulus magnitude.[5] A quantitative correlation between the objective intensity of stimulus and the pattern of neural activity was subsequently demonstrated by physiologists recording from individual fibres.[6] Since the work of S. S. Stevens in the 1930s and later, it has been recognised that, although the Weber–Fechner law holds for many sorts of sensory experience, the exponent varies widely – from 0.33 for luminance to 3.5 for electric shock. The relation between the intensity of the stimulus and that of the experienced sensation is therefore better described by a power function; for example, subjective loudness measured in 'sones' increases as the 0.3 power of the physical sound power. This power function also holds for the relationship between the frequency of firing in individual fibres and the intensity of the applied stimulus. The principle of a quantitative correlation between external stimulus, neural activity and experienced sensation thus now appears to be well-established. This has encouraged physiologists and certain philosophers in their belief that 'our sensations are simply identical with, say, a set of stimulation levels (spiking frequencies) in the appropriate sensory pathways'.[7]

CRITIQUE OF PSYCHOPHYSIOLOGY

It would seem, therefore, that physiologists, working within the common-sense assumptions that we experience the world because it impinges upon our bodies and that what we experience is what, directly or indirectly, impinges on our bodies in the form of energy transfer, have made considerable progress in explaining how 'the diversity of working produceth the diversity of experience'. Or have they? In the discussion that follows, I shall question whether:

1. scientific, and in particular physiological, observations have provided any additional, independent evidence in support of the impingement theory of perception/experience;
2. the impingement theory, with its physiological embellishments, goes any way towards explaining perception.

One might expect, a priori, that no *empirical* (i.e. perception-based) observations could provide evidence in support of a fundamental theory of the basis of perception. By unmasking the circularity of physiological explanations of perception that have been developed within the framework of the idea of the 'impingement', I shall show that that a priori expectation is upheld.

According to the Müller doctrine, sensory endings are particularly sensitive to certain types of energy – light energy in the case of retinal endings, sound energy in the case of cochlear endings, and so on – and that when they or their central connections are stimulated, a specific modality of sensation is experienced. The differential sensitivity of sensory pathways is remarkable. Whereas it requires a good deal of mechanical energy to trigger impulses in the visual system, retinal receptors may respond to as little as one quantum of light.[8] According to the Weber–Fechner law, there is a correlation between the intensity of the energy incident on the sense ending and the magnitude of the corresponding subjective experience. These laws seem (a) to provide empirical support for the neurophysiological account of perception, and (b) to contribute to its explanatory force. I will argue, however, that both (a) and (b) are apparent rather than real.

Do the Laws Provide Empirical Support for the Neurophysiological Account of Perception?

Both laws are derived from observations and there can be no doubt about their empirical status. The pertinent question, however, is whether their empirical credentials suffice to sustain the metaphysical implications they are thought to have. Empirical observations may generate laws that correlate one type of experience with another; but can they take us 'beneath' experience to its basis? It seems unlikely that experience can take us outside the closed circle of experience to reveal that upon which experience – experience in general, rather than particular experience – is based. Nevertheless, some writers seem to think that the laws do just that; and that the quantitative observations summarised in them take us beyond (subjective) experience because they are based upon objective measures of physical energy, utilising scientific instruments.

The objectivity of the psychophysical laws – or the extent to which they take us beyond the closed circle of (subjective) experience – is more apparent than real. For the scales on the 'objective' measuring devices used to generate the relevant scientific data are not validated independently of subjective experience. In the final analysis, the scientific estimate of the intensity of light, for example, is rooted in subjective experience of brightness. Objective measures of light intensity would be discarded if they *universally* or *consistently* gave answers that contradicted our subjective experiences. Scientific measurements may 'correct', 'reform' or at least question individual unaided observations but there cannot be a systematic, universal discrepancy. The truth of scientific observations in this context must therefore be based ultimately upon subjective experience and cannot transcend it. Although we may use physical methods of measuring intensity that are apparently independent of our subjective experience – e.g. photosensitive cells – such methods are accepted only because they correlate to a greater or lesser degree, under normal circumstances, with subjective experiences of brightness. If there were simply no correlation whatsoever between the electrical output of a photoelectric cell and some other measure of light intensity directly or indirectly related to experience, this output would not have been used as a way of quantifying light intensity; indeed, it would not have even occurred to anyone to use it in this way. However indirectly related to sensory experience a laboratory quantification of a particular form of energy may be, in the end the rate of exchange between one form of energy and another – the way in which we compare the quantity of one with the quantity of another – reposes upon the gold standard of subjectivity. From this it follows that the Müller observation that a sensory system has a relatively low threshold for the form of energy which it transforms into experience is not only a pre-scientific empirical observation but also one that science could not reform – if reform were necessary – or independently validate. And the same applies to the Weber–Fechner correlations between the 'objective' magnitude of the physical stimulus and the subjective experience of its intensity.

It would seem therefore that the contingent or empirical links uncovered by experimental science between the nature of the stimulus and the intensity and distribution of neural activity on the one hand and between the properties of the stimulus and those of the evoked sensation on the other are not based on discoveries that go beyond, or arise outside of, ordinary experience. Ultimately, the two variables of impinging stimulus and evoked sensation are internally rather than externally related; for our estimate of the properties of the impinging stimulus – and the decision as to whether or not those properties 'justify' the sensation they give rise to – is based upon the norms of, necessarily subjective, experience. The psychophysical laws relate sets of experiences, rather than relating experiences to something external to experience. They do not take us beneath or beyond sensation to its basis.

Interestingly, the psychophysical laws may be even more explicitly embroiled in subjectivity than I have suggested. Recent work[9] has confirmed that it is not possible to measure intensity of subjective sensation in a way that is distinct from and independent of measurement of the physical stimulus from which it is derived; that Fechner's logarithmic transform exists only as a mathematical construction to link reports of sensations with measurements of stimuli; and an experimental subject's conformity to Steven's power law depends on his getting the experiment 'right'.

Whether or not these more recent observations hold up on further investigation and analysis, it remains indisputable that, even if the laws of psychophysics are empirical laws in the sense of correlating one type of observation or experience with another, they are *not* laws about the relationship between experience and something – such as 'pure', objective, material energy – that lies outside of experience in the sense of being its trigger or basis. Psychophysical laws, in other words, provide no independent information about or evidence for a physical basis of perception.

To assert this is merely to reiterate a point that should be obvious: that science, however sophisticated its instrumentation, cannot generate observations – experiences – that somehow enable us to look at the relationship between experience and the world as it were from outside. The relationship between scientific observation and ordinary experience has been well described by Max Born:

> the feeling of hot and cold was not sufficiently precise for a theory of heat to be built upon it; it was replaced by thermometers, therefore, where a thermal difference could be observed as the length of a mercury column, or by some similar device. There are innumerable cases where one of the senses has been replaced, or at least checked, by another. In fact, the whole of science is a maze of such cross-connections whereby the purely geometric structures, such as given by vision or touch, are preferred because they are the most reliable ones. This process is the essence of *objectivisation*, which aims at making observations as independent of the individual observer as possible.[10]

Scientific observations become objective, 'scientific', by virtue of being independent of the individual observer, *not* in virtue of observation. (Indeed, *the elimination of the unobservable* has been a fundamental principle of contemporary physical science, with increasingly interesting consequences regarding the role of the observer in the most objective observations. See Chapter 7.)

Do the Psychophysical Laws Have Explanatory Force?

Perhaps more worrying than the doubtful empirical status of those physiological or psychophysiological laws that are supposed to explain how the individual gains accurate qualitative and quantitative access to external reality is their actual lack of explanatory force. This is especially evident in the case of the Müller doctrine which, ultimately, boils down to a circular restatement of the obvious: Why did I experience those vibrations in the air as sounds? Because they stimulated my auditory, rather than my visual, system. But why do those particular nerve endings count as part of the *auditory* system? Because they are connected with the part of the cortex that is designated the auditory cortex. But why is that particular area of the cortex designated the *auditory* cortex? Because it is concerned with the reception of sound. But what evidence is there that this bit of the cortex *is* concerned with the reception of sound? Well, there is the fact that it is connected to sensory endings that are designed specifically to respond to vibrations in the air. And so we are back to the beginning . . . Once it is teased out, the circularity is undeniable. The destination of the particular sensory pathway defines/explains the starting point, the starting point defines/explains the destination.

Neither the Müller doctrine nor the Weber–Fechner law, nor the physiological researches that have derived from them, furthers our understanding of how 'the diversity of working produceth the diversity of experience'. The Müller doctrine merely refines the observation that we have different senses but does not provide an explanation – or even the framework of an explanation – as to why excitation at different endings by different forms of energy should produce different sensations. While it is easy to explain the special sensitivity of retinal receptors to light and that of the endings in the Organ of Corti to vibrations in the air in terms of their respective physical or biophysical properties, physiology has nothing to offer in explanation of why the relevant sensory pathways, once excited, should be associated with a particular modality of experience. Likewise, there is no a priori reason why increased frequency of firing should be experienced as increased intensity of experience – especially as that increased frequency is not represented in any direct way centrally where neural activity is supposed to become experience.

This lack of explanatory force is explicitly admitted by some scientists and has been especially well expressed by Richard Dawkins:

> The sensation of seeing is for us very different from the sensation of hearing, but this cannot be directly due to the physical differences between light and sound. Both light and sound are, after all, translated . . . by the respective sense organs into the same kind of nerve impulse. It is impossible to tell, from the physical attributes of a nerve impulse, whether it is conveying information about light, about sound or about smell.[11]

Locke made a similar point and saw this as an insoluble mystery. Richard Dawkins, however, feels he has an answer. He asserts rather cryptically that:

> It is because we *internally use* our visual information and our sound information in different ways and for different purposes that the sensations of seeing and hearing are so different. It is not directly because of the physical differences between light and sound.

This is hardly a convincing escape from the circularity of the psychophysical laws. On the contrary, it underlines the explanatory weakness of the Müller doctrine, if the latter is offered as a means of advancing our understanding of the origin of different modalities of sensation, of why the world feels as it does; and, even more, if it is thought to contribute to explaining our being able to feel the world at all.

Which brings us to the fundamental difficulty. Consider the physiologist's intuition that an increased neuronal firing frequency *explains* increased intensity of experience. This depends for its *prima facie* plausibility, for its explanatory force, upon the assumption that there can be – or indeed, should or must be – a correlation between the quantity of energy incident on nervous tissue and the intensity of experience; that the currency of energy must be translatable into the currency of sensation. But to *begin* with this assumption is to bypass, rather than explain, the mystery of perception as it presents itself to us if we assume that perception occurs because the perceived object impinges directly or indirectly upon the nervous system. The mystery that it bypasses is that of *how energy is transformed into sensation, experience, information* or whatever. Only when *that* has been explained might the Weber–Fechner law and the Müller doctrine have any explanatory value. The specific observations of neurophysiologists, correlating stimulus properties, neural activities and the characteristics of subjective reports of sensation, contribute to explaining how 'the diversity of working produceth a diversity of experience' only if we have already explained how 'working' produceth 'experience' at all. Or how energy impinging on the nervous system is transformed into information in, or addressed to, the nervous system. I would argue that physiologists of perception, operating within the framework created by the Müller doctrine and the Weber–Fechner law are in a position of dotting the i's and crossing the t's in a text that has not yet been written.

METAPHYSICAL PROBLEMS

The neurophysiologist's account of perception is an infinitely more sophisticated version of the common-sense CTP. It is therefore appropriate to look at the unresolved problems that, despite its enormous intuitive appeal, beset the CTP.

How are the Neural Events Related to the Mental Events?

This is the question that has dominated recent discussion of the mind/body problem; indeed it is to be counted as the most typical modern formulation of that problem. The CTP can be summarised as follows:

Object $\longleftarrow$ of $\longrightarrow$ Perception

E_o $\longrightarrow$ Causes $\longrightarrow$ E_p

where E_o stands for the event(s) in the object causing the object to be perceived and E_p for the event(s) in the brain that are in some way responsible for perception. What is the relationship between E_p and perception (P)? There are three main answers to this:

(a) E_p causes P (a causal version of substance dualism);
(b) E_p and P are two aspects of the same thing (property dualism);
(c) E_p and P are identical (materialist monism).

Each of these accounts of the relation between E_p and P is associated with different problems.

E_p causes P
There are two interpretations of this:
(i) The causal chain forks, thus

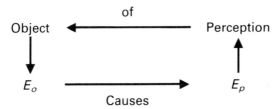

etc. $\rightarrow E_o-1 \longrightarrow E_o \longrightarrow E_p \rightarrow E_p+1 \rightarrow$ etc.
$\downarrow$
P

in which case, the perception, P, is, to use Herbert Feigl's term, a 'dangler'. This interpretation brings us close to a purely epiphenomenal view of consciousness: it is an effect but not, apparently, a cause.[12] Mind becomes an impotent reflection of the world, a metaphysical mist or phosporescence on the sea of reality. This is hardly consistent with the biological view that explains consciousness in terms of its use to the organism possessing it, its role in bringing about states of affairs advantageous to the organism. And it is counter to the common-sense experience of the apparent efficacy of consciousness. We seem to know from direct experience that states of consciousness – moods, pains, pleasures, etc. – influence our behaviour. This, of course, could be accommodated by assuming that the behaviour is itself an effect of E_p (rather than of P) and that the apparent causal relation between consciousness (perception, P) and behaviour (B) is really between physical events that are merely reflected in consciousness:

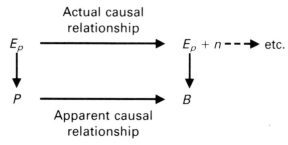

Perception P (of E_p) is followed ultimately by perception B (of behaviour-event $E_p + n$). The causal relationship may look to the subject as if it is between P and B or between P and $E_p + n$; as if, as a result of perception P, he was prompted to enact behaviour $E_p + n$. The actual causal relationships, however, bypass the succession of perceptions altogether: they are between E_p and $E_p + n$; and, separately, between E_p and P (the perception of E_p) and between $E_p + n$ and B (the perception of the behaviour event). The succession of perceptions, and indeed consciousness itself, in so far as it is made up of perceptions, is thus only apparently causally efficacious; in reality, it merely passively reflects material events which alone have causal power.

(ii)   Alternatively, we may envisage the causal chain relevant to perception passing into and then out of a 'mental phase':

Physical	Mental	Physical

etc. ➤ $E_o - 1$ ➤ E_o ⟶ E_p ➤ P ➤ $E_p + 1$ ➤ etc.

It then becomes very puzzling why the causal chain should behave in this way, undergoing two metaphysical changes when other causal chains of a very similar nature remain stubbornly non-mental throughout. For those who adhere to the CTP agree, along with pretty well everyone else, that only a small subset of neural processes is actually associated with mental processes. There is, moreover, little or nothing to distinguish those neural processes that are from those that are not associated with mental processes – apart from their location within the nervous system. And it is very difficult to see why location should be so crucial; why, in short, a nerve impulse should be rewarded for travelling from one place to another with becoming or causing a mental process; and why it should have to commute in this way to become a cause of a mental process.

Some of the difficulties of these two interpretations of the CTP arise because they at least implicitly acquiesce in a dualism of substances: the causal chain either gives off a branch into, or passes through, non-physicality.

E_p and P are Two Aspects of the Same Thing
An alternative approach is to deny a duality of substances and opt for a duality of properties. There is no additional substance beyond the physical brain but the brain has a special set of (non-physical) properties whose instances are mental phenomena, subjective experiences. E_p and P are not two different things (events/processes) but two aspects of the same thing (event/process):

$$\text{etc.} \rightarrow E_o - 1 \rightarrow E_o \longrightarrow \boxed{\begin{array}{c} E_p \\ P \end{array}} \rightarrow E_p + 1 \rightarrow \text{etc.}$$

In most versions of property dualism, the subjective inner experience is regarded as *emergent* with respect to the neural events in the brain. The fact that introspection reveals an absolute difference between objectively observed neural activity and subjective experience is discounted as an argument against emergent property dualism on the grounds that one cannot tell by simple inspection (or introspection) whether or not a property is emergent from some other property;[13] nor can introspection predict whether or not it will in future be reducible to something else. The introspectionist is

not in a position to say whether or not his introspectible experiences may one day turn out to be properties of physical events.

The emergentist position – which asserts that complex neural
networks may have properties or generate events that have
properties utterly different from those of the physical material
upon which they are based – has been widely championed. The
examples most commonly used to illustrate, and so argue for, the
concept of emergence (and the inverse concept of inter-theoretic
reduction) are derived from the physical sciences: the relation of
the liquidity or blueness of water to the microphysics of H_2O
molecules; of heat to molecular kinetics; of light to electromagnetic
energy; etc. The relata, it is argued, are totally different and yet
they turn out to be aspects or properties of the same thing.

The problems of dual aspect or property dualism have been
extensively discussed[14] and the discussion has focused on the
question of whether or not mental phenomena and the neural
events that are supposed to relate to them could conceivably be
aspects of the same thing and whether it is possible to have two
descriptions of the same thing that present it as both physical and
as mental. There has been a good deal of confusion in this area, as
is well illustrated by John Searle's defence of his own version of a
dual aspect or property dualism.[15]

In *Intentionality*, Searle claims that he can 'demythologise' the
whole mind/body problem by considering the relation of the liquid
properties of water to the behaviour of the individual molecules.
He points out that we cannot say of any individual molecule that it
is wet, 'but we can say both that the liquid properties of the water
are caused by the molecular behaviour, and that they are realised
in the collection of the molecules'. The *causal* relation seems to hold
because, if we change the behaviour of the molecules, we lose
liquidity and get something quite different – steam or ice. It seems
equally valid to say that the liquidity is *realised* in the behaviour of
the molecules since the liquidity

> is not some extra juice secreted by the H_2O molecules . . . The
> liquidity, though not epiphenomenal, is realised in the molecular
> structure of the substance in question. So if one is asked "How can
> there be a causal relation between the molecular behaviour and the
> liquidity if the same stuff is both liquid and a collection of mo-
> lecules?", the answer is that there can be causal relations between
> phenomena at different levels in the very same underlying stuff.

Such relations, Searle asserts, are very common in nature; and he instances the solidity of the table he is working on and the elasticity of the tyres on his car as examples of causal properties that are themselves both caused by and realised in an underlying micro-structure. The general principle is that 'two phenomena can be related by both causation and realisation provided that they are so at different levels of description'. He then applies this principle to the relation between neural activity and subjective experience. It would appear that, according to Searle:

Liquidity : Molecules H_2O : : Mental phenomena : Neural events

or

Molecules H_2O	Neural events
Liquidity	Mental phenomena

The mental phenomena and the neural events are the same phenomena described at different levels.

Searle's is a particularly complex version of the dual aspect theory, since the two aspects are both (a) the same phenomena at two different levels of description, and (b) also causally related to one another. As a result, Searle's property dualism has all the vulnerability of the dual-aspect theories, which I shall come to presently, along with some vulnerabilities of its own. Let me deal with Searle's particular problems first.

Searle appears to believe that a phenomenon can relate causally to itself if it is described at two levels; that, in other words, description can itself generate causal relations. For (although he is not very clear on this point), it would seem that it is only through descriptions that the two aspects of the phenomena are distin-guished and, as it were, separated, so that they can then interact. This is of course absurd. How has this absurdity arisen? Because of Searle's tendency (a tendency he is not alone in suffering from) to merge descriptions with levels of observation and levels of observation with the phenomena observed. As a result, the levels are seen to be inherent in the object and the descriptions, confused with the levels, also inherent in the object. Searle, I am sure, doesn't believe this; even less does he believe that *descriptions* causally interact; but the muddle that has led him to seem to believe this is necessary to make his version of emergent/property dualism seem even half-way plausible. One would think it would hardly be necessary to point out that levels and descriptions exist only after the emergence of consciousness (and a rather sophisticated one at that) making sense of the phenomena presented to it. Levels and descriptions at different levels cannot therefore be invoked in explanation of the emergence of consciousness itself or of the manner in which consciousness appears to be connected with that from which it seems to emerge.

Searle's misuse of the concept of levels and of levels of description is, as I have indicated, not unique to him. Patricia Churchland,[16] for example, is similarly muddled when, in order to advance her own brand of reductionist physicalism, she considers the relationship between the blueness of liquid water and the microphysics of H_2O molecules. In order to undermine the idea that blueness is a self-contained and irreducible property that appears *in addition* to the microphysical features of aggregated H_2O, she advances the following argument: the microphysics of H_2O molecules entails that liquid aggregates of them will preferentially scatter incident electromagnetic radiation at a wavelength of about 460 nanometres. This microphysical property affects both human observers and non-human instruments in all the same ways as does blueness. Because of these systematic parallels, the blueness of the object may be *identified* with its disposition to scatter electromagnetic waves preferentially at about 460 nano-metres.

One can construe this as an argument in favour of either a property dualism or (as Churchland herself does) an identity theory. For the present purposes this is less important than the flaw in the argument; namely, that it accepts that there are viewpoints on (cf. levels of observation of, descriptions of) objects or events that may see them differently without appreciating that the assumption of the existence of such viewpoints presupposes precisely that which is being explained, explained away or reduced. Churchland accepts the two distinct properties arising out of the microphysics of water – a tendency to scatter light of a certain sort and a tendency to bring about certain subjective experiences – and then tries to deny that these properties are different. Of course, there is a viewpoint from which they *are* the same – that of physics. To the physicist, or rather the physical instruments with which he performs his physics, the effects of subjectively blue light and that of radiation identified, by means other than subjective experience, as having the same wavelength as blue, are identical. The non-human instrument does not discriminate between these two things. But that is precisely the point the *non-reductionist* would wish to make: namely that, in the absence of consciousness, there is no blueness (or, indeed, other secondary qualities) only scattering of light and the latter is *not* itself a subjective experience.

We can think of the blueness of water as having two aspects:

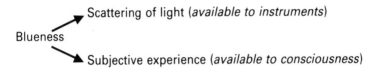

Scattering of light (*available to instruments*)

Blueness

Subjective experience (*available to consciousness*)

Of course these two aspects are aspects of the same thing only to *consciousness* – indeed to a higher order consciousness that has mastered the principles of optics.

The general difficulty with dual aspect theories is that while it is easy to imagine the two aspects – or levels or descriptions – it is equally easy to forget that those aspects – levels and descriptions – require the existence of two viewpoints (the objective and the subjective) and so of consciousness. Most discussion of property dualism therefore bypasses the fundamental problem; namely, the origin of the two aspects (levels, descriptions). It is, of course, possible that a given material object may look totally different from two different aspects. A cat from the rear may look like a tail and from the front like a pair of whiskers. Likewise the same physical phenomenon may appear rather different when presented to the naked eye or to a non-human physical theory. But these differences are differences in the *appearance* of the object and such differences must presuppose a consciousness to which it appears. The difference between one aspect or appearance of an object and another cannot be used as a model of the difference between the object and its appearance to consciousness, between the physical object and its viewpoint-dependent appearings. Aspects are established within consciousness; they cannot be used to establish the relationship of consciousness to that which is not conscious. We cannot readily conceive of a cat that has a physical rear end and a mental front.

Property dualism, or two-aspect dualism, is an elusive theory as will be apparent from the examples I have given; for Searle is really arguing for a causal dualism, and Churchland uses what seem like property-dualist tactics to champion her own purely physicalist, mind-body identity theory.

E_p and P are Identical

The currently most popular view of the relationship between E_p and P – the mind-brain, or mind-brain processes identity theory – asserts a strict identity of P and E_p so that perceptions are physical events in, or states of, the brain:

$$\text{etc.} \longrightarrow E_o - 1 \longrightarrow E_o \longrightarrow E_p P \longrightarrow E_p + 1 \longrightarrow \text{etc.}$$

Identity theories may assert either type-type or token-token identities. According to type-type mind-brain identity theories, a law-like relation holds between mental phenomena and the types (locations and patterns) of nerve impulses identified with them; so that, for example, all the instances of the thought of the type 'I hate Monday mornings' will correlate with brain processes of a certain specific type. Token-token theorists make claims that seem at first sight to be less vulnerable since they merely assert that a given mental phenomenon will be identical with a given brain process, without the further claim that all the instances of a certain type of mental phenomenon will be embodied in the same type of brain process. Under different circumstances, the thought 'I hate Monday mornings' may be identified with, or embodied in, widely different brain processes. Indeed, functionalism (discussed in Chapter 5) allows that the same type of mental phenomenon may be embodied in processes that are not neural at all. Much has been made of the difference between these two forms of identity theory; for present purposes, however, it is sufficient to discuss the important vulnerabilities they have in common.

The assertion that mental processes are numerically identical with certain physical processes faces the obvious difficulty that brain processes and mental phenomena seem utterly unalike. Claims for such strict ('Leibnizian') identity fall foul of Leibniz's law which states that $a = b$ if and only if a and b have every property in common. For one can say of a brain process that it occupies a particular point in space or that it can be displayed on an oscilloscope screen; whereas neither of these things could be said of the subjective sensation of the colour blue or the thought that I hate Monday mornings. These differences between mental phenomena and brain processes seem incompatible with an identity theory; for it is difficult to comprehend an object that is utterly unlike itself. This difficulty is dealt with by proposing that mental phenomena and brain processes are the same stuff viewed within different theoretical frameworks. The recognition that the brain processes uncovered by neurophysiological research and the mental phenomena presenting to introspection are identical then becomes an example of 'intertheoretic reduction'.

Intertheoretic reduction of this kind has many parallels in the history of science, as was pointed out by the early supporters of the theory.[17] Place, for example, stated that the assertion 'Consciousness is a process in the brain' is a reasonable scientific hypothesis, in the way that the statement 'Lightning is motion of electric charges' is a reasonable scientific hypothesis. The identity between the lightning – or the subjectively experienced flash – and the motion of electric charges is strict, Leibnizian, identity and yet contingent. The flash and the motion of the electric charges are exactly the same thing and yet it is possible that the flash could have turned out to have had a different basis.

It seems to me that the identity theory, as defended in this way, becomes a version of the two-aspect dualism or, more precisely, two-description dualism, inasmuch as we have two descriptions of the same thing rather than distinct aspects intrinsic to it. The two aspects of the mental-process-brain-process – the subjective experience, the perception, or whatever, and the objectively observed physico-chemical processes in the neurones – boil down to two types of description of the same thing, just as macroscopic clouds and the fine droplets of which they are made, or heat and the molecular movement with which it is identical, are the same things differently described. Instead of two aspects, we have two theoretical frameworks or two descriptive levels.

We have already dealt with the problems that the two-description approach creates. Explicit identity theories have additional problems of their own. The most important of these is the paradox of an identity (between perceptions and the brain processes) which is at once contingent (so that it could be the subject of a genuine scientific discovery) and, since it is a strict Leibnizian identity, necessary. Kripke made much of this problem in *Naming and Necessity*:

the correspondence between a brain state and a mental state seems to have a certain element of contingency. We have seen that identity is not a relation which can hold contingently between objects. Therefore, if the identity thesis were correct, the element of contingency would not lie in the relation between the mental and the physical states. It cannot lie . . . in the relation between the phenomenon . . . and the way it is felt or appears . . . since in the case of mental phenomena there is no 'appearance' beyond the mental phenomenon itself . . . Materialism must hold . . . that any mental facts are 'ontologically dependent' on physical facts in the straight-forward sense of following from them *by necessity.*[18]

It is counter-intuitive to assert that there is such a necessity. For it seems strange that the discovery that 'red is red' should have been such a late entry into human knowledge.

Kripke's argument is based upon a hostility to the idea of 'contingent identity' and a refusal to accept that, for example,

$$H_2O : water :: brain\ processes : sensations.$$

or

$$molecular\ movement : heat :: brain\ processes : sensations.$$

At the heart of Kripke's argument is his assertion that though *descriptions* can be used to make *contingent* identity statements, this is not possible where the identity is asserted to hold between named objects picked out by rigid designators; that is to say, by terms that have the same reference in every possible world. Kripke argues that the items being identified in the mind/brain processes identity theory can be rigidly identified in precisely this sense. From this it follows that the only identity which could link them is *necessary* identity. It is, however, logically possible for the brain state to exist without the mind state existing. In short, the identity theory requires that the identity should be both necessary (and not contingent) and contingent (and not necessary).

One way out of this impasse for the identity theorist is to accept that the identity is, indeed, a necessary one which only seems to be (but is not) merely contingent. Kripke does not allow this and, in doing so, points to a fundamental flaw in the analogies used by identity theorists. Consider this analogy:

$$Heat : Molecular\ motion :: Pain : C\ Fibre\ firing$$

Could the identity theorist assert that pain is identical with C fibre firing in precisely the way that heat is identical with molecular motion if it were accepted that in both cases the identity was necessary though it seemed to be contingent? In the case of heat : molecular motion, the assertion seems admissible. 'Heat might not have consisted of molecular motion' could be interpreted 'Someone could have sensed a phenomenon as heat even though the phenomenon was not molecular motion'. In the case of pain : C fibre firing, however, this saving interpretation is not available; for pain, unlike heat, exists only as a sensation of pain.

This final point underlines the essential flaw in the idea that the identity theory depends upon a reduction comparable to the intertheoretic reductions that take place when a natural phenomenon is reinterpreted within a new theoretical framework. The lightning flash and the motion of the electrical discharge are, or are at least detected via, two aspects of the same thing: the impact of the phenomenon on the eyes and its impact on recording instruments. The sensation and its supposed physical basis cannot be 'two aspects' in the same sense. Such plausibility as the identity theory has, it enjoys by virtue of exploiting the intuitive appeal of the dual-aspect theory while distancing itself from it. The appeal of the dual-aspect theory – its seeming to make sense – depends, as I have already indicated, on crude analogies:

FRONT : BACK : : HEAT : MOLECULAR MOTION : : SENSATIONS : BRAIN
(as of a house)   PROCESSES

or

Aspects of object ≡ Levels of description of phenomenon ≡ Mind/Brain

Far from addressing the problems associated with dual-aspect theories, the identity theory (from which, as I have suggested, it is not clearly distinguished) is more deeply embroiled in them. For identity theories are essentially 'dual-description' theories. Perceptions and the neural processes that underlie them are not so much the same things approached from different angles as the same things described differently or brought under different theoretical paradigms. But, as already pointed out, the idea of different paradigms, or different descriptions, presupposes consciousness, indeed a very highly developed consciousness, and so cannot be employed to account for the difference (only apparent, it is claimed) between 'unconscious' neural processes and conscious mental events. It may be a recognition of the inadmissability of the

analogy between the different aspects of an object and the difference between the mental and the physical that in part lies behind
Nagel's insistence on the irreducible difference between the objective view that yields neural processes and the subjective one that
experiences phenomenal, inner reality.[19] However, Nagel's objection doesn't go far enough back – as will be discussed in Chapter 5.

Further Problems

These, then, are the apparently insuperable problems which we
encounter if we believe that perceptions are in some way identical
with neural processes. But the difficulties with the CTP begin
further back than that. Let us look at the theory again:

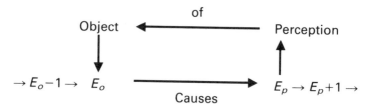

and consider some of these further difficulties.

The Boundlessness of the Causal Chain
The diagram above depicts a causal chain that stretches from the
events in the object to those events in the nervous system that
constitute, or are directly related to, perception of the object. E_o is a
kind of beginning and E_p is a kind of end. But, of course, every
cause is an effect of some prior cause and every effect is a cause of
some further effect; in short, a causal chain has no intrinsic
beginning or end. These limits arise only within an established
viewpoint – that of the perceiving subject for whom the piece of
matter 'out there' is already assumed to have the status of an object
(or, indeed, of an object of perception). Without this presupposed
viewpoint, there is nothing to determine that E_o should count as a
beginning or E_p as an end. Unless, however, E_o and E_p are,
respectively, beginning and end, there is no explanation of why E_p
(rather than E_p+1, or E_p+2, etc.) should relate to P or why P
should be *of E_o* (or O) rather than of E_o-1, E_o-2 etc. If there is
no objective basis for the status of E_o and E_p as limits, there is no
compelling reason why E_p should be the event that reaches back

to E_o (rather than say $E_o+10{,}000$) nor why, if it does reach back, it should reach to E_o rather than $E_o-10{,}000$, or, indeed, to the origin of the causal chain, at the beginning of time. The chain $E_o \longrightarrow E_p$ seen in objective perspective – that is from no perspective, from the viewpointless view implicit in the physicalist framework of the CTP – would appear as a not terribly distinguished fragment of a boundless causal net, as in Figure 3.2.

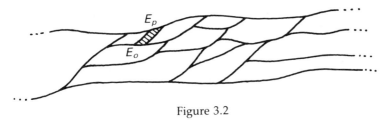

Figure 3.2

Perceptual Events and Perceived Objects

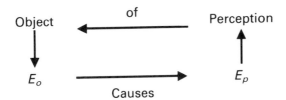

The causal chain links events with events – E_o with E_p. But it is *objects* that I perceive – and *events in objects*. Indeed, I perceive both objects and events and can separate – and relate – them. In other words, the basis of perception is (to use Hume's phrase) 'perishable impressions' caused by change; and yet I perceive enduring objects as the background to changes also perceived. The diagram should therefore be modified as follows:

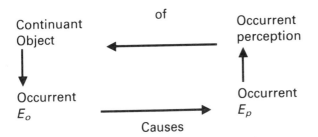

How is the enduring object (not to speak of the contrasts between enduring objects and the changes they undergo) constructed out of a flux of events – events in the object itself and in the brain?

Many solutions have been proposed to this problem but none has proved satisfactory. In fact, it has seemed so intractable that even some materialist philosophers have resorted to the desperate strategem of denying that material objects are the source of perception. They have espoused varying forms of phenomenalism, suggesting that the object itself does not exist independently of perception; that, indeed, it is a construct out of perceptions:

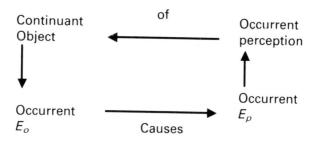

E_o no longer arises out of, or in, a pre-existing stable object. All is flux; continuants are artefacts of consciousness. Even if stable objects did exist independently of consciousness, there could be no empirical evidence for this and such objects would not be the same as the objects constructed by consciousness. Phenomenalism is, of course, incompatible with the CTP and impingement views of perception which begin with solid objects colliding with a solid body.[20]

Perceiving Causation

If all perception is itself the product of causation, how is it that we are able to perceive, or to identify, certain causal tracks through the perceived world? This puzzle has two facets:

(a) If causation informs the whole of perception, then specific causal tracks should not be evident in the perceived world. Causation should be no more *focal* than space – or perception itself.

(b) It may be argued that we are talking about two different dimensions of causation: a vertical dimension in which the perceived world is linked with the brain of the perceiver; and a horizontal dimension in which perceived events are linked:

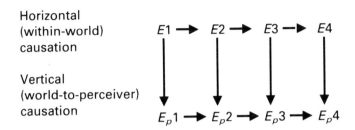

Horizontal (within-world) causation

Vertical (world-to-perceiver) causation

It is difficult to imagine a unified theory that would encompass both of these dimensions of causation, let alone a physicalist one. At the very least, it would have to give some explanation of the emergence of these two dimensions of causation. Even more intractable is the problem of seeing how the causal relations so central to the CTP are themselves perceived.

Monotonous Nervous System, Infinitely Various World
The perceived world is infinitely various, within and across modalities of sensation. Moreover, there is a clear distinction between present and past perception (memory); between memory and thought; between passive and active states of mind (day-dreaming versus active recall; association of ideas versus directed meditation); and between the content and the level of conscious-ness. For causal theorists there are only nerve impulses all of which are essentially the same. Perception, that is to say, boils down to the passage of sodium, potassium and other ions across semi-permeable membranes. It is legitimate, therefore, to ask what it is that is special about flea-bitten membranes that they should open up one object (the body) to all others, to a world? That they should make of one body a site where the variousness of all other bodies is in some way received.

There are several responses to this puzzle. They all involve the use of terms of concepts that are illegitimate within the physicalist framework of the CTP. Yes, it will be conceded, there *is* an apparent discrepancy between the rather simple impulses in the nervous system and the complex representations of the world they afford us. This discrepancy, however, disappears when we recog-nise that it is not in individual nerve impulses that we must seek our representations of their world, but in their patterns. We must think of the nervous system encoding the perceived world; and in trying to understand this process we should consider not individual spikes but their potentially infinite combinations. The monotony of the individual neurones is irrelevant; what matters is the infinite variety of their combinations, of their patterns, which will become evident when we look at the nervous system at the right level.

I shall have something to say about the language of neurophysiological description shortly. However, it is necessary to say a word or two here to refute this seemingly compelling argument. We are so used to hearing talk about the nervous system 'encoding' the outside world that it is easy to forget that this is a metaphor and it is one that has no place in serious philosophical discussion of the mind–body problem or the philosophy of perception. The reason the coding metaphor has such currency in contemporary talk about perception is that it seems to suggest a way in which very simple and apparently homogeneous elements such as nerve impulses can generate the richness and variety of consciousness.

Consider Morse code. Using this very simple system, constructed out of dots and dashes, it is possible to encode a text of any degree of richness – even, for example, the works of Shakespeare. We may imagine therefore that neural dots and dashes – trains of impulses – can encode the variousness of experience. The analogy is attractive, but illegitimate. For the richness of morse code is a borrowed richness. First, morse is parasitic, as all codes are, upon a primary, natural language. The meanings of morse are borrowed from the meanings of, for example, English and messages encoded in it are meaningful only when they are interpreted, that is, decoded. Where is the decoder in the nervous system? In so far as it translates at all, the nervous system translates only from nerve impulses into nerve impulses, from sodium fluxes into sodium fluxes. This would not count as decoding unless muscular activity and other outputs were regarded as translations out of 'impulsese' into an interpreted language. But to understand decoding in this way would be to espouse behaviourism and to bypass consciousness altogether. To 'translate' from afferent to efferent impulses, or from afferent impulses to motor activity, is not to 'translate' from nerve impulses into experience or consciousness.

There is, however, a second, even more profound objection to the coding metaphor. For translation from Morse into natural language does not take us all the way to consciousness; and, in the absence of consciousness, language is merely variegated sound, rather than the rich varieties of meaning that are embodied in, for example, Shakespeare's texts. No one outside of the wilder sects of the AI fraternity would suggest that a device that translated Morse into natural language characters on the screen of a computer was releasing the consciousness implicit in morse. Natural languages such as English in turn owe their meanings to the conscious experiences of language users. Codes, in short, ultimately owe their meanings – and the variety that is constructed out of their monotonous elements – to consciousness. If the nervous system, therefore, owes the richness of the experiences which its activities embodies to the complexity of its codes, it must, ultimately owe its consciousness – to consciousness; for this will be required to turn its codes into complex experienced meanings; into experiences.

The coding explanation is another example of an explanation that depends upon assuming the thing that has to be explained. The appeal to 'levels' and 'patterns' – the claim that the richness of the experienced world is represented in patterns of impulses visible only if one examines the nervous system at the right level – is similarly flawed. Consider levels. Neural activity, it is argued, consists of individual nerve impulses only at a certain level of observation or description, just as a picture in a newspaper consists of individual dots of print only at a certain level of observation or description. And just as we have no difficulty in understanding how complex and very different pictures can be derived from different combinations of very similar dots, so we should have no difficulty understanding how complex experiences can be built up out of similar, rather simple, nerve impulses. This appeal to levels is inadmissible for the same reason that 'aspects' (discussed earlier) are not allowed in the dual-aspect theory. Just as different aspects cannot be the basis of the difference between the world of nerve impulses and that of subjective experience because the concept of an aspect is internal to the realm of perception, and so posterior to the emergence of consciousness, so levels cannot be the basis of the difference between the individual nerve impulses, which are all the same, and the infinitely various world of subjective experience. And what of 'patterns'? A similar objection holds: patterns are not inherent in multiples of nerve impulses; they have to be extracted by perception; they have to be perceived, to be made explicit in order to come into being. Consider this array of neurones in a state of activity:

$$\begin{matrix} \star & \star & \star & \star \\ \star & \star & \star & \star \\ \star & \star & \star & \star \end{matrix}$$

What is the pattern of this activity? Is it

★　★　★　★　＋　★　★　★　★　＋　★　★　★　★　?

Or is it

$$\begin{matrix} \star & \star & & \star & \star \\ \star & \star & + & \star & \star \\ \star & \star & & \star & \star \end{matrix}$$

Or is it a collection of six pairs? There is simply no answer to this question. Intrinsically, or from the physicalist standpoint, it is none of these. The fact that a vast number of possible patterns could be extracted from this simple collection should make this shiningly clear. A consciousness is required to make the necessary decision in order that one pattern may emerge rather than another. If the nervous system is to be viewed as a physico-chemical system, as something that has no viewpoint, then the events in it have no more intrinsic patterns than do the events in a stone, or an avalanche.

The Unities of Consciousness
Human consciousness is characterised by unities at different levels. There is the unity of the moment. Different tactile and proprioceptive sensations amount to a coherent body image. Different visual sensations cohere to a visual field. And then sensations from different modalities converge to a general sensory field, an organised moment-by-moment presence of a world, so that the feeling in my hand as I hold a stone, the sight of the sea and the sound of the seagull behind me are all not merely present but co-present. Beyond this synchronic unity, there is a unity across time: current sensations converge with knowledge and memory and desire to make sense of the sensory experience of the present. At the lowest level, this diachronic unity is manifested in

the fact that I not only experience this object but I recognise it – as something belonging to a certain kind; I identify it as yours, as mine, as something I have seen before; and it means something to me in terms of my appetites and needs and ambitions. Above and beyond this, the object carries an aura of familiarity. At a higher level, there is the unity of the self that coheres over time, so that a person P_2 at time t_2 is in some sense identical to the person P_1 at time t_1. This identity operates at a conscious level above that of the mere identity of the body or continuity of habits. It is an explicit sense of continuing self which includes a sense of responsibility over time ('*I did that*') and, beneath this, a deep sense of psychological continuity ('I remember that experience', 'I was there then'). Sensations and memories converge to create a continuing, if interrupted, sense of a coherent self. This sense of self is quite robust: when we wake up, we not only remember what we know, but also who we are. We are able to resume ourselves after sleep, after an alcoholic stupor, after an epileptic fit, after prolonged coma. In the light of these unities, it seems necessary to postulate a systematic set of relationships between the patterns of memory and the sense of 'I', the qualitative interior of mental experience.[21]

The basis of these unities does not seem to lie within the nervous system as it is currently conceived. Since Sherrington's famous book,[22] there has been much talk of the integrative activity of the nervous system, based upon the convergence of nervous pathways. But the scattered activity of different parts of the nervous system seems to converge only at the cost of merging and so losing the components that came together in the process of convergence. Typically convergence takes place at synapses. This may be illustrated as in Figure 3.3.

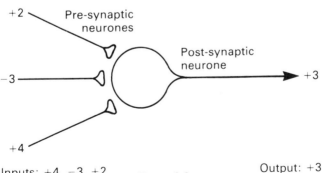

Inputs: +4, −3, +2   Figure 3.3   Output: +3

This is clearly a simplification of what may take place in many millions of neurones simultaneously. Nevertheless, there is no neurophysiological model of the kind of convergence that would seem to be necessary for the many different sensations of the moment to be synthesised into the instantaneous sense of 'being here' without loss of the distinctiveness and specificity of the individual components; or of how the experience of many different moments can be synthesised into a sense of continuing self without those moments losing their separateness in memory. As for the recovery of consciousness, or wakefulness, there is no imaginable physiology of this 'light dawning over the whole'.[23] Neural activity, temporally and spatially dispersed, has nothing within itself to create the basis of these fundamental unities of consciousness.

Intentionality
The causal theory of perception relates the object and contents of perception in two directions: there is an afferent limb connecting the object with the nervous system in which perception is generated; and an efferent limb in virtue of which the neural events 'reach out to' or 'are about or of' the object. The efferent limb carries the intentionality or aboutness that is fundamental to perception:

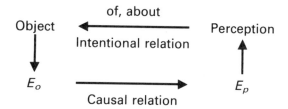

We have a circuit of what Searle has referred to as 'intentional causation'.

Intentionality is usually overlooked by causal theorists who tend to see their job as being to deal with the afferent limb. It is ironic, however, that one of the features of the CTP – its locating the basis of perception literally in the head, at a particular place, a measurable distance, away from the perceived object – actually italicises, exacerbates, the mystery of intentionality.[24] Whatever other barriers intentionality may raise to the understanding of perception, or consciousness, in biological terms (which is, after all the ultimate purpose of the CTP), there is one thing that cannot be denied: there are no other causal chains in nature in which events causally downstream refer back causally upstream to the objects that are involved in producing their causal ancestors. The intentionality of perceptions – and indeed of other mental phenomena – makes them non-analogous to material phenomena outside of the nervous system. And nothing that takes place within the nervous system can explain why intentionality should emerge there rather than elsewhere.

APPARENT ATTRACTIONS OF THE CTP

In the light of what has been said, the consensus in favour of some version or other of the CTP might be a source of wonderment. It will be appropriate, therefore, to consider why the CTP is so attractive. I shall look at this under three headings:

(a) the way in which it seems to account for ordinary and not-so-ordinary observations about the dependence of mind function and mind contents on brain function and brain position;
(b) the way in which the CTP seems to constrain perception to be true and so ensure the survival value of consciousness;
(c) the language of neuromythology.

The fundamental attractiveness of the theory is that it promises to biologise consciousness and seems to point towards a unified account of the world that encompasses not only physical events but also apparently non-physical, or mental, events. The causal thread that reaches from the perceived object to the perception and on from that to the motor activity of the perceiver acting on the material world symbolises an ontological homogeneity in the world. In other words, the CTP, or something like it, is central to the project of describing the whole of reality in terms of a single set of (physico-chemical) mechanisms.

Observational Basis of CTP

The evidence for the belief that we perceive the world because energy arising from it impinges on our bodies, and more particularly our brains, ranges from the simplest observations of everyday life to the most sophisticated neurophysiological enquiries. Here is some of this evidence:

(i) Brain Position Determines Experience Content

Where our head is (in space and in time) is the most important determinant of the content of our consciousness. If my head is in Manchester in 1990, it is samples of Manchester-1990 that I experience. *Which* samples, will depend on precisely where and when my head is. The direction of my head, which will fix the direction of my eyes, etc., will be another determinant. And so, also, will be the position of other objects. The street cannot become part of the present content of my consciousness because the walls of the house intervene between my brain and it, preventing me from hearing or seeing it.

In short, the dependency of what I experience perceptually upon what is there to impinge on my senses is amply demonstrated by the fact that the position of my head (and hence my brain and its sense endings) determines what I perceive.

(ii) Sense-Ending State Influences Experience Content

If I cover my ears I do not hear. If I close or cover my eyes, I do not see. If my eyes or ears are destroyed or removed, I do not see or hear. And damage short of destruction may dramatically alter the experienced quality of what is seen or heard.

(iii) Physiological Changes in Brain Function Lead to Changes in Content of Consciousness

If, for example, there are changes in the brain associated with sleep or drowsiness, there are dramatic changes in the content and quality of consciousness. These may be correlated with changes in the electrical activity of the brain as recorded in an electro-encephalogram.

Points (ii) and (iii) fit with the idea that perceptual experience is dependent not only on the energy impinging on the nervous system but on the neural media through which it is refracted on its way to those central places where it becomes perception – on the state of the brain and its sensory connections.

(iv) Correlation Between the Intensity of the Impinging Energy (e.g. Physical Luminance), the Distribution and Intensity of Spiking Frequencies and the Subjective Sensation

We have already dealt with this earlier. It is simply reiterated here as part of the apparent evidence for the CTP.

(v) Brain Dysfunction Leads to Abnormalities of, or Absence of,
Perception

Observations under this heading range from the crude to the most refined. Decapitation, with associated brain removal, leads to a perceptible decline in IQ in most instances. Indeed, brain removal leads to mind removal. Brain injury, due for example to trauma or to stroke, or to experimental lesions, seriously interferes with perception and may remove perception completely, either temporarily or permanently. There are rough correlations between the kinds of brain injury and the deficits observed in perception, as is described in a vast neuropsychological literature. Brain dysfunction – due to uncontrolled electrical discharges as in epilepsy or to the effects of drugs or toxins damping down electrical activity – will lead to disturbance or loss of consciousness. Contrariwise, pseudo-perceptions, ranging from crude, unformed noises and flashes of light through to complex scenes with accompanying meanings and emotions, can be generated by spontaneous discharges of the brain or in the laboratory by stimulating electrodes.

All of these observations seem to fit with, and to give support to, the idea that perception is the result of the impact of the perceived objects on an appropriately tuned nervous system.

The CTP Seems to Constrain Perception to be True

The CTP seems to constrain perception to be true and thus to ensure the adaptive or survival value of consciousness.

I have related the CTP to the wider project of 'biologising' consciousness. In the previous chapter, we looked at the explanation of consciousness in evolutionary terms. It is clearly an evolutionary imperative that perception should be generally true. The CTP, by apparently guaranteeing the general truth of perception, even if it does not ensure that perception is true on all occasions, seems on the whole to satisfy that evolutionary imperative.[25] Let us therefore look critically at this apparent constraint-to-truth that the causal connection between the content of perception and the perceived object seems to impose on perception.

The impingement theory has as its fundamental tenet that what we perceive is also the *occasion* of our perceiving: the object that I see now is, in part, responsible for my seeing. My seeing is thus occasioned by the content of what I see. This at once seems to

constrain perception to be *of what is 'really there'*. The impingement thus seemingly provides a kind of explanation of the 'truth'
of normal perception and a basis for distinguishing between
normal and pathological perception, or between perceptions and
hallucinations:

Normal (True) Perception

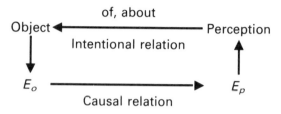

Hallucination

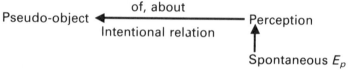

In the case of normal perceptions, experience is triggered by that
which is the external object of the experience; in the case of
abnormal perception, experience is not so occasioned, being triggered by, for example, events internal to the body, or more
specifically the brain, of the subject.

Ultimately, the framework of physiological investigation and
discourse is that of common sense. This takes as read – and
overlooks the inexplicability of – the fact that I have access to that
part of the world where I am; that I perceive *this*, rather than
something else, because it is actually here – in virtue of really
existing and being in my vicinity – while other things are not here;
that I perceive what is actually 'there'. The belief that the impingement theory ensures that we usually perceive what is really there –
so that perception is consequently usually true – is a potent one but
it is also naive in so far as it takes as self-evident something that a
true explanation of perception would have to explain. Let us
examine more closely what is meant by 'really there'.

There are many things that are 'really there' – i.e. exist – which I
would not be entitled to perceive. For example, New York is 'really
there' but I cannot, at present, perceive it. Any naked eye vision I
(currently in the United Kingdom) had of New York would be an

hallucination – perceptually untrue. In other words, it is not enough that an object or event exists for it to count as 'really there' in the sense required to give the impingement theory its attraction. The constraint that I shall perceive only what is 'really there' boils down on further analysis to the guarantee that I shall perceive only what is actually present to my senses. And this, of course, is circular.

Or is there some way of analysing 'present to my senses' to make the constraint that I shall perceive only what is present to my senses other than trivially tautologous and no constraint at all? 'Present to my senses' implies 'falling within my current or present sensory field'. In the case of touch, the sensory field at any given moment is an area conterminous with the surface of my body so that 'present to my senses' means 'touching my body'. In the case of other senses, however – such as vision and hearing and, even more problematically, smell – the sensory field is not so readily defined. The visual field, for example, will depend not only upon the distribution of opaque objects in relation to my eye, but also upon the background illumination, the properties of distant objects relative to their surroundings (determining sharpness of contrast) and (more damagingly still) upon the visual acuity of the perceiver. The idea of 'an acoustic field' is even more perplexing, being defined by the surface connecting the locations of all the objects that can be heard at a given moment.

It does not, therefore, help the impingement theory to redefine 'present to the senses' as 'falling within the sensory field' – not only because the latter is enormously variable but also because it is ultimately dependent upon the senses themselves. The visual field consists of whatever I can see at a given time; the overall sensory field of whatever I can sense. At best, the constraint arising out of the impingement theory could be reformulated as follows: 'We shall perceive/sense only whatever we might expect ourselves to perceive/sense under the conditions in question'. Since these expectations are also based upon (previous) sense experience, the triviality of the 'constraint' returns. The constraint may guarantee the *coherence* of sense experience (though I am not sure even of this); *but it will not guarantee that perception is of and only of what is truly there, where 'there' is defined independently of sense experience.* It will not, in other words, provide independent support for a 'correspondence' theory of perception.

The attractiveness of the CTP, that it explains perception in such a way as to provide an objective basis for its general truthfulness, and so for its survival value, is thus illusory. It gives no basis for the belief that mind is part of nature, or, more generally, that consciousness is ontologically continuous with unconscious matter.

The Language of Neuromythology

Twentieth-century neurophysiologists have shown in considerable detail how the nervous system transforms the energy impinging upon its receptors into patterns of nerve impulses and how those impulse patterns correspond to the presence of objects or the occurrence of events. The elegant experiments of Adrian, Wald, Granit and Iggo – to choose a few names at random – have demonstrated how sensory endings behave as transducers, transforming various forms of incident energy into the electrochemical activity that eventually gives rise to propagated nerve impulses. But it has been mistakenly thought that these kinds of observations – which merely describe how one form of energy is transduced into another – contribute to an understanding of how we perceive the world. The hidden assumption – absurd as soon as it is made explicit – is that the process by which energy is transformed into information or events, gives rise to experience, is somehow analogous to that by which one form of energy is transduced into another. Without this assumption, it would be impossible to sustain the illusion that contemporary neurophysiology begins to offer any kind of explanation of (to use the title of Adrian's famous book[26]) 'the basis of sensation'.

It is of course self-evident that the transformation of, say, light into electrochemical energy and the subsequent redistribution of electrochemical activity in the nervous system is in no way analogous to the transformation of energy into information, to the process by which unconscious events become conscious experiences so that one type of body (the living human body) is 'worlded' in the way that other bodies (e.g. rocks) are not. There are many transducers that are not sense organs – for example photo-electric cells – so transduction is not itself sufficient to create sensations out of the impingement of energy arising from one body upon another. Since this *is* so obvious, we have to ask ourselves how the illusion that the events in sensory endings and their proximal connections explain perception could have been sustained for so long.

The power of neuromythology resides in the subtlety with which it juggles descriptive terms. Neurophysiological observations seem to provide an explanation of perception only because those observations are described in increasingly mentalistic terms as one proceeds from the periphery to the centre of the nervous system. The gap between the physical and the mental is bridged by describing end-organ events in rigidly physical terms, and events occurring more centrally in psychological terms. As a nerve impulse travels along an afferent fibre, it also propagates from one part of Roget's *Thesaurus* to another, a process that is accelerated when it manages to leap over a synaptic cleft and join its colleagues on the other side. As the impulse propagates centrally, it leaves the world of 'energy transformations' and enters the world of 'signals' until, two or three feet and two or three synapses later, it has become 'information', or part of a pattern of impulses that count as information. In short, electrochemical activity leaves the sense-ending as physical events and arrives somewhere in the cortex as information. No explanation whatsoever is offered as to how this happens – and yet it cries out for explanation as all parties are agreed that the electrochemical activity remains electrochemical activity throughout.

The lack of explanation is sometimes frankly admitted: Peter Nathan's 1977 article in *Brain*, reviewing certain aspects of pain,[27] contains the following passage:

> It should be emphasised that the spinal cord is not concerned with sensation, with the final sensory act that appears in consciousness. It is the part of the nervous system concerned with immediate reflex responses. What we call sensation is added by the cranial end of the central nervous system.

Such candour is by no means universal. More often the curious process by which a propagated potential picks up mentalistic descriptors and sheds physical ones – rather in the manner of a high-speed mail-train collecting and dropping mailbags – is accepted without question.

The problem is to some extent concealed because of a certain flexibility in the terminology used to describe an impulse at any particular point in the sensory path. Prolepsis and regression are the important rhetorical devices here. An event in a sensory receptor may sometimes be described quite mentalistically – as a 'signal', for example – in anticipation of its causal successor's ultimate spiritual elevation (prolepsis). Alternatively, the most central events, which are supposed to be identical with, or the basis of, perceptions are described in unreconstructed physicalistic terms (regression). Mentalistic descriptions are sometimes taken even further back than the most peripheral neural events, into the energy in the outside world even before it impinges on the nervous system. The metaphysical duties of the nervous system are thereby greatly lightened; for the energy/information barrier – or the body–mind gap – may be crossed simply by referring to, for example, light not only as 'energy' but also as 'information', so that at the very least, it possess *intrinsically* the subjective qualities of the experience of it, such as brightness. This may sometimes reach the point of absurdity; for example, Johnson-Laird quotes J. J. Gibson to the effect that 'light reflected from surfaces and focused on the retinae contains a large amount of information'.[28] On the other hand, events in the cerebral cortex – even in the 'highest levels' of the cortex – sensory association areas or whatever – may be described in brutally physicalistic terms: as electrochemical events, or more mentalistically as 'complex information processing'.

Since it is rarely made clear at what place in the nervous system a train of nerve impulses is supposed to pass over spiritually to the other side, it becomes more difficult to pinpoint the absurdity or explanatory weakness of neuromythological discourse. It used to be said that nerve impulses 'entered consciousness' in the thalamus, but this suggestion has been quietly shelved. Even neurophysiologists find the idea of the thalamus as the back door or ground floor of consciousness somewhat embarrassingly naive. But superficially more cunning neurophysiological theories of consciousness suffer from the same fundamental naivety. They are rooted in the belief that the transduction of unconscious energy understood in physicalistic terms from one form to another and its redistribution within the nervous system somehow accounts for the emergence of consciousness out of that energy, for its transformation into information; that energy transduction will explain how, in the human body, matter becomes conscious of itself.

CONCLUSION

The impingement theories of perception – which seem so inescapably tied to common sense, to scientific investigation and to currently mainstream English-language philosophical thought – are quite insufficient as explanations of perception, or even as a framework in which such an explanation might be sought. If they have apparent explanatory force, it is because they narrow the scope of perception, of consciousness, of being worlded, of being situated, to a state of being in receipt of a discrete stream of information. And they solve the problem of the transformation of physical events into consciousness, of energy into information, by using these and other key terms interchangeably at almost every stage in the processes that are supposed to lead from one to the other.

If it were not for these two types of move – the narrowing of the scope of consciousness and the elision of the difference between energy and information – the various forms of the CTP would not even begin to look like explanations of consciousness. It would be observed that:

(a) consciousness – the dehiscence or opening up of matter into a (someone's) world – is not a mere stream of information (or data required to solve problems); and

(b) it is a tautology that we perceive that which impinges on us.

Point (b) is worthy of further comment. To be aware of something is to be aware of it as present and of oneself as present to it. A thing has presence only in so far as it is present to someone; in so far as it has entered the present tense of someone's consciousness. I think enough has been already said to justify profound doubts that presence can be intelligibly described as being caused by the direct or indirect impingement of one object on another (e.g. a brain understood as a physical object). Nor can 'thereness' be inherent in an object in the absence of a subject: things are not sufficient, or even necessary, causes of their own presence. For this reason, there must be a circularity implicit in the CTP: it boils down to the claim that a thing becomes present in virtue of its presence to the nervous system. The causal relationship (between for example a material object and the nervous system) cannot bring about presence, at the very least because causation is essentially a relation between presences. It is posterior to, rather than under-lying, presence.

What is the implication of this? If we imagine that physiologists have brought us any nearer to explaining how perception is possible – how you and I are 'worlded' – then we are seriously deluded. But does this imply that the enormous progress that has seemingly been made in sensory physiology over the last two hundred years is only apparent rather than real? It does not. Physiologists – and psychologists – have greatly advanced our real knowledge of the conditions (both inside and outside of the body) under which perception is possible, and of the influences that constrain what we perceive. No doubt we shall, in the future, sufficiently understand the cerebral constraints on perception to be able to manipulate them to the advantage of the brain-injured. Even so, the situation of neuroscience is most fairly compared to that of a developing child learning that it can, in part, influence the experiences that it has by moving its head or its entire body. Further development and experimentation leads it to have an increasingly sophisticated ability to manipulate the contents of its sense experiences. At no time, however, would anyone claim that the child is getting anywhere nearer to an understanding of the basis of perception. The physiological community is like an enormously more sophisticated version of that child. It knows more and more about the processes involved in perception but has learned nothing about why there is perception at all, how those processes lead up to, or come to be, the 'worlded' state of certain objects – namely living human bodies. For there is nothing in what has been discovered of the properties of the brain – understood in terms of the physico-chemical laws physiologists and physicalist philosophers usually appeal to – that answers to the philosophical mystery of perception whereby the chain of material events gives rise to consciousness of those events. The laws relating physical events 'out there', neurophysiological events, and perceptual experience do not explain perceptual experience. Nor would one expect them to do so, since they arise out of, and are ultimately validated by, perceptual experience. It should not surprise us that the observations of physiology do not reveal how observation is possible at all. That perceptions, however sophisticated, have not uncovered the metaphysical basis of perception. We do not yet have a neurophysiology of mind, nor even the beginnings of it.

None of this, I would emphasise again, invalidates sensory physiology; nor does it detract from the great advances that have been made in the study of the neural processes apparently required for perception. Which points up another mystery: how can we be making such advances in our detailed account of perception when we do not understand how perception is possible at all? How is it that neuroscientists are able increasingly to relate neural events to subjective experiences while they have no explanation for the fact that the brain appears to be the seat of subjective experience; that they seem to be able to sort out the details of the relations between neural and other events even though the framework of explanation within which these details make sense is valid only in so far as it is a tautology? It seems that we do not as yet have any idea how to relate the specific soluble problems of perception – addressed by physiologists and psychologists – to the mystery of how the world is present to us – how we are 'worlded'. The relation between physiological problems and their solutions and metaphysical mysteries remains itself shrouded in mystery.

The contrast between the physiologists' increasing ability to explain details while the metaphysical framework of their activities remains profoundly unsatisfactory is not unique within science. They are not alone, that is, in working within an unexplained framework of explanation. The same is true of physicists. The unintelligibility of the concept of matter does not cancel the validity – or the practical value – of Newton's Laws of Motion or the General Theory of Relativity. Our bridges and planes and machines are no less safe and effective for having been built by human beings whose conception of matter remains profoundly unsatisfactory. Even less does the unexplained explanatory framework of sensory physiology imply that there is anything fraudulent about psycho-physical correlations between the quantity of energy impinging on sense endings and the intensity of the resulting subjective experience even though there is no explanation of how, in the brain, mere energy becomes awareness (of that energy).

The present chapter, therefore, has not been intended as a critique of sensory physiology as such – nor does it question the value of physiological investigation in this area – only of certain claims regarding its metaphysical implications. In a sense, this chapter merely reiterates the unsurprising and, one would have hoped obvious, fact that physiology has not discovered – nor will it discover – the 'basis' of perception; nor do, or will, its discoveries explain perception at a metaphysical level. Physiology begins after the metaphysical issues have been settled or shelved. The impingement theory provides a framework for physiological investigation and the interpretation of observations. It is not been proved or supported by physiology. The great advances made by modern sensory physiology, resulting from the refinement of recording techniques, add nothing to the respectability of, say, materialism. The *metaphysical* attractions of the impingement theory of perception – in either its common sense or hi-tech scientific versions – are as illusory as its explanatory force. They have rendered humoral theories of perception, but not say dualism or Berkeleian monism, untenable. Thinking by transferred epithet has encouraged the false belief that the CTP offers a metaphysical explanation of how it is that there is such a thing as perception. It will take us a long time and a lot of seeing to undo that belief.

We can summarise the burden of this and the previous chapter by stating that the biological accounts of consciousness have contributed nothing to furthering our understanding of its essential nature or helping us to understand how it is possible or how it relates to the other phenomena of the world. On the contrary, they have constructed a great wall of pseudo-explanations within our intellect, preventing us even from seeing what consciousness is.

APPENDIX:
SOME FURTHER OBSERVATIONS ON THE LANGUAGE OF NEUROMYTHOLOGY WITH SPECIAL REFERENCE TO 'INFORMATION'

A *picture* held us captive. And we could not get outside of it for it lay in our language and language seemed to repeat it to us inexorably.

Wittgenstein[29]

Thinking by Transferred Epithet

Both biological and computational models of consciousness depend for their apparent plausibility upon the use of certain terms that have a multiplicity of meanings. These terms are popular with theorists because within the shades of their voluminous connotative folds arguments that would not stand up in broad daylight may seem to carry conviction. The reader or listener, in allowing the use of the terms, does not know what he is taking on. The most important characteristic of these terms is that they have a foot in both camps: they can be applied to machines as well as to human beings and their deployment erodes, or elides, or conjures away, the barriers between man and machine, between consciousness and mechanism. The usual sequence of events is that a term most usually applied to human beings is transferred to machines. This begins as a consciously metaphorical or specialist use. The special, restricted, basis for the anthropomorphic language is however soon forgotten: the metaphorical clothing in which thinking is wrapped becomes its skin. Machines described in human terms are then offered as models for mind (described in slightly machine-like terms).

To see what is wrong with the vast majority of philosophical discourse in the field of cognitive science, and what is amiss with physicalist accounts of the mind generally, we need to look particularly carefully at the first step: the application of human terms to machines. In most cases, as we shall see, the process of epithet transfer is no more valid (or no less metaphorical) than referring to the place used to house candidates for execution as 'a condemned cell'. When we hear of a man who has spent the last year in a condemned cell, we know that it is the man, not the cell, who faces execution. It is the man, not the cell, who should have right of appeal. It is the man, not the cell, on whose behalf we grow indignant. When we are told that a telephone receives information, however, we fail to notice – or at least fail to be alerted by – the fact that it is we, not the telephone, who require, are able to receive, and are glad of, information. This is not because there is more justification in taking the transferred epithet literally in the case of the telephone than in the case of the prison cell but because 'information' has a multiplicity of meanings that 'condemn' does not. In the case of the telephone, the transferred epithet adopts a protective colouring to suit its new surroundings.

It is not too much of an exaggeration to claim that the greatest advances in breaking down the mind–body, consciousness/ mechanism, man/machine barriers have come not from neuro-biology or computer science but from the use of transferred epithets. The engineer's customary courtesy in his dealings with his machines (not qualitatively different from that which prompts sailors to refer to their ships as 'she') has permitted many asser-tions to pass 'on the nod' that would otherwise be challenged. Indeed, such courtesies have come so to dominate our language that it is almost impossible to look critically at the idea that machines have memories, that they 'store information' and do calculations, or that different parts of the nervous system 'signal' to one another. We are accustomed to hearing that radar 'sees' an enemy plane or that it 'hunts' a target. We cease to notice that we are conferring intentionality upon systems that are themselves only prosthetic extensions of the conscious human body.

Epithet transfer is, I have indicated, two-way: machines are described anthropomorphically and, at the same time, the terms in which they are described get machinised. The same terms, modified by their life among the machines, can then be re-applied to minds and the impression is then created that minds and machines are one. In other words, to get across the machine/mind barrier, it is not sufficient to machinise the mind; one must machinise the mind using terms that have already unobtrusively mentalised machines. If you make machines into minds by describing them mentalistically, you are already half way to making minds into machines. The awaiting terminology is more friendly. As a result of this process, it is possible to overlook, for example, that a computer viewed in any way other than mystically is an unconscious automaton.

This journeying of terms between the mental and the physical realms lies at the root of the myth that modern neurological science has somehow explained, or will explain, or has advanced our understanding of, what consciousness truly is. Neuromythology exploits the justified prestige of neuroanatomy, neurophysiology, neurochemistry and the other legitimate neurosciences. The terms that seem to me the most important among those that are responsible for carrying discourse painlessly – indeed almost unconsciously – across the man/mechanism divide include: calculations (or computations); complexity; goals; grammar; interpretation (translation); instructions; code; level; logic; memory; pattern; representation (model); rule; and information. They are vital to the illusion of explanatory force that machine models of consciousness – whether biological or abstract computational – seem to have. Indeed Janus-faced words like 'memory' and 'information' – which look in the direction of both man and machines – seems to dissolve the very problems that philosophically are most interesting. In consequence, most neurologically-based biological and computational explanations of consciousness begin beyond the point where the real questions are to be found. The terminology begins, as it were, on the far side of the answers. A critical examination of such terminology, by showing the hollowness of the answers built into it, should restore the questions and the sense of the mystery of the object of our enquiries: of consciousness.[30]

Information (Knowledge)

'Information' is by far the most important term in the language of neuromythology. It is an absolutely key term in cognitive science and much contemporary thought about brain function, the mind and the relationship between them. According to popular thought, what, above all, the mind-brain does is acquire, process and store information.

What is information? 'Information' is a term that has a variety of senses, some every-day, some highly specialised and technical. Much of the explanatory force of 'informational' explanations of consciousness and the mind-brain depends upon unobserved shuttling back and forth between these various senses.

Let us begin at the beginning. The Oxford English Dictionary lists numerous senses of the word 'information'. The most important of these is 'Knowledge communicated concerning some particular fact, subject or event; that of which one is apprised or told; intelligence, news'. This ordinary sense is very different from that used widely in cognitive and other sciences. At first the specialised sense of information was kept quite separate from the ordinary sense, as was made clear by the communication engineers who first introduced it.

The specialised sense was occasioned by the need to quantify information, in order to evaluate the work done by, and the efficiency of, communication channels charged with transmitting it. One important measure of the information content of a message *in engineering terms* is the amount of prior uncertainty it resolves. If there are only two possible messages, then the successful transmission of one of these – the actual message – will convey a selective information content of one bit or binary digit. The amount of information carried by any message will be determined by the number of possible alternatives that have been selected from and the prior probabilities of the different messages. The more unexpected, or unexpectable, a message is, the greater its information content. A totally expected message, one that resolves no prior uncertainties, is redundant and, in engineering terms, has no information content: it is not worth paying for. Redundancy is both good and bad. It is good, inasmuch as it allows for a degradation of the message without loss of information transmission. The redundancy in written messages permits accurate decipherment of the most appalling handwriting, despite our inability to read certain individual letters. It is bad in so far as it may be uneconomical.

It will be clear from this that the engineer's sense of information, and in particular information content, has little to do with information in the ordinary sense. Weaver, one of the first to think of information in the way just described, emphases this:

> Information in this theory is used in a special sense that must not be confused with its ordinary usage. In particular, *information* must not be confused with meaning. In fact, two messages, one of which is heavily loaded with meaning, and the other of which is pure nonsense, can be exactly equivalent from the present viewpoint as regards information.[31]

Indeed the meaningful statement may have less information content than the meaningless one. Supposing A asks B if she loves him. B's 'Yes' is one of only two possible alternatives and, assuming he has no idea in advance of the answer, will have an information content of one bit. Consider, by contrast, a meaningless message composed of randomly generated letters of the alphabet: even a single letter 'message' of this sort will have an information content of between 4 and 5 bits. It is all a matter of the range of alternatives from which the message has been selected and their prior probabilities. As Shannon, who originated the mathematical theory of communication, wrote, 'the semantic aspects of communication are irrelevant to the engineering aspects'.

In the specialised technical sense, information is measured by the reduction of uncertainty; the number of possibilities and their prior probabilities becomes a way of measuring information. Before long, this objective way of measuring information (which is quite separate from how informative it seems to the informee) becomes a definition of information itself, the method of measuring the thing defines it: information is uncertainty reduction. This uncertainty may not be experienced as such by the individual but is inherent in the multiplicity of objectively-observed possibilities presented to the him.

The engineering notion of information entered the sciences of the mind via the psychology of perception. From the early 1950s onwards, sensory perception was interpreted as the acquisition of information and sensory pathways were seen as channels transmitting information from the outside world to the centre. These channels had limited information handling capacity; they could cope with only so much at a time. Using the notion of information in the engineering sense, it was possible to make certain predictions that proved to be true. For example, Hick[32] found that the reaction time of human subjects to a stimulus depended on its selective information content; it depended, that is to say, not upon its actual content but upon the number of alternatives that had to be selected from. This, in turn, determined how much information had to be processed before the subject could react.

From this, it was but a short step to see perception as 'information processing' and to regard the function of the nervous system as that of transmitting information from one place to another. It is a strange and contradictory move because it both dehumanises perception and anthropomorphises the organs of perception. The perceiver is placed on all fours with a telephone receiver, while the sense organs are treated as if they were devices that had certain goals and aims and functions. Nevertheless, over the last twenty years, the rhetoric of information has dominated thought about mental, cerebral and neuronal function. The apparent success of this mode of thought depends upon an almost continuous unacknowledged vacillation between the engineering and the ordinary senses of information. The information-theoretic account of perception makes intuitive sense because we think of the bearer of the nervous system as being informed in the ordinary sense by what is going on in his nervous system as well as acquiring information in the narrow sense of selecting between alternative possible states. By narrowing the conception of consciousness or awareness to that of being in receipt of information and widening that of information way beyond the engineering sense that gives it scientific respectability, and not acknowledging (or noticing) either of these moves, it seems possible to give a scientific, information-theoretic account of both consciousness and the nervous system. We can speak without embarrassment of consciousness as being the outcome of the information-processing activity of the nervous system.

The inappropriateness of reducing consciousness to information will be further discussed in the next chapter. It amounts to expanding information to encompass the whole of awareness. Under this interpretation, an ordinary conscious being is literally steeped in information; his perceptual field is a multi-modal sphere of information. Not everyone is able to see the absurdity of this consequence of extending the engineer's use of the term information outside of its legitimate provenance – that of devices designed by human being to help them communicate with other human beings. Although engineering-type information-content is distinct from meaning, it does not make sense beyond places where people are, ultimately, trying to convey meaning, or to resolve uncertainty through the transmission of meaningful events. If we remove this essential element of human intentionality, in particular its involvement in acts and instruments of conscious and deliberate communication, then 'information states' or 'information-bearing states' can encompass pretty well everything that happens or exists. Under such circumstances, the information-theoretic account of perception not only tries to have its conception of information in the aseptic, semantics-free scientific sense while eating it in the ordinary sense (otherwise the events in the afferent pathways would not count as perceptions), it also stands at the top of a slippery slope at the bottom of which lies the lunacy of those who claim that the entire universe is a process of transmitting and receiving information.

The first step down the slope carries information beyond the body, and even beyond devices that are designed to serve the information needs of human beings, into the energy incident upon the body. If one really believes that consciousness arises out of the interaction between the nervous system and objects outside of it, that it is the transfer of energy from external objects to sense endings that accounts for perception, then one has a problem. How does the energy impinging on the nervous system become transformed into consciousness? For, although the nervous system seems quite good at transducing various forms of energy into its own dialect of energy (propagated electrochemical changes), it doesn't seem to do anything corresponding to the transformation of energy into information.

One 'explanation' is that, while the events in the periphery of the nervous system are indeed energy-to-energy transductions, those that take place centrally somehow add up to a pattern and this adding up to a pattern is an energy-to-information transformation. I have already discussed why this is a non-explanation. I mention it here only to draw attention to the particular difficulties encountered (but not apparently experienced) by those such as Patricia Churchland for whom 'nervous systems are information processing machines'.[33] Clearly you can't process something you haven't got: a stomach isn't a dinner-processing machine unless there is such a thing as dinner to be got from somewhere. If the impulses in the nervous system convey information rather than making it themselves (as we are conventionally told) where does the information come from? According to some it is actually present in the energy that impinges on the nervous system! The job of the nervous system is simply to extract and transmit it.

Johnson-Laird who, as we noted earlier, endorsed J. J. Gibson's claim that 'light reflected from surfaces and focused on the retina contains a large amount of information' – gossippy stuff, light – also asserts, astonishingly, this has been 'demonstrated' by Longuet-Higgins' analysis of the projective geometry of images.[34] There are, however, no entirely free gifts: 'no matter how much information is in the light falling on the retinae, there must be mental mechanisms for recovering the identities of things in a scene and those of their properties that vision makes explicit to consciousness'. He also adds that this information has little or nothing to do with consciousness:

> No matter how much information is in the light falling on the retinae, there must be mental mechanisms for recovering the identities of things in a scene and those of their properties that vision makes explicit to consciousness. Without such mechanisms, retinal images would be no more use than the images produced by television cameras, and, contrary to the naive view, *they* cannot see anything.

It appears that you can have all the information in the world and still not be informed; or that you can be well-informed but unconscious. Still, the information in the light is a flying start and it must provide one of the easiest solutions to the physicalist's puzzle of how (to use his own terms) energy is transformed into information: the information is *in* the energy; it simply has to be 'extracted' from it. The older magic thinking – 'mind among things' – has been updated: 'information in energy'.

This is not the bottom, only the top, of the slippery slope. For some writers, information among things does not have to be extracted by the nervous system: it is there for the taking. Or, rather, it is there whether it is taken or not, irrespective of whether the information bearer interacts with the nervous system. According to some authors, not only are unconscious organisms information-processing devices, but the individual parts of them are as well. Indeed, information is embodied in all organisms, most notably in the genetic material. For example Richard Dawkins (whose views on this matter are by no means heterodox), asserts that DNA is information, and embodies instructions for transmitting and preserving information. 'If you want to understand life, don't think about vibrant throbbing gels and oozes, think about information technology'.[35] 'The information technology of the genes is digital . . . since we receive our inheritance in discrete particles'. The difference between DNA and a floppy disc is merely a question of the storage medium used – chemical as opposed to electronic – but the essentials are the same. 'Each individual organism should be seen as a temporary vehicle in which DNA messages spend a tiny fraction of their geological lifetimes' (pp. 126–7). And what an enormous number of messages there are! DNA is ROM (Read Only Memory) and it is comparable to a laser disc in terms of the amount of information it packs into a small space (pp. 152–3): 'at the molecular genetic level, every one of more than a trillion cells in the body contains about a thousand times as much precisely-coded digital information as my [Dawkins's] computer' (p. xiii).

Such anthropomorphism – which makes the cells of my body infinitely better informed than I could ever hope to be – is not unusual and, indeed, it takes its rise from a whole cluster of notions about the relations between information, entropy and order. Entropy is the degree of disorder in a system; living systems, which are (according to the conceptual schema of one particular species of living system) uniquely ordered, entrain a high degree of negative entropy. They are highly improbable because, according to the Second Law of Thermodynamics, the degree of disorder in a system tends to increase. The ideas behind the relationship between information, entropy and order are well summarised by Colin Cherry:

> Entropy, in statistical thermodynamics, is a function of the probabilities of the states of the particles comprising a gas; information rate, in statistical communication theory, is a similar

function of the probabilities of the states of a source. In both cases we have an *ensemble* – in the case of the gas, an enormous collection of particles, the states of which (i.e. the energies) are distributed according to some probability function; in the communication problem, a collection of messages, or states of a source, again described by a probability function.[36]

The idea that information is equivalent to negative entropy derives from Szilard's discussion of the Maxwell demon problem. The demon is conceived as 'receiving information' about the particle motions of a gas, this information enabling him to operate a heat engine and so set up a perpetual motion machine. The demon, in making use of his information in this way, was seemingly violating the Second Law. However, he is not merely an observer of the system, he is also a participant; he is part of the system because he must receive energy in order to make his observations; he must be affected by the system in order to observe it. Szilard demonstrated that the selective action represented by the demon's observations result in an increase in entropy at least equal to the reduction in entropy he can effect by virtue of this information. There seems to be a trade-off between entropy and information; from which it is concluded that information is, in a sense, negative entropy.

This analogy has a certain amount of intuitive attraction, as Cherry, upon whose account of Szilard's thought experiment the above paragraph has been highly dependent, explains:

> In a descriptive sense, entropy is often referred to as a 'measure of disorder' and the Second Law of Thermodynamics as stating that 'systems can only proceed to a state of increased disorder; as time passes, 'entropy can never decrease'. The properties of a gas can change only in such a way that our knowledge of the positions and energies of the particles lessens; randomness always increases. In a similar descriptive way, information is contrasted, as bringing order out of chaos. Information is then said to be 'like' negative energy.

Cherry, however, warns against too literal an interpretation of these analogies and, even more severely, against too wide an application. Entropy is 'essentially a mathematical concept and the rules of its application are clearly laid down, and 'any likeness that exists [between negative entropy and information] exists between the mathematical descriptions which have been set up'. Moreover, the term entropy is usually applied to closed systems, which are utterly isolated and unable to exchange energy with their surroundings, are in a state of near-randomness and are enormous. This hardly applies to the communication systems in which humans and other organisms participate. Cherry's final comments on this matter are especially worth quoting:

> Mother Nature does not communicate to us with signs or language. A *communication channel* should be distinguished from a *channel of observation* and, without wishing to be too assertive, the writer would suggest that in true communication problems the concept of entropy need not be evoked at all. And again, physical entropy is capable of a number of interpretations, albeit related, and its similarity with (selective, syntactic) information is not as straightforward as the simplicity and apparent similarity of the formulae suggests. (p. 217)

Such warnings have gone unheeded by psychologists, for whom the sensory pathways as a channel of communication (and indeed the entire nervous system as an information transmission device) is an apparently undislodgable received idea; by biologists; and by philosophers for whom the equation between order and information and information and mental function is beyond dispute.

The idea that order is information (and the preservation of order is the transmission of information through time – or memory) is implicit in Dawkins's description of DNA as ROM. The equation between organic order and higher mental function is explicit in Paul Churchland's use of the entropy/information metaphors. Churchland at times seems to espouse a conventional behaviourist account of intelligence: 'the possession of a complex set of appropriate responses to the changing environment'.[37] Such a definition is interactionist, as befits an evolutionary outlook which sees intelligence as an instrument to help the organism survive on a potentially hostile planet. Under the influence of a series of metaphors derived from ectopic thermodynamics and information theory, Churchland's conception of intelligence moves inwards until it becomes inscribed in the actual order or structure of the organism:

If the possession of information can be understood as the possession of some internal physical order that bears some systematic relation to the environment, then the operation of intelligence, abstractly conceived, turns out to be just a high-grade version of the operating characteristics of life, save that they are even more intricately coupled to the environment . . . Intelligent life is just life, with a high thermodynamic intensity and an especially close coupling between internal order and external circumstance. (p. 174)

A system has intelligence just in case it exploits the *information* it already contains, and the energy flux through it (this includes the energy flux though its sense organs), in such a way as to *increase* the information it contains. Such a system can *learn*, and it seems to be the central element of intelligence. (p. 173)

The 'especially close coupling between internal order and external circumstance' does not seem to be a distinctive feature of life; according to the physicalist world picture within which Church-land writes, it is the common condition of all existents. Far from being the great achievement of life, one would have thought that it was precisely the kind of thing that life – and intelligent versions of it in particular – has been trying to escape. So one is left with 'thermodynamic intensity' which, if it means anything, is the high level of information and negative entropy which Churchland and others think is embodied in complex structures.

What is there to say about the idea that there is information implicit in systems, that *order is embodied information?* There are two types of problem with this very popular and potently misleading belief. The first concerns the latent anthropomorphism inherent in the use of terms such as 'complex' and 'ordered' to discriminate between portions of matter. From the physicalist standpoint, all pieces of matter are both random and highly ordered, depending upon how, or at what level, they are viewed. Order, ultimately, means explicit, visible or perceived order; and this, in turn, means order according to a human viewpoint. Without consciousness-born criteria of order (of what shall count as ordered or as disordered), material entities are neither ordered nor disordered. (This is not an idealist position: I am merely pointing out that man does not impose order on the world, he merely finds it according to his criteria; or, rather, he imposes order only to the extent that he imposes chaos.[38])

A rather different and even more serious criticism of the idea that the structure or internal physical order amounts to information (as if one's material assets can be capitalised as information flow) is that, quite apart from the dubious thermodynamics upon which the metaphor is founded, the structure of an organism is not available to that organism in the way that information is. It is certainly not part of consciousness. If one's structure were equal to information (about that structure?), then being a crystal would be a sufficient condition of being an at least primitive crystallographer. A pebble's 'experience' may change its structure but that changed structure does not embody the experience. And the same applies to any organism where learning (and acquired information) is not thought to lead to conscious memory.[39]

Once information is uprooted from consciousness – and from an informant or from the experience of being informed and of wanting to be informed – then any kind of nonsense is possible. Valid thermodynamics and information theory that is valid within its area of appropriate use converge in a form of pataphysics whose fundamental tenet is that things embody information in virtue of their observed or observable structure – as if they were tools, and tools embodied the spirit of the toolmaker. According to the information theorists we have discussed so far, the unconscious structure of organisms contains information and the energy impinging on the nervous system contains information. It is possible to go further than this: for the fully paid-up theorist, information is simply and literally everywhere. The 'informationalisation' of the universe has been taken to its logical conclusion by writers such as Fredkin for whom the fundamental particles that make up the world – atoms, quarks, etc. – boil down to bits of information.[40] The universe is made up of combinations of such binary digits; and atoms are 'information-processing systems'. The universe it seems is not only incredibly well-informed about itself – a huge polymath set out in boundless space, an infinity of omniscience – it *is* information. Fredkin's 'digital physics' has a further twist: it is based on the hypothesis that the universe no longer processes information like a computer but that it *is* a computer, still processing a programme that was installed at the beginning of time, possibly by a 'Great Programmer'. Whether or not this Computiverse is carried on the back of an elephant has not yet been determined.

This is what lies at the end of a long chain of unchecked

metaphors. Little by little, we arrive at lunacy. As is so often the case, the first steps on the path to lunacy are often innocuous. The most important and the seemingly most innocuous is that of accepting the idea that information can be 'stored' – outside of the human body, outside of conscious organisms – in books or on discs. In the loose sense of 'inform', I, who have derived a lot of information from a book I have read, may regard it as 'informative'. Likewise, the book I am writing may be informative; so (again, in a very loose sense, I am filling my book with information. The books I read inform me and the books I write are informed by me. Once the books are born, surely they can inform one another: information may be passed from book to book. If this is accepted, then information, informing and being informed start to be liberated from a *consciousness* being informed or wanting to inform. If it sounds odd to talk of one book informing another, consider what is often said about 'information stored on discs': information may be copied from one disc to another; information may be transmitted from disc to disc. This is perfectly normal computer talk; and it seems to suggest that information can be given and received without the involvement of consciousness. This is, of course, misleading: the information in a book, or on a disc, is only *potential* information. More generally, it is not information but only *potential information* that can be inscribed outside of a conscious organism. It remains potential until it is encountered by an individual requiring and able to receive information, to be informed. In the absence of such a (conscious) organism, it is loose talk to refer to the states of objects as 'information'; but such loose talk is the beginning of a very long journey.

In conclusion, 'information' is an absolutely key term in establishing the conceptual confusions so necessary to the seeming fruitfulness and explanatory power of much modern thought about the mind and the brain. By playing upon different meanings of the terms, it is possible to argue that minds, brains, organisms, various artefacts such as computers and even non-living thermodynamic systems are all information-processing devices. Because they are essentially the same in this vitally important respect, they can be used to model each other; homology and analogy can run riot. Once the concept of information is liberated from the idea of *someone being informed* and from that of *someone doing the informing*, anything is possible.

4

Computerising Consciousness

The central nervous system is an information processor of almost incredible complexity . . . and in order to understand the mental processes it supports we are going to need the most sophisticated notions of information technology.[1]

A NEW ORTHODOXY[2]

The prevalent biological model of consciousness identifies mental phenomena with certain brain processes. The view to be examined in this chapter is that while those processes have so far been embodied in biological systems, they are only incidentally or contingently biological; they are, however, essentially computational. The sensory systems, for example, are symbol-manipulating systems rather than just physical transducers. There are many positions along a spectrum of views that extends from a neurophysiological model of mind, in which the brain computes but is not just a computer, through the idea of mind as a neural computer, at once specifically neural and essentially computational, to a conception of mind as essentially a logic machine that is only accidentally and unimportantly embodied in the wetware of the brain.

It is often difficult to know how seriously or literally those who advance computational models of the mind mean us to take them. On the whole, it would seem pretty seriously and pretty literally. Sometimes, however, there is a revealing uncertainty as to whether computer modelling of mind is at least in part a heuristic device, a methodological tactic. For example, Johnson-Laird, whose excellent review of cognitive science[3] will act as our main source-text for the current orthodoxies, writes as follows:

102

Is the mind a computational phenomenon? No one knows. It may be; or it may depend on operations that cannot be captured by any sort of computer . . . *Theories* of the mind . . . should not be confused with the mind itself, any more than theories of the weather should be confused with rain or sunshine. And what is clear is that computability provides an appropriate conceptual apparatus for theories of the mind. (p. 51)

The interpretation of this statement will be crucially dependent on how 'appropriate' is read. If it means 'accurately reflecting the nature of the object the theories are about', then one must assume that Johnson-Laird thinks that minds are 'computational phenomena'. If 'appropriate' means only 'likely to produce results' (e.g. to generate publishable data) then the computational approach to consciousness will be merely a metaphor, a heuristic device, that may be fruitful even if untrue. Elsewhere in the same book, Johnson-Laird writes that 'cognitive science tries to elucidate the workings of the mind by treating them as computations' (p. 9) which is nicely, and puzzlingly, ambiguous. Clearly one could not elucidate the workings of the mind by treating them as if they were something they were not; and yet the 'as if' suggests some doubt as to whether these 'workings' are or are not computational. By the time we have reached the end of his book, this ambiguity is still unresolved, though he asserts quite plainly that, 'for cognitive science, mental processes are the computations of the brain', and one assumes that, as a cognitive scientist, he has not elected for what he considers to be untruth.[4] The blurb to his book speaks of the 'central metaphor' behind cognitive science – that 'the mind depends on the brain in the same way that the execution of a "program" of symbolic instructions depends upon a computer'.

Others are less ambiguous. Patricia Churchland[5] bluntly asserts that 'nervous systems are information processing machines' (p. 36) and that the mind is 'essentially a kind of logic machine that operates on sentences'. And for Paul Churchland[6] neurons are 'information-processing devices' (p. 133) and seeing is 'optical information-processing' (p. 114). While Longuet-Higgins states that for David Marr (whose contributions to the psychology of vision are a paradigm of cognitive science) vision was 'an ongoing process of computation, which begins with the optical images formed at the back of the eye and culminates in a spatio-temporal world model, useful for picking things up and getting about'.[7]

There is, therefore, a highly influential contemporary school of thought which holds that the mind, cognition, consciousness etc., are identical with certain types of operation which are in the broad sense computational; and that actual operations that take place in the brain and constitute mental phenomena are more important than the material out of which the neural machine is composed. The brain is merely an embodiment of a logical system and any other object that embodied that logical system would share the brain's ability to sustain consciousness.

This idea derives ultimately from Alan Turing's famous paper of 1937 *On Computable Numbers, with an Application to the Entscheidungs-problem*. Turing's biographer (quoted in Johnson-Laird[8]), describes Turing's vision of the brain as an embodied instance of the universal computational machine:

> To understand the Turing model of 'the brain', it was crucial to see that it regarded physics and chemistry, including all the arguments about quantum mechanics . . . , as essentially irrelevant. In his view, the physics and chemistry were relevant only insofar as they sustained the medium for the embodiment of discrete 'states', 'reading', and 'writing'. Only the *logical* pattern of these 'states' could really matter. The claim was that whatever a brain did, it did by virtue of its structure as a logical system, and not because it was inside a person's head, or because it was a spongy tissue made up of a particular kind of biological cell formation. And if this were so, then its logical structure could just as well be represented in some other medium, embodied by some other physical machinery, but one that did not confuse logical patterns and relations with physical substances and things, as so often people did.

Searle, who has specifically argued against the view that consciousness is only incidentally embodied in the biological brain and that it could be embodied in anything that instantiated the right formal system,[9] has distinguished between weak and strong artificial intelligence (AI): weak AI claims only that the computer is a useful tool in the study of the mind; while strong AI makes the much more powerful claim that 'the appropriately programmed computer really *is* a mind, in the sense that computers given the right programs can be literally said to *understand* and have other cognitive states'. The view to be examined in this chapter – and one favoured by cognitive scientists – goes beyond this; it is that naturally occurring mind, real intelligence and not only the artificial stuff, is identical with certain computational activities of the brain. This could be described as 'super-strong AI'. But the principle is the same: appropriately programmed computers are minds and it doesn't really matter what material – biological or industrial – the programs are embodied in. The mind is essentially a logic machine, an enormously complex software system that could be implemented (with the relevant changes having been made) on any machine, biological or non-biological. The brain is merely the hardware in which the mind's software programs run. The mind's software – a set of instructions or algorithms – could be embodied in quite different, biological or non-biological, types of hardware.

It is easy to appreciate the initial intuitive attractions of Turing's vision: its account of mind seems convincingly mental inasmuch as it is disembodied or, at least, separate from its embodiments; the embodiments are external to the mental essence. There are three sorts of ground for the current popularity of this way of conceiving mind:

1. First of all the Turing principle (of universal computability) itself, which seems to have proved to the satisfaction of many cognitive scientists that all brain-mind events and phenomena can be seen as input–output relations and that these input–output relations are computable.
2. The demonstration that, as computers become more advanced, they can simulate more and more behaviours that previously seemed to require the control of a conscious mind. In other words, as the capabilities of computers become more and more like those of beings with minds, so computers are becoming more and more mind-like.
3. The observation that various systems discerned in the brain can be described not too tendentiously in computational terms.

The cumulative weight of seeming evidence and the apparent conceptual support for the computational theory of mind is quite impressive. Add to this the conscious or unconscious interpenetration of the languages in which mind and computers are discussed (see Appendix to Chapter 3) and we have a picture that it is very difficult to see round, never mind to question. In order to demonstrate its inadequacy, however, it is necessary only to look at it more closely; to this end, I shall reconstruct a middle-of-the-road computational theory of mind.

A COMPUTATIONAL THEORY OF MIND

In order to establish what a computational theory of mind actually boils down to, let us begin with a simple description of the object upon which mind or consciousness is modelled: the computer.

A computer is a machine for processing what is, in a very extended sense of the term, called 'information'. In order to do this, it has to have an input module (e.g. a keyboard) where the information can be entered, and an output module (e.g. a screen, a printer or some other device whose behaviour is controlled by the results of the processing) through which the outcome of the computer's operations can be expressed. Between the two is the central processing unit (CPU) where the processing takes place. The CPU will operate on material currently entered into it and also upon stored material previously entered into the computer and held in 'memory'. *What* it does to the entered information will be in part determined by the instructions entered with the information and in part by the instructions built into the processor or extracted from that part of memory where programs are stored. Information processing consists essentially of the rule-governed transformation of formulae into other formulae.

At the heart of the computer is the central processing unit (CPU), composed of the Control Unit and the Arithmetic-Logic Unit (ALU). The Control Unit receives instructions from the programs in the main memory, decodes them, and sends signals in the appropriate units in the computer to execute the instructions. It directs the units of the computer as a whole. It is through the control unit that the computational activity of the CPU is controlled and the 'software' – the sequence of instructions or programs that exercises that control – exerts its influence. But the Control Unit is not absolutely central. It is in the ALU that the actual business of computing gets done. And what does this business consist of? Arithmetical and logical operations; number- and logic-crunching. The most typical operation at the heart of the most sophisticated computer – whether it is digital-serial or parallel – is the execution of *calculations*; the transformation of a quantitative input into a quantitative output, as the result of the operation of certain general rules.

The analogies with what goes on in the human brain, and with human consciousness, seem at first sight very persuasive, indeed inescapable. The input modules are the senses (eyes, ears, temperature receptors, joint receptors, etc.). The outputs are the visible movements and invisible physiological and biochemical adjustments that take place in adaptive response to the inputs. The highest levels of the brain constitute the ALU, the Control Unit and the memory modules in which previous inputs and programs are stored. The manner in which the neurones are connected corresponds to the wiring on circuit boards. And so on.

So what is wrong with taking this analogy as seriously as cognitive scientists and others appear to take it?

AN UNFOCUSED ANALOGY

First of all, it is very difficult to be sure what, in terms of the computational model, consciousness, mind, mental states, etc. are actually supposed to be. Are they information? Or information processing – i.e. what is done with the information? And if the former, is information the stuff that goes in or the stuff that comes out? Or is the mind, etc. the software, i.e. the instructions for processing the information? There are no definite answers to this question, never mind consistent ones. Secondly, as already discussed (see note 2 above), it is rarely clear what, at any given time, is being modelled. Consciousness in the broadest sense? Mind in the narrower sense of certain intellectual capacities? Mind in the broader sense of consciousness plus the unconscious processes that make consciousness possible and determine its shape? Mental states? Mental contents? Mental processes?

The lack of focus in the analogy (which makes it difficult to argue against and so is its greatest strength) is illustrated by Johnson-

Laird's different accounts of the computational theory of the mind in his book. A typical account revolves round his assertion that 'the mind depends on the brain in the same way that the execution of a "program" of symbolic instructions depends upon a computer'. Elsewhere, we are told that 'Simple consciousness – bare awareness of events such as pain – may owe its origin to the emergence of a high level monitor from the web of parallel processes' (p. 356). And, a few pages on, that 'the conscious mind is the result of a special mode of processing that creates the subjective experience of awareness. Once an operating system had evolved, it could take on such a function, and this mode of processing, I believe, is our capacity for *self-awareness*'. It would seem, then, that the computational theory of mind encompasses a group of quite different theories, in which any one of the items in the left hand column below may be related to any one of the items in the right hand column (see also note 2):

Consciousness	Information
Mind	Information processing
Mental processes	Product of information processing
Mental states	Software
Mental contents	Instructions, algorithms, etc.
Conscious mind	Function of operating system

If we consider only pairs of items from the left and right hand columns, thirty-six possible theories emerge. For example, it has been variously held that mind is: information; the processing of information (Patricia Churchland: 'Mind is computation over sentences'); the *product* of information processing; something half way between process and product (Johnson-Laird: 'Vision is rather like the problem of finding the value of x in the equation $5 = x + y$'); the processor – e.g. the software installed in or operating in the brain's hardware; and the instructions or algorithms of which the software is composed. As I have said, the unfocused nature of the theories makes it difficult to target one's objections; indeed much of the theories' robustness in the face of seemingly devastating criticism lies in their essential vagueness. Clarification, to the point where one risks the charge of simplification, is therefore an essential preliminary to a critical examination.

WHAT ACTUALLY GOES ON IN A COMPUTER?

Let us look at what a non-neural computer might spend its time doing. In essence a computer is an electronic device for performing high-speed arithmetical and logical operations, calculating quantities, truth tables and weights. These operations lie at the heart of the most sophisticated or powerful computer – irrespective of whether it is digital-serial or a parallel-processor. They have nothing to do with thought, occurring in virtue of the way in which logic gates, half-adders, hidden units and so on are connected to one another. Everything that goes beyond these calculations – for example, translations in and out of machine code into ASCII characters, lines, or natural language statements, the production of graphics, and the control of robotic movements – are secondary to this. So, although computers do infinitely more than perform simple calculations, or simple logical operations on non-arithmetical symbols, the latter are central. Removing the razzmatazz of peripherals will put us in a better position to address the important question 'whether the activities that constitute conscious intelligence are all *computational procedures* of some kind or other', (Paul Churchland, p. 105) and assess 'the guiding assumption [of AI] . . . that they are', and the aim of AI 'to construct actual programs that will simulate them'.

The following is a typical computational event or 'act':

$$2 + 2 = 4$$

or:

$$\left. \begin{array}{c} 2 \rightarrow \\ 2 \rightarrow \end{array} \right\} \rightarrow 4$$

Here is another:

$$\left. \begin{array}{c} 1 \\ 1 \end{array} \right\} - \text{NAND} - 0$$

Upon such simple operations, mighty calculations and the infinitely refined control of peripherals are based. What is wrong with the idea that mental processes are essentially the same, that the neural mind is essentially computational?

WHY COULDN'T WHAT ACTUALLY GOES ON IN A COMPUTER MODEL CONSCIOUSNESS?

There are several reasons why:

1. Events in the ALU

The events in the arithmetic-logic unit are intrinsically neither computational nor logical. They are electrical. The structure of the ALU may enable us (the conscious human users) to add 2 + 2 and make 4 or to draw the following inference:

$$T \qquad\qquad T \qquad\qquad F$$
$$p \qquad\qquad q \qquad\qquad not\ (p+q)$$

But the events in that structure do not count as addition or as logical inference except to someone who is interpreting them. In themselves, they are simply the passage of electricity. One could imagine an identical passage of electricity across a similar circuit taking place in the absence of an interpreting consciousness. Under such circumstances, it would not count as a calculation or a logical operation. Two things are necessary to turn the electrical events into arithmetical or logical ones: the peripherals required to make the output of the logic circuit visible; and a conscious someone to interpret that visible output. Cognitive scientists usually remember the first but seem invariably to forget the second.

That the events in the ALU seem to be intrinsically calculations or logical operations reflects only our habit of reading back from *our* consciousness of what machines can do for us into the events which take place within machines. Although it is a useful short-hand to speak of an ALU 'performing calculations' or 'logical operations', it is obvious that what is going on in the ALU is not by itself either calculation or logic. In order to count as performing a logical operation or a calculation one has to know what one is doing – one has to understand the significance of it. This under-standing, this awareness, is denied the ALU. Anyone who is inclined to claim that the ALU *does* have this understanding has stepped on to a slippery slope at the bottom of which are a lot of awkward and silly consequences – such as having to attribute consciousness not only to pocket calculators but to even more primitive devices such as a mechanical abacus.

2. Consciousness is Not Number- or Logic-Crunching

All right, granted that the events, in particular the computations, in the ALU are not themselves primitive 'atoms' of consciousness, could they not *model* whatever it is that constitutes consciousness in human beings? Many cognitive scientists seem to believe this. We have already quoted Johnson-Laird to the effect that 'vision is rather like the problem of finding the value of X in the equation $5 = x + y$'.

Suppose we took seriously the idea that consciousness is like a mass of calculations or in some non-trivial sense analogous to it. What is it about the calculations themselves (as opposed to someone doing the calculations) that is consciousness-like? What is quasi-conscious about $2 + 2 = 4$? (I have chosen a short calculation because I see no reason why a short calculation should be less like consciousness than a long one. Or a calculation with many steps spread over a period of time be closer to consciousness at any given moment than a one-step calculation). Why is $2 + 2 = 4$ more conscious, or nearer to consciousness, than 2 alone? In what does the model of consciousness reside. The individual symbols? The plus sign between them? The result, i.e. 4? If consciousness is a matter of computation, on which side of the equation is it to be found? Is *moving towards* a result consciousness? Or is consciousness the result itself? (And what of my consciousness of doing a sum – as when I consciously calculate the square root of 81 – is this a meta-sum, a sum of sums, or a sum that manages, mysteriously to be about itself?)

It is enough to ask these questions, to take the computational model with sufficient literalness to denude it of the enveloping vagueness, to discredit it. Clearly consciousness resides in none of the things considered in the preceding paragraph; or not, at least, in any of them more than any others of them. Nor in all of them together. Nor is there any reason for believing that consciousness resides in the operation of the sentential calculus or any other kinds of mathematical or logical operations such as vector-to-vector transformation.[10] Patricia Churchland's suggestion that mind is 'a kind of logic machine operating on sentences' raises a third, even more implausible possibility – namely that mind, or consciousness is to be located not in the operations of the ALU – the events that occur in it – but in the ALU itself; either the material of which it is made or the electronic structure that can be abstracted from it. (If, that is to say, mind includes consciousness; but I won't go over the ground covered in note 2.)

It might be felt that I have caricatured rather than described computers and that an account of computing that showed greater respect for their complexity might present them as less unconvincing models of consciousness or mind. But computation – addition and other arithmetical operations, the operation of logic on sentences, vector-to-vector transformation – is the essential activity of the computer. Anyone who feels that I have misrepresented the computational theory of mind by grotesque simplification must produce a form of the theory that is not reducible in this way. One that, for example, does not start from the assumption that computation is the central business of a computer.

OTHER REASONS WHY CONSCIOUSNESS IS NOT NUMBER-CRUNCHING

Once computers are demystified and one actually looks past the magic word 'computer' to the events that take place inside them, the inadequacy, indeed absurdity, of the computational model of consciousness is exposed. But the model is intuitively so powerful (because it is now sealed into the very language in which the nature of both minds and machines are described) that it has enormous regenerative powers. Further counter-arguments must therefore be deployed – lest, in particular, there is talk of 'levels' and 'emergent properties' and it is suggested that what goes on in an ALU is, after all, conscious or consciousness, if it is looked at from the right distance (i.e. from far enough away to be seen unclearly). Or someone suggests that the events in an ALU amount to consciousness if an enormous number of sums are going on in it at the same time and all of these somehow get together or merge or aggregate; that one sum is not consciousness – of course – but the sum of a lot of sums is so that (in Johnson-Laird's words) vision, for example, becomes 'rather like hundreds of problems of finding the values of X in equations like: $5 = x + y'$.

Let us, therefore, look harder at the other reasons why sums – singly or in gangs, logical or numeric – do not look convincingly to be the elements of mind or models of it.

1. Sums are Made up of Uninterpreted Symbols

It has been emphasised that digital-serial computers are not simply number-crunchers in the narrow sense but general symbol manipulators, systems which combine and modify symbols according to instructions encoded in programmes. According to Johnson-Laird, the cognitive computer (the brain-mind) 'is a device for converting energy into symbols, symbols into symbols and symbols into actions' (ibid., p. 391). Where the cognitive computer is the brain of a conscious individual, the transformation of energy into symbols is the function of the sensory pathways; the conversion of symbols into symbols is the job of the central processors, located mainly in the cerebral cortex; and the conversion of symbols into actions is the work of the motor pathways. The passage from energy into action is thus really a passage from energy back to energy; the overall outcome should therefore cause little physicalist or scientific embarrassment.

The status of the intervening symbols, however, is another matter altogether. We have already in Chapter 3 discussed the illegitimacy of thinking of the sensory pathways – which, after all, seem only to convert one form of energy into another – as devices for converting energy into information. The conversion of other forms of energy (light, sound, etc.) into electrochemical energy and the latter's propagation along sensory pathways does not seem a sufficient account of the conversion of energy into information. It seems equally inadequate as a model of the process by which representations of the world, or symbols, emerge.

Let us suppose, however, that we could accept that the central events in the sensory cortex count as symbols. Would they, on that basis, amount to consciousness? Hardly; for consciousness is inherently meaningful (the things we are conscious of make sense to us) while the symbols in the cognitive computer are simply converted into other symbols and it has often been pointed out – for example by David Lewis[11] – that symbols are meaningless until they are assigned an interpretation. The manipulation of meaningless formulae is unlikely to provide the basis for meaning-filled consciousness. But the situation is worse than this; for without being assigned a meaning, or at least being suspected of having a meaning, electrical events do not even count as *empty* formulae, since they do not count as formulae. The symbols, unrecognised as such, fail even to symbolise that they are symbols. As Peirce pointed out, an event may or may not be a sign, depending on how it is taken. It certainly can't be a sign if it isn't 'taken'. The processes that lead up to consciousness cannot terminate in or be constituted out of (uninterpreted) symbols. If the symbols are to symbolise, if in short they are to be symbols, they must be interpreted. And if interpretation is not merely to imply conversion into other (uninterpreted) symbols, it must presuppose consciousness. Symbols *per se* fall short of consciousness; they are, at best, the possibility of consciousness, or the possibility of shaping consciousness; such possibilities can be realised only through an interpreting consciousness. The temptation to suggest that the behavioural output triggered indirectly by the events in the sensory cortex counts as an interpretation of the cortical symbols and provides the missing semantic dimension – see McGinn, discussed in note 9 – must be resisted, though it is implicit in functionalism. The non-symbolic muscular events seem even further away from consciousness, and conscious meaning, than the uninterpreted symbols in the brain's central processes. Moreover, such an account of consciousness reduces its intentionality to causal consequences; worse still, the direction of this 'intentionality' is causally downstream, away from causally upstream events the sensory events are supposed to be consciousness of.

There is a further sense in which numeric and logical symbols are seriously incomplete – in a way that consciousness is not. By itself, '4' means little or nothing even when someone is conscious of it; at best, it is a shell providing a location for possible meanings. In isolation, numbers convey nothing – even of the qualitative aspect of size. 1000 is neither big nor small, without it being understood what it is a 1000 of. And transforming one set of numerical and logical formulae into another – rule-governed or not – brings us no nearer definite meaning. The output of an ALU is as meaningless as its input. '4' has no more meaning than '2 + 2' nor does '2 + 2 = 4' mean more than either of them. As Popper said, 'It is our human brains which may lend significance to the calculator's senseless powers of producing truth'.[12] The meanings the 'symbols' have do not mean in, to or for the computer.[13]

One way of closing the gap between senseless symbols and meaningless manipulations of uninterpreted formulae on the one hand and meaningful consciousness on the other is to re-describe the contents of consciousness as if they also were composed of symbols. In this way, the meaninglessness of the operations and output of the computer *to the computer* will not cause embarrassment to those who would wish to model consciousness on computational activity. For example, Johnson-Laird says:

> What do mental processes process? The answer, of course, is a vast number of perceptions, ideas, images, beliefs, hypotheses, thoughts and memories. One of the tenets of cognitive science is that all of these entities are mental representations or symbols of one sort or another. (p. 28)

Elsewhere, he asserts that 'the mind is a symbol manipulating device . . . (p. 35) and 'a symbolic system' (p. 34). The reader, startled by this, may wonder whether perhaps symbols are meant here in some saving Pickwickian sense. Not a bit of it. Johnson-Laird means symbols in the ordinary sense and, in a discussion that embodies a spectacular confusion of levels, illustrates the kinds of symbols he means with a road traffic sign. (This example is considered to be so apt that it actually features on the jacket of his book, superimposed on an intracranial floppy disc.) If all of the contents of consciousness really *are* symbols – so there is no point of rest and consciousness is continually pointing past itself to that which it will never be, to meanings and references it will never reach – one wonders what they are symbols of, and where, or by whom, they get interpreted.

Some of the points just made have been expressed forcibly by Searle in his classic paper:

> Because the formal symbols manipulated by themselves don't have any intentionality, they are quite meaningless; they aren't even *symbol* manipulations, since the symbols don't symbolise anything. In the linguistic jargon, they have only a syntax but no semantics. Such intentionality as computers appear to have is solely in the minds of those who program them and those who use them, those who send in the input and those who interpret the output.[14]

> Intentional states are not that way formal . . . They are defined in terms of their content, not their form. The belief that it is raining, for example, is not defined as a certain formal shape, but as a certain mental content with conditions of satisfaction, a direction

of fit. Indeed, the belief as such hasn't even got a formal shape in this syntactic sense, since one and the same belief can be given an indefinite number of syntactic expressions in different linguistic systems.[15]

The position that the mind is a device for manipulating un-interpreted symbols, in short 'a syntactic machine', is not always arrived at inadvertently. This conception of mind has been positively championed by several philosophers and psychologists in recent years, notably Daniel Dennett and Stephen Stich. Dennett has specifically asserted that the brain is a syntactic engine, not a semantic engine.[16] For him, this means that it proceeds from state to state as a function of the causal properties of the antecedent states, not as a function of what the states are 'about' or whether they represent something true about the world.[17] (Interestingly, according to McGinn, as I have already alluded to in note 9, the causal relations of the cerebral symbols actually furnish them with the requisite semantics.)

Stich – for whom also causal relations are syntax rather than semantics – develops a position that is more radical, more interesting and ultimately more absurd. Stich has advocated a Syntactic Theory of Mind (STM) in specific opposition to the propositional attitude (PA) psychology he associates with the pre-scientific psychology.[18] The STM also helps to define the proper scope of a fully-fledged cognitive science that has at last emerged from its roots in 'folk psychology' and its atavistic entrapment in those roots. It is not very clear whether in fact the STM is the result of a methodological decision about what can be fruitfully and 'scientifically' studied or whether it is really intended to be a theory of the mind.

Psychology, Stich argues, should be concerned only with the intrinsic properties of the mind. He identifies these intrinsic properties with the causal roles of mental states in interaction with other mental states, stimuli, and behaviour. In particular, the cognitive psychologist is concerned with predicting behaviour. If this is the case, Stich says, he should not take into account mental contents, especially those contents composed of propositional attitudes such as beliefs. He gives two reasons for this. The first is that there is no objective, or definitive, description of such contents. The beliefs we ascribe to someone have sources of variation that are independent of any variation in the mental state. They will depend on the context of the beliefs, on our interests, on the aims of our description, etc. There is, in other words, no clearly defined notion of content and no means of stabilising our idea of content. There would, for example, be no way of *counting* the number of beliefs a person had. For this reason, beliefs, and other propositional attitude contents, are not appropriate subjects for scientific enquiry. But there is a more intimate worry about mental contents understood from the PA standpoint. It is that, if we consider truth, meaning or reference, we shall find that they are not internally fixed. The content of my belief does not determine whether it is a true belief. Nor does it determine its referent or even, according to Stich, its meaning. This last point is best illustrated by referring to Putnam's Twin Earth Thought Experiment.[19]

Putnam imagines a planet, called Twin Earth, which is a mirror image of the Earth in every respect except one. On Twin Earth, there is a substance 'twater' which looks, tastes, feels, etc. like water but it is made not of H_2O but of XYZ. It is indistinguishable from water but is not water. Everyone on Earth has a *Doppelganger*, identical to him in every respect, on Twin Earth. There will, however, be a set of significant differences, arising out of the differences in the two earths. When Earthling Sergio is in a belief state which he sincerely expresses by saying 'This is drinkable water' he is not in the same belief state that Twin Earth Sergio would express by uttering a phonologically and syntactically identical sentence. Earthling Sergio would be talking about water and Twin Earth Sergio would be talking about twater. In other words, the meaning, and the reference (not to speak of the truth) of the mental contents is not internally determined. For Putnam, this argues that 'meanings are not in the head' – for there are external, as well as internal, determinants of what one means.

Stich finds in this thought experiment another reason for unlinking a mature, fully scientific, cognitive psychology from mental contents. The functional relations of both Earthling Sergio's belief and Twin Earth Sergio's belief – understood in terms of the behaviour and the other mental states they determine and the stimuli by which they are themselves determined – are the same, despite the fact that the two beliefs have different contents. In other words, there are aspects of content that are irrelevant to their causal role: some of the propositional content is causally inert. Content, therefore, is too impure an object to be considered by the purified cognitive psychology of the future which should be concerned only with the rules connecting stimuli with behaviour. These latter, rather than context-sensitive semantic contents, capture the intrinsic properties of mind and provide the appropriate material for scientific psychology.

Stich's proposed purification of cognitive psychology is like a kind of inverted, though half-hearted, phenomenological reduction. Whereas the Husserlian phenomenologist focuses on the contents of consciousness because he is agnostic as to the real existence of the external entities posited in those contents, Stich's purification ignores mental contents in favour of their observable causal relations because of the contents' uncertain relation to objectively observable (or scientifically investigatable) realities. His claim that 'the cognitive state will wither away' and that entities such as beliefs will vanish (described as a 'breakthrough' by Patricia Churchland) is, however, unfounded; or, rather it is based upon a confusion between a methodological principle, legislating over what is susceptible to satisfactory scientific investigation, and a truth about the world. Stich may have the reasons given above for finding mental contents unsatisfactory as objects of scientific investigation but, even if these reasons were valid, they would not constitute proof of non-existence of these entities or a case against the folk psychology that believes in their existence.

Moreover, it is not even clear that Putnam's conclusion that meanings are not in the head is supported by his Twin Earth thought experiment. The correct conclusion is that *referents* are not in the head; or that truth – understood as propositions plus their truth conditions – is not in the head. Stich is entitled to conclude from Putnam that the referents of mental contents cannot be safely determined by inspection of those contents. He is certainly *not* entitled to conclude that contents are not in the head – or intrinsic to the mind – and are consequently not a suitable subject for a mature psychology.

In short, the Syntactic Theory of Mind, like Watsonian Behaviourism before it, is the result of a confusion between a methodological decision – to make science easier or more fruitful or more scientific – and a discovered truth about the world. The initial attraction of the STM for a hard-headed physicalist is obvious: it gets rid of the awkward customers, in particular the intentional relation between the mental content and its objects. But this attraction is more apparent than real; for it is difficult to see how a non-content-based psychology of the future, in which the mind is

seen as a system of causally interacting, but semantically uninterpreted, syntactic tokens, will actually progress.

As Flint Schier points out,[19] there is no method of forming
plausible hypotheses about the syntax of a mental state that
wouldn't require an ascription of content – just as one couldn't
parse a sentence without having at least some idea of the meaning
of the individual words. This point is developed by Simon
Blackburn:[20] 'Believing as I do that semantics rule syntax (the
syntactical organisation of a sentence, or indeed the identity of
anything as a sentence, is a reflection of the *kinds* of semantic
power of its various components), I think it is equally artificial to
talk of encodings possessing a "syntax".'[21]

2. Placing Logic-and-Number-Crunching at the Root of Consciousness Inverts the Actual Order of Things

For syntactic theorists, indeed for most computational theorists,
the mind is primarily a device for manipulating symbols and
its most important structures are the rules governing the combination of symbols. Of far less, or no importance, are the rules
for, or ways of, assigning meanings to those symbols. These may
be implicit in the material embodiment of mind, in causal or other
aspects of its contact with an extra-mental world, the expression
of its output in the behaviour of peripherals such as the body, or
the (qualitative) content of its states. Nevertheless, they have the
status of mere afterthoughts. In short, the essentially syntactic
computational model of mind turns the world upside down. This
can be illustrated by looking at how it: (a) places higher-order
mental phenomena below lower-order ones, and vice versa; and
(b) puts abstract qualities and/or variables before concrete
qualities.

(a)   Inverting the Hierarchy of Levels
It seems intuitively true that sensations are more primitive than
perceptions; that perceptions are more primitive than abstract
ideas; and that abstract ideas are more primitive than the operations (logical or numerical) performed upon them. The idea that
the very medium of mind is logico-numeric runs counter to this
intuitive ordering. Since, moreover, logico-numeric operations
must presuppose sensations if the mind is to get a purchase on the
actual world, computational theories of consciousness seem to

embody a kind of Escher Staircase where the most sophisticated function of mind is found to underpin the most primitive:

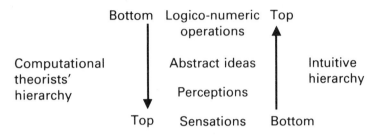

The most obvious fruits of such inversions are absurd notions, of the kind illustrated by Patricia Churchland's bald assertion, cited earlier, that 'the mind is a kind of logic machine operating on sentences'. It is surely counter-intuitive to think of sentences and logical operations as the very basis of mind itself, and as under-lying even such relatively primitive, basement awareness as the appreciation of light, rather than to think of them as achievements of the more advanced forms of consciousness. Of course number-crunching and the performance of logical operations on sentences are comparatively simple tasks for a *computer*: hardly surprising as they are computational, in the literal sense of the term, in their essence. Ordinary perception, by contrast, is not a simple task for a computer; even distant approximations to 'vision' may present themselves as computational tasks of insuperable difficulty. In other words, the order of magnitude of apparent achievement is inverted for computers compared with everyday consciousness. A primitive human being (e.g. a young child) can perform what an advanced computer cannot (e.g. recognise objects and retrieve information under unfavourable conditions, on the basis of incom-plete, unpredictable and noisy data); while a primitive computer (e.g. a pocket calculator) can perform what few mature adults can carry out after years of education and none can carry out with a hundredth of the speed and accuracy. The assumption that mind is computational requires this hierarchy to be overlooked, indeed inverted.

(While it is convenient shorthand to speak of a computer 'calculating' or 'performing logical operations on sentences', it is, for the reasons given already, misleading to think of computers in this way. The events in computers are not, of themselves, calcula-tions, etc.; the computer is not a stand-alone mind. All that a computer may do is to *help minds* perform logical operations on sentences; but it is, of course, minds that make the electrical events in the computer into logical operations on sentences.[22])

Another common result of inverting the hierarchy of phenomena is that more complex and deliberate operations, displaced from the higher levels of consciousness, reappear surprisingly at lower levels. Consider this account of vision by Johnson-Laird:

> Your visual system constructs a description of the perceived object and compares it with some sort of mental catalogue of the three-dimensional shapes of objects. It can recognise them from particular viewpoints and then make automatic extrapolations about the rest of their shapes.[23]

This sounds a darned sight more difficult than simply seeing the object and recognising it. Johnson-Laird's account is a striking example of the tendency – widespread among computational theorists of mind – to displace explicitness and deliberate action from the places where it is usually considered to be, to other places, underlying the unconscious mechanisms postulated by the theories, where it has no place. This is accompanied by the use of terminology appropriate to conscious activity (and higher order conscious activity at that) precisely where, according to the theory, consciousness is absent. That it should be absent is evident from Johnson-Laird's belief, expressed on the same page, that 'the machinery of [visual] identification is unconscious in the Helmholtzian sense'. Whenever you try and drive out consciousness from where it is usually thought to be, from its rightful place, it will return in places where it obviously has no right to be – a non-Freudian example, perhaps, of 'the return of the repressed'.

(b)   Inverting the Relationship between the Abstract and the Particular
Numbers, words, equations and calculations are abstract. They are incomplete, requiring something else to give them a determinate sense. They do not exist except in so far as they are embodied in particular physical symbols – in numerals, tokens, etc. They are general; they are variables; they are the (empty) forms of possibility. And because of this, they are secondary rather than primary: the general is secondary to the particular, just as the possible is secondary to, indeed ontologically parasitises, the actual. Particularity and actuality have primacy over generality and possibility.

The computational account of mind inverts this relationship; it places abstract equations handling general possibilities above particular qualitative contents.

Quine's aphorism that 'to be is to be the value of a variable' is a joke but a revealing one. For variables – and indeterminables and (general) possibilities – come into being only with a fully-developed consciousness and come explicitly into being only at a very high level of consciousness. The variable cannot, therefore,be at the root of being itself. Quine's joke illuminates the aberrant mode of thinking that informs the computational model of mind; indeed, presents it in its starkest, and so obviously vulnerable, form. This mode of thinking derives ultimately from one of the great intellectual projects and glories of the human mind: the mathematisation of nature. So long as this project is directed towards summarising the relations between variables and para-meters, it is valid. But as soon as it attempts to reduce, or interprets its ultimate aim as reducing, material reality (and consciousness) to variables, then it begins to drift towards absurdity. The crucial false step is the move away from discerning laws of nature linking material facts towards thinking of material facts themselves as reducible to abstract equations. The way is then open to the displacement of quality by quantity, of things by formulae that capture the abstract order of things, of the stuff of things by the abstract ghost of this stuff. The digitisation of consciousness itself is the latest phase in the mathematisation of nature.

Descartes was an early prophet of misplaced digitisation, as evident in his insistence that scientific explanations should invoke 'nothing apart from that which the geometricians call quantity, and take as the object of their demonstrations, ie that to which every kind of division, shape and motion is applicable'.[24] It seems self-evident that quantities, abstractions, equations, generalities cannot be logically or ontologically prior to qualitative experiences of particulars; nor can they have meaning, except in so far as they are rooted in particulars. In the end, the phenomenal character of our experience cannot be digitised, in the sense of being represented in, or identical with, or reduced without remainder to, purely quantitative relations; for digits, and the formulae that connect them, are in themselves empty.[25] Symbols – numbers, sentences, crunched or uncrunched – however numerous, would not tot up to the experience of being here, of knowing where and that and who and even what one is. To be is not to be the value of a variable;

even less is it to be a variable. The actual does not boil down to the possible.

Computational theorists of consciousness might counterattack as follows:

(i) 'The computational activities of the mind/brain are not like the sums we are eventually (long after we have learned to find our way round the world) taught to carry out. Nor are they like the logical operations and other symbol manipulations that take place in computers.' This may be so; but until someone says precisely what the mind/brain's calculations *are* and in what fundamental way they are different from the calculations and other logico-numeric operations we are familiar with, the computational theory remains absurd.

(ii) 'The computational activities of the brain are implicit and not explicit.' This leads, alas, to a first-minute own goal; for if the brain is not conscious of the computational processes, these computational processes, though they may underlie conscious-ness, are not themselves consciousness. This does not rule out the possibility that there is an unconscious computational basis of consciousness. But the concession that consciousness is different from computational processes (see, for example, Boden quoted in note 2 to this chapter) is fatal for the computational theory as a theory of consciousness, of actual experience.

OTHER ARGUMENTS AGAINST THE COMPUTATIONAL
THEORY OF MIND

Consciousness is not just an Information Processor and nor are Machines (in the Absence of Consciousness) Information Processors

Cognitive scientists and others repeatedly tell us that the mind is a device for processing information. This sets the scene for an implicit argument that goes as follows:

Premise 1
Computers are essentially information processors;[26]
Premise 2
The mind is essentially an information processor;
Conclusion
Therefore minds are essentially the same as computers.

The premises are incorrect.

The assumptions implicit in Premise 1 have already been examined in Chapter 3 and, especially, in the discussion of 'information'
appended to that chapter. Ascribing the status of information
processor to a machine depends on the transferring of epithets
(and properties) from minds to machines, from their users to
computers. To anyone who is not misled by transferred epithets, it
is obvious that, in the absence of conscious human beings, for
whom the computer is performing a function and who are able to
interpret the symbols on the screen of which they (but not the
computer) are conscious, the events occurring in the computer are
not information, nor are they information processing.

Premise 2 is also incorrect; for mind is not simply information
processing. Certainly those parts of it that are conscious are not. It
is slightly odd, to say the least, to think of me, as I sit here in this
room, as being in a three dimensional information-state, or sitting
in a sphere of information. Being situated is not merely being
informed – otherwise merely being conscious would be to be
well-informed to the point of saturation. The extended sense of
information (discussed in the Appendix to Chapter 3), to include
whatever resolves uncertainty, and indeed all awareness, is the
result of a long and confusing journey taken by the word. In the
course of that journey, 'information' has passed out of conscious
human beings into unconscious machines and then back to
consciousness. The rationale of this journey could be briefly
summarised as follows: any transmission of consciousness though
a machine must involve its being encoded, and so transformed into
what could be justifiably described as information; from a machine's
point of view, therefore, all consciousness takes the form of
information. But this is a distorted image of consciousness: consciousness, reflected in the mirror of machinery, reduced to
trickles of information; all-encompassing being-here narrowed to
streams of data.

The Illegitimacy of the Use of the Terms Input/Output in a Physicalist Context

The concepts of 'input' and 'output' are fundamental to computational theory; and if we look at what the computer is doing *for us*, it
is easy to assign events to the 'input' and 'output' modules.
Looked at as a purely physical entity, however, – that is, on its

own, unrelated to (conscious) users and their needs – the computer does not have inputs and outputs; no more, at any rate, than a pebble or any other physical entity does. Strictly, the physical world, in the absence of viewpoints, does not have inputs and outputs. We require a point of view, available only from conscious-ness, to turn events in the physical world – whether inside a computer, inside an organism or inside a volcano – into inputs and outputs. For every input is an output to elsewhere and every input is an output from elsewhere, so neither is intrinsically either. The output from a machine, for example, is an input into the machine-outside. And if we break down the consciousness-derived distinc-tion between machines and non-machines, we could regard a pebble as having inputs and outputs. A consistent physicalism, which will not allow us points of view, will not allow us inputs and outputs either. Consciousness cannot, therefore, be understood in terms of the input-output relations of a (cerebral) machine, or of any other machine-like entity, because consciousness, a viewpoint, is required to turn events which are intrinsically neither into either inputs or outputs. More specifically, to see the mind as a computa-tional device whose input is perception and whose output is action, and to imagine that this way of seeing could provide a framework for understanding the basis of mind, is to overlook the fact that events in the sensory pathways count as inputs, and events in the motor pathways as outputs, only if we presuppose consciousness, and the viewpoint it generates, as being already available.

The constant reference to 'neuronal circuits' betrays this problem. A circular process has no intrinsic input or output; beginnings and ends of circles are by fiat.

The Fallacies of Simulation Arguments

Turing's famous 1950 paper[27] has confused discussion about the relations between computers and human intelligence, between computational processes and genuine thought, for forty years. The argument in his paper was that if a machine could produce a performance on a particular game (the imitation game) that was indistinguishable from that of a human player, it was effectively thinking. In Turing's own words, the question '"Can machines think?" should be replaced by "Are there imaginable digital computers which would do well in the imitation game?"' – that is, sufficiently well to simulate a human being. The question of whether a computer could think would be settled by an operational test: can a computer imitate the performance of a human being so well that no one could tell the difference between them?

By transforming the question in this way, Turing made the definition of thought, or the criteria for identifying thought, dependent upon how willing or liable the observer was to be fooled into confusing the computer with a human being. More importantly, he made successful *simulation* of human faculties – thinking, consciousness – the criterion of their presence. He inaugurated the following mode of thinking about machine 'intelligence': 'If computers can do this' (or, more often, 'If there is no reason why computers won't one day be able to do this'), 'then computers must be intelligent/conscious/have minds' (or 'will, one day, be intelligent/conscious/have minds'). Moreover, all things that have minds (are intelligent/conscious, etc.) must be computational in essence, as must minds, etc. themselves.

The imitation or simulation argument is flawed, for at least two sorts of reasons:

(i)   The Concept of Simulation is Profoundly Ambiguous[28]
Simulate can mean 'represent' or 'model' as in, for example, war games. No one thinks that a war game is a real war, so if a computer were able to simulate mental processes in this sense, this would not prove that it was actually performing mental processes, thinking, etc. Simulate can mean 'represent dynamically and pictorially' – as when a model is used to simulate an incident in a football game. Again, no one thinks this 'action replay' is itself an incident in the match, an episode of football. So, if a computer could simulate mental processes in this sense, this would not prove that it was thinking, had a mind, etc. Simulate can mean 'be easily mistaken for' – and this seems to be the sense deployed in the imitation game. A *trompe l'œil* painting simulates its subject in this way but, however good it is, no one would claim that it *was* the thing it depicted. Finally, simulate can mean 'does the same job as'. An automatic shoeing machine might do the same job as a blacksmith but no one would claim that the machine was the same as the blacksmith. (Someone might argue, against this latter example, that if function is what identifies x as a blacksmith and other characteristics, such as physical composition, are irrelevant, the automatic shoeing machine really *is* a blacksmith. This would

be to assume a functionalist position on the matter and I shall deal with this in the next chapter.) In summary, successful simulation of objects, events or processes, in any of its many senses, does not permit us to infer identity of the simulator with the simulated.

(ii) The Simulation Argument Tends to Rebound
There are at least four possible responses to the discovery that computers can simulate tasks usually carried out by human beings and usually requiring conscious thought to do them:

(a) such computers are thinking – they possess consciousness;
(b) consciousness is itself a computational activity;
(c) all the activities that seem to require consciousness can be managed without consciousness – consciousness is therefore epiphenomenal; or it cannot, at least, be explained in terms of its functions.
(d) consciousness is a doubtful, quasi-mystical concept left over from folk psychology, folk anthropology, theology, etc.

The most sensible response to the increasing power of computers is (c): the more complex the tasks that a computer can do in the absence of any independent evidence that it is conscious, the less should computational power be regarded as having anything to do with consciousness. There are computers now that have considerably greater power than Turing could have anticipated and they can perform operations he could scarcely have dreamt of. We are not, however, inclined to grant them consciousness. Independently-conscious computers, free-standing machine-minds, the ones that we shall have to treat with the kind of respect we owe to a conscious creature, are always 'the next generation', or 'the generation after next'. In the case of the present generation of computers, we never doubt that the necessary consciousness is provided by the human context in which they operate (which makes their inputs and outputs quasi-intentional), by the minds of whom they are a prosthetic extension. If we found a very sophisticated computer operating by itself and having no apparently human origin (and not originating from other advanced consciousnesses, e.g. Martians), we might perhaps be inclined to consider granting consciousness to it. Until we find such a stand-alone artificial mind, we will take spectacular human performance simulations for what they are: simulations. Instead of concluding, from the increasing power of computers to perform (or simulate) complex tasks, that computers are approximating consciousness more and more closely, we conclude that the same tasks – or the movements of which they are composed – can be made to occur either consciously (as in the case of human beings) or unconsciously (as in the case of computers).

A computer that can simulate some of the behaviour of – that is, make the same context-dependent movements as – a conscious human being simply underlines the irreducibility of consciousness to behaviour. A successful computer simulation of large sections of human behaviour would, moreover, support the point made in Chapter 2 that the origin of consciousness cannot be accounted for in evolutionary terms; in terms, that is to say, of its role in promoting adaptive behaviour; for there is no reason why such behaviour could not be secured mechanically – by means of unconscious electronic mechanisms. The postulated *uses* of consciousness can therefore explain neither its origin or its nature. Mind or consciousness cannot be understood solely in relation to certain behavioural functions – as if consciousness were a set of programs for bringing certain (useful) things (goals) about; nor is it the process of achieving them.

That is why even the artificial intelligentsia are more inclined to grant the possibility of consciousness to some future, as yet ill-defined, computer than to any actual computer, whatever its capabilities. It isn't a question of the goal-posts being moved: the computers carry the goal-posts with them. Confronted with actual computers we are more impressed with how much a computer can achieve without mind than how mind-like the computer is.[29]

The Failure of the Alternative Architectures Argument

Some afficianados of AI believe that, if the mind is identical with certain computational activities of the brain, the computer in question is going to be rather different from the kinds of computers that have so far been designed. At first it was a matter of power and complexity: the cerebral computer was going to have to be 'incredibly' powerful and 'incredibly' complex. Out of this power and complexity the emergent properties of consciousness would emerge. Power and complexity came, however – and in the case of Cray super-computers they do seem 'incredible' – but nothing mind-like came with it. Our attitude towards a super-computer is not all that different from our attitude to a pocket calculator; we are no more likely to grant the former consciousness and personhood than the latter.

Next, it was suggested that it was not so much a question of needing more power as of requiring different organisation. Mind-like computers would have different architecture from the ones currently available. For example, their elements would be connected, and would operate, in parallel rather than in series. This would not only speed things up enormously but would move us closer to the connectedness and integrated activity of the cerebral computer. Parallel Distributed Processing (PDP), in particular, would permit learning by computer networks to take place and with impressive speed. Moreover, the knowledge would be held in an holographic fashion throughout a network, in a way that seemed to model the manner in which, according to some, memories are held holographically in the human brain. Furthermore, PDP would permit a network to continue functioning despite the fall-out of a proportion of its elements ('graceful degradation' and 'adaptive reorganisation'), just as the brain continues to function in the face of continuing neuronal depletion. Finally, PDP does not seem to have to begin with particular structural rules; it simply learns as it goes along. Neural networks are 'trained up' by exposure to examples, from which they extract rules, rather than having pre-training built into their software in the form of explicit rules.[30]

In PDP, information processing is achieved by a large number of highly interconnected units that affect each other's levels of activation through signals that are modified by local connection strengths. Learning consists of the modification of these connections and connection strengths and this in turn modifies the manner in which outputs are related to inputs. Information processing takes the form of change of activation of the network under the influence of external input, current state and internal connections. When, for example, the output of the system deviates from the output expected if it were responding correctly to a given type of input, the difference between correct and incorrect output is fed back into the system and this resets the connection strengths. By means of this 'backward error propagation', the network 'learns' to respond correctly. Unlike digital-serial systems, PDP systems are not defined by a formal syntax of symbol manipulation but by the way they interact with their environment and this seems to some (e.g. Phillips[31]) to suggest that they can evade Searle's Chinese room problem.

PDP systems have created an enormous excitement among cognitive scientists. According to Phillips, they have transformed our understanding of the mind-brain:

> Until recently, the way in which mental functions arise from neural activity was a complete mystery. Now computer simulations of neural networks are helping to resolve that mystery. What is becoming clear is how properties of computational value can arise from the collective activity of groups of neurons.

The analogy between 'backward error propagation' and brain-based learning in living systems seems persuasive: the modification of weights or connection strengths in the light of backward error propagation seems to model learning embodied in synaptic plasticity:

> Despite their limitations, simple auto-associative memories show many of the valuable properties of neural computation. What they remember is the pattern of activity created across their units by the external input. All learning rules store some aspect of the pairwise co-occurrence statistics in the units in the weightings on their connections (Phillips).

On the basis of the extraordinary achievements of systems that seem able to learn to distinguish letters and words, spoken and written, with remarkable rapidity, it has been claimed that our ordinary ability (hitherto beyond the reach of the most powerful computer) to recognise objects and retrieve information on the basis of unpredictable, partial, and noisy data can be explained in terms of the dynamics of neural nets.

Alas, PDP does not seem to provide a convincing model of consciousness, as Johnson-Laird concedes.[32] And Phillips, despite his claim that computer simulations are 'helping to explain' the mystery of the way in which mental functions arise from neural activity, admits that PDP casts no light on the properties of networks 'required for deliberate conscious control'. It remains, he agrees, 'a complete mystery' how this arises from neural networks. Moreover, neural nets [i.e. PDP networks thought to simulate neural function] 'provide an endless source of post hoc explanations. Unconstrained, they predict little'.

Johnson-Laird gives several specific reasons for doubting the explanatory power of PDP: the brain does not appear to be wired up in a way that matches current connectionist suggestions; it does not seem to possess any mechanism like the backward error propagation so central to PDP learning; and it can learn from correct responses as well as from errors. Next, a learning programme requires either considerable knowledge or considerable instruction. Since a network can start with no knowledge at all, the secret of its learning regime lies in the nature of its instruction, that is, the amount of information that it receives from its feedback. There are very few ordinary learning tasks that could be accomplished in this way. This is a major limitation of backward error propagation as a means of learning:

> When you learn to skate, could your performance be controlled by backward error propagation? Almost certainly not. There is no way in which falling can yield sufficient information about what has gone wrong in the performance. The procedure needs a more sensitive index of performance than a crude 'right' or 'wrong'.[33,34]

The procedure is even more limited when it comes to learning, for example, the rules of arithmetic. Denied access to the underlying principles, allowed to learn only by being alerted by mistakes, the brain would have to be taught each of an infinite number of arithmetical calculations separately.

Connectionist devices have demonstrated impressive abilities to discriminate between types of objects when they have a finite range to chose from – rock versus mine; the letters of the alphabet, etc. Beyond this they are severely limited and, as a model of learning, recognition, memory and understanding, connectionism seems to combine the worst of associationism with the worst of operant conditioning. Connectionist devices cannot cope with an infinite array of possible objects which may have an almost infinite variety of presentations (different lights, shades, distances, proximities etc.) and susceptible of almost infinite re-classification. Parallel architecture does not create search procedures that can reduce to a finite requirement the apparently infinite capacity required by a cerebral computer to carry out the ordinary business of consciousness – ordinary learning and ordinary access; ordinary recognition of objects; making sense of whole, continuous scenes and connecting them with the sense made of previous scenes. This last faculty will be considered further presently.

Perhaps more important than these semi-technical criticism of the claims of PDP is criticism that stems from pointing to the implicit anthropomorphism it shares with other computational theories about consciousness. For example, PDP systems' ability to discriminate between one type of item and another – evidenced in a different output – is described as 'recognition'. But what, in conscious organisms such as ourselves, is recognition? Absolute identification of a particular, accompanied by the sense of familiarity, by the feeling that *I* have encountered this individual before. Recognition, in other words, is not identical with its external symptom – discriminant behaviour – but includes the subjective sense of familiarity and the feeling that the object before me is *this* object and no other. The greater power of discrimination of the PDP circuits does not bring them nearer to conscious recognition than digital-serial systems. Excitation of a particular 'face unit', for example, does not amount to recognition in the important sense just described.

The Total Openness of Consciousness, the Closed-Offness of the Computer

Johnson-Laird (p. 151) points out that 'people . . . appear to be equipped with a long-term memory that is both easy to access (like Random Access Memory, RAM) yet relatively permanent (like tape or disk)'. This observation takes us half-way to an important truth. If our memory were to be understood in computational terms, it would seem that we retain the entirety of our retrievable past in RAM or something like it. Now the past that has to be retrieved is, if measured in terms of computerised information, absolutely vast. The computing load corresponding to ordinary recall and ordinary experiences was first discussed by the mathematician Sir James Lighthill, who argued that it would overwhelm any conceivable computer.[35]

Lighthill's argument originates out of a mathematical investigation of the dependence of the computing load upon the size of the task for a variety of problems. One of these is the double exponential, of the type $(2^n)^n$.

This, as has been pointed out, is 'like an exploding explosion'. For n somewhere between 8 and 9, the value of this function passes 10 raised to the power 100, exceeding by far the number of particles in the known universe.[36] And it has been argued that ordinary human pattern-recognition problems may be in this category and so be described mathematically by combinatorial spaces of this type. Any attempt to solve such problems on a computer would lead to a 'crisis in computability'.

Now this crisis would arise only if we assume that the mind, unlike existing computers, has unbounded openness. And of course it has such openness. We are able to identify objects without prior warning or preparation – for example the face of someone we have not seen for many years and whom we have no reason to expect. We can, moreover, make instantaneous absolute identification of such objects even when they are presented to us from angles and distances at which, and in lightings and settings in which, we have never encountered them before; when, that is to say, they have a phenomenal appearance unlike any they have previously presented to us. This is totally beyond the reach of any conceivable computer, in which the relevant data area has to be mobilised and accessed before the process of 'recognition' can begin. Such a process of mobilisation can take place only with prior warning. The computer has to be in some sense 'set' or initialised and its sorting task predetermined in order that, for example, a search can be advanced over a finite universe. The correct disk, the appropriate data area, the correct search terms and search routines have to be pre-selected in order that the relevant data are loaded into the working memory of the computer. In the case of the commonplace task of recognising particular objects, the search terms required to specify the object (which must allow for all the variations in phenomenal appearance) would be extremely complex. There is no guarantee that the requisite description would be finite. But without these and other constraints, the cognitive computer would be faced with the exploding explosion situation described by Lighthill.

However, there does not seem to be any way in which these constraints could be mobilised to assist the computational mind. For consciousness is not tidied away into a finite number of labelled disks whose contents are in turn tidied away into discrete, labelled files. The world that surrounds us is a continuous field of recognised objects and events. The unrecognised stands out against that background of recognition, the incomprehensible against the continuum of comprehension. And yet most of our sensory encounters are unscheduled, unplanned, unexpected.

Any computational model of single object recognition (ordinary object recognition) would require an ability to select an individual from a population of possible candidates that exceeds the number of particles in the known universe.

We must contrast, then, the continuous, boundless, catholic, informal hospitality to all-comers that characterises ordinary consciousness and is most obviously exemplified in the openness of sensory space and the ever-changing perceptual fields we inhabit, with the files, programs, disks, user areas, etc. of computers; the radically unspecified moments of unfolding consciousness with the carefully prepared recognition and action schedules of the computer. Granted, there is a certain amount of pre-setting of our mental functions, determined by contextual cues, prior warnings, etc. – so that we recognise things faster if we know to expect them – but this does not in any significant way foreclose perceptual possibility. We are open to the unexpected and, more tellingly, to the utterly irrelevant. My waiting for a particular individual at a station does not prevent me from seeing, perceiving or recognising any other individual, or from noting the colour of a coat worn by an utterly irrelevant passer-by, or from seeing the dust on the floor and recognising it for what it is. Most of the contents of a given visual field are (behaviourally) irrelevant, even though more of it may be potentially relevant. A sensory field is nothing like an agenda for behaviour and it cannot be foreseen what may set the agenda for our behaviour.

Sensory space is utterly different from the deceptively metaphorical 'space' (or 'vector space') of the feature detector, of the 'classifying' automaton. Consciousness is not merely an all-purpose detector, classifier, responder or whatever; it is also all-purposelessness. It is not merely tied to goals but is open to the setting of the goal, the journey to the goal, and the unabstract context of the goal that has nothing to do with it. Vision, for example, is not merely problem solving on the basis of information given. Of course, we may solve visual problems (e.g. Is this shadow the edge of an object or a stripe across an object?) but the following (quite ordinary visual activities) could hardly be described as visual problem-solving:

(a) being enclosed (as we usually are) in a three dimensional visual field. (Is such a field a large spherical problem?);
(b) looking at an object I have already identified;
(c) enjoying a splash of sunlight on the object.

Yes, there are hypothesising and inferential and problem-solving elements to perception but perception goes beyond them. Perception is not a series of discrete tasks, and the continuum of perception – the temporally and spatially continuous perceived world – is not a discrete task, the result of solving discrete problems; it is not a mosaic of solved problems or of solvings. At most, one could say that perception is a state that comes about when these preliminaries have been accomplished. The perceptual field is not a discrete vector space with a finite number of dimensions and loci but a continuum with an uncountable number of dimensions and loci. Moreover, the conscious mind is quite unlike a physical computer inasmuch as the latter does not enjoy its states: the computer is not *in* the vector space that the observing scientist can construct out of its behaviour, or out of the behaviour of its feature detectors.

Reflection on the ordinary achievements – and, even more, the ordinary states – of consciousness must lead one to conclude that the mind is unlike any conceivable computer.[37] If mind is 'the sum of the computational activity of the brain' that computational activity is of a kind that could bear little or no relationship to computational processes as they are currently understood. It has been pointed out that consciousness is content-driven, rather than address-driven; content-accessible, rather than address-accessible. But even this seems to concede too much to an analogy which the considerations discussed above render non-viable.

The calculations about the non-computability of most of our ordinary acts of identification also demonstrate how recognition of particulars cannot take place by a process of successive classifications and sub-classifications. I cannot, for example, cone down on an individual person I recognise by approximations, through progressively narrower or more highly specified categories: 'objects', 'animal objects', 'human animal objects' 'human animal objects I know', 'human animal objects I know as colleagues', 'Fred', etc. Recognition is immediate and direct. This directness seems also to follow from the fact that the kinds of recognition that humans execute at a glance occur in a period of time corresponding to no more than a single 'pass' through the neuronal network. It might be objected that this immediacy is only on the surface and that it depends on numerous unconscious processes executed in parallel in this single pass. Possibly. But this directness also follows more fundamentally from the fact that successive classifications would not reach the particular: there is no class whose specification can guarantee that it shall have only one member. Or, there could never be a built-in guarantee that a finite series of sub-classifications would take the mind or brain down to a single member class. This is particularly true of, say facial recognition (where absolute identification is all), since the classes with which any recognition device dealt in would have to be very baggy and tolerant in order to take account of the fact that the same face may have very different appearances. A uniqueness rider, to be deployed automatically when a certain level of sub-classification had been reached could not solve the problem for the same reason. One cannot, that is to say, reach down to the particular by successive approximations from the general. The intuition of singularity – that this is *this* and no other – which derives ultimately from the intuition of actuality as opposed to possibility, cannot be built into a classifying device or, indeed, any device that begins from generality.[38]

The Particularity of Perception

This argument brings us back to a point made earlier, in relation to the claim that consciousness consisted of number-and-logic-crunching: the primacy of the particular. The particular is primary, the general is secondary, is derived. If absolute (that is to say ordinary) identification were the result of progressive sub-classification, the instrument by which it was performed would require infinite storage capacity. The mind does not operate in this way, so absolute identification is possible for it; whereas absolute identification – and so most elementary perceptual feats – is not possible for any conceivable i.e. finite computer. Perceivers do not gradually *come down* on the actual, *derive* its particularity, its unique identity. They *begin* from the here and now with the particular, the unique. Computers, in contrast, begin with general possibility. They are not here and now in the way that minds primarily are: minds are surrounded by, are embedded in, the actual, the particular, the here and now. Computers lack this basis for deixis; most, fundamentally, they lack the here-and-now intuition.

The absolute particularity of the referents of ordinary consciousness is importantly overlooked by many philosophers. This oversight may result from an excessive emphasis on the generalising or classifying tendency of perception. That we perceive examples of general types is indisputable but this should not be taken to imply that perception is in a fundamental sense inherently general, and that its particularity is an optional extra, something added on. And yet it is often taken to mean precisely this.

Colin McGinn[39] points out that the content of an experience does not uniquely identify its object: for example, many books in the world may 'fit' the content of an experience as being of a book with certain features. We cannot deduce the identity of an *object* of a perceptual experience from knowledge of its *content*. The conditions which constitute respectively the content and the object of a perceptual experience are logically independent: experiences could have the same content but different objects (or the same objects and different contents). An accurate description of the phenomenological content of experience will employ only *general* terms to specify how the experience represents the world; or, more simply, the content of experience is to be specified in terms of general concepts alone. So the answer to Wittgenstein's question[40] 'What makes my image of him into an image of *him*?' would not, according to Colin McGinn, be the fact that the perceptual content looked like or was unique to him.

This argument, if it is used to support the idea of an intrinsic generality of perception, is fundamentally misconceived, in a way that is closely connected with the belief that perception can be understood in terms of (inherently general) computational functions. It is dependent on a confusion between the content of experience – which must always be singular – and the *description* of that content, which is general and may have to be so in order to be intelligible. The fact that the content of perceptions of two distinct objects might have the same description is due to description being composed of general terms. The precision, or degree of specificity, of description is finite. If this were not the case, then no two objects, or the percepts corresponding to them, would have identical descriptions. Nevertheless, two objects, even if they were identical in respect of all their properties, would, if they were distinguishable, be occupying different sectors of space-time. And the experiences of them would be correspondingly different, as would the content of those experiences.

McGinn seems to regard generality as the starting assumption of the perceiving consciousness, and the particular, singular object, as something it gains access to secondarily to via increasingly precise specification. The truth is that we directly experience particulars (even if under the aspect of their general types) rather than universals. The fundamental intuition of perception is that this object I am perceiving exists: it is here and now, actual. Which means that it is not merely possible, general, nowhere in particular. The object or perception is a particular beneath its various forms of generality; it has *haecceitas* as well as *quidditas*: 'thisness' as well as 'whatness'. The object that I see as 'a dog' presents itself to me as 'this particular dog' as well as 'instance of dog'. It is, as Duns Scotus famously put it 'an intelligible singular' – singular as well as intelligible.

Perception is informed by the underivable intuition of actuality (and so singularity) unavailable to any classifying machine; or, indeed, any machine. Computers deal in possibility (even though they are themselves particulars and their peripherals engage a particular world). Computer possibility cannot be narrowed down to actuality because computers lack the subjective view that underpins deixis; deictic co-ordinates are required to bring the general possibilities envisaged in a computational system down to the level of actuality. In the case of a conscious human being, the relation of the observed objects to the body of the observer – itself perceptible and informed with the unprovable and underivable sense that 'I, the perceiver, *am* this' – provides the essential basis of deixis and maintains the presupposition of perceptions that their reference is to singulars, that they have an intentional relation to singulars. There can be no singularity without such deixis. Perhaps this is what Aristotle was driving at when he asserted that it is one's perceived status as a sensible particular that enables one's intellect to get a purchase on individuality. At the root of this intuition of the identity and the real existence of the other is the sense of oneself as a particular.

The fundamental intuition that the object exists, that it is particular, that it is 'here' and 'actual' (so that, among other things, it is available for indefinite re-classification) is not afforded a computer. A computer could not have such a particular in its 'mind'. Or no computer could be programmed to experience particulars: in a computer's 'mind', generality is primary and particularity the asymptote, the unreachable target, of successive sub-classification. By contrast, the uniqueness of the perceived object is the founding intuition of perception; it is connected with the sense of the object's actuality (rather than its mere possibility), its being there.

Those who try to reduce consciousness to 'mental operations' and who see mental operations in formal terms as computational processes end up by emptying consciousness of particular content, of qualitative experience, and the perceived world of its particularity. The purely formal consciousness envisaged in computer models of mind is often justified by evidence of formal features in thought. But thought – and especially formal thought – arises against a background of already established perception; indeed logically presupposes it. It would otherwise have no reference or any material to operate with or through. Formal thought takes its rise from a consciousness which is not formal and which is most of the time closer to, say, the state of looking, whose contents are spatio-temporally connected particulars, than to a page of logically connected symbols. Despite the protestations of the artificial intelligentsia, the substance of Searle's criticism remains: computerised consciousness is rather like language reduced to syntax, to a set of rules for combining terms, without reference to the meaning of those terms or their use in everyday life. It is emptied consciousness; or a consciousness in which the presence or absence of qualia, of experience, of being there, in short of consciousness, makes no difference.

CONCLUSION

Enough evidence has been adduced in this chapter to justify the conclusion that actual computing processes are nothing like actual consciousness and that nothing that takes place in a computer would warrant describing it as conscious.[41] An increase in computing power, either by increasing the number of elements or deploying novel architectures, is unlikely to remove the difficulty that computers do not do – or even simulate – what ordinary consciousness is doing, and being, all the time. Now it may be argued that these objections to computational theories of mind or consciousness are valid only if one confuses the computational infrastructure – or an infrastructure that could plausibly be described in computational terms – necessary to support consciousness with consciousness itself. But, in fact, this is precisely what most strong AI theorists do. And this is implicit in their assumption that anything that has the computational infrastructure of the brain – or one analogous to that of the brain – must itself be conscious.

For some, the computerisation of consciousness presents an appalling vision of an essentially machine world. For others, it seems to leach the mystery from human beings and their conscious processes. Both of these objections are irrelevant; or at least they cut no ice, appealing to preferences rather than to argument. For yet others, among whom I number myself, computational theories simply miss the nature of consciousness. In particular, computer models, in so far as they are intelligible (and they get less intelligible, the harder one looks at them and the less they are allowed to parasitise anthropomorphic terms), seem to have two negative effects:

(i)   they empty consciousnesses. The idea of 'mind as a kind of logic machine operating on sentences' traduces the rich plenitude of experience – the sensations from our clothes, the willow tree silvering in the breeze, the smell of oranges, the sensation of sadness or fatigue, the sound of an orchestra, the continuum of presence that fills our moments.

(ii)   they marginalise consciousness – though consciousness denied its usual location tends to pop up just where it shouldn't.

These are the themes of Chapter 5.

5

Emptying Consciousness: Functionalism

The biological (causal) and computational theories of consciousness have the common outcome of reducing mind to a set of input/output relations. In the biological model, the emphasis is on the causal links between perception and its external occasions – the objects of perception – and active peripherals such as muscles and glands. In the computer model, the emphasis is on computational procedures whose essence is the rule-governed transformation of formulae into other formulae. In both cases, consciousness is curiously emptied. Traditional mental contents disappear and the mind itself becomes an unremarkable and unspecial site in causal chains and computational procedures that begin before consciousness and extend beyond it. Indeed, mind is scarcely a locus in its own right and certainly does not have its own space. It is a through road (or a small part of one) rather than a dwelling. Consciousness is voided of inwardness.

This feature of modern theories of consciousness is brought to the fore in functionalism which explicitly asserts that consciousness is a set of external relations rather than a collection of phenomena with inner qualities. Functionalism – which can be mapped on to biological, computational or neurobiological-computational theories of consciousness, and which fuses causal and algorithmic elements – must be regarded as a logical and, to the vast majority of physicalist philosophers and scientists, a desired outcome of, rather than an unexpected result of, current trends in thinking about consciousness. Consciousness has features that are an embarrassment to science and it is not therefore surprising that functionalism in one form or another – which effectively *eliminates* these features[1] – is probably the most widely held theory of mind among cognitive psychologists, AI researchers and philosophers sympathetic to their objectives.

According to functionalism, mental states are functional states; by this is meant that the defining, indeed essential, features of any

141

type of mental state are its *causal relations* to the effects of the environment on the body, to other types of mental states, and to bodily behaviour. Mental states are defined, in other words, not by reference to inner subjective qualities, but by their unique causal roles in a complex of states mediating between sensory inputs and behavioural outputs. Pain, for example, consists in entities that have a certain relation to inputs characteristically associated with pain (e.g. damaging stimuli) and to behavioural outputs characteristically associated with pain (e.g. avoidance, cries of woe).

Since, according to the theory, the essence of mental states lies not in some intrinsic 'inner' content but in their causal relations, any events that have the right causal pedigree, the appropriate causal ancestors and descendents, would count as mental states. Functionalists are therefore happily committed to the consequence that a Martian made of silicon could have pains like ours. For a Martian's brain could be conceived of as sustaining a system of internal states whose mutual relations paralleled precisely those relations that, according to functionalism, define our own mental states, including pains. Such a brain would have wishes and hatreds and pains and beliefs just as we do. Systems sustaining mental states need not be biological in origin; they can be artefactual. A computer whose internal organisation was functionally isomorphic with our own in all the relevant respects would also be the subject of mental states like our own. What matters is not the material of which the brain is made but the structure of the internal activities which it sustains.

It can be seen how functionalist interpretations of mental states fit with the Turing model of the brain, according to which it is the logical pattern of the states, not the material in which they are embodied, that matters. The emphasis is on processes – or the logical structure of processes – rather than substances; on how the stuff of a system is organised rather than the substance of which it is made. In contrast to the mind-brain identity theory, consciousness is identified not with physico-chemical states or events (nervous activity) in the brain but with certain 'higher-order' properties of the brain; these, however, (surprisingly, as we shall later discuss) are particularly identified with the *causal properties* of the physico-chemical states of the brain. Functionalism individuates mental states by reference to their causal roles.

Putnam's version of functionalism explicitly analyses cognitive states as the realisation of the logical states of a Turing machine.[2]

Such software descriptions do not logically require neurons. Mental properties are understood relationally, and in abstraction from the physical substance of their bearers; their essential characteristics are independent of their physical realisation. Mental states will emerge wherever the appropriate pattern of relations is realised – in an intact human brain, a Martian brain or in a computer. For example, following damage to the brain, an individual may recover and have the same types of experiences as he had before, using alternative neural networks. Particular types of mental states are not necessarily dependent on particular organisations of matters – only on types of organisations. Whatever central state is typically triggered off by the kinds of damage that cause pain in us and itself triggers off the kind of behaviour we exhibit when we have pain will count as pain. Pain *is* a set of functional relations.

Pain is also, under the same definition, whatever serves a certain type of *function*[3] – in the sense of promoting, or tending to promote, a certain type of behaviour. This would seem to make functionalism simply an updated version of logical behaviourism, in which mental events are dissolved into behaviour or in dispositions to behave in certain ways. However, functionalists, by insisting that the function of a mental state may include the production of other mental states, feel that they have sufficiently distanced themselves from both crude Watsonian behaviourism and logical behaviourism. This may not be so. As Robinson points out,[4] the chain of states must eventually terminate in behaviour. If the mental state is interpreted in terms of the function of producing a further mental state, 'then we await the elucidation of that before the significance of the first can be made plain or "cashed"'. In other words, the inclusion of the production of further mental states in the function of a mental state only postpones, but does not resolve, the difficulties associated with behaviourism. Functionalism remains the heir of behaviourism and inherits all its problems. These are not, however, our immediate concern.

Functionalism provides an explicit theoretical framework for the biologist and machinist reductions of consciousness we have discussed in earlier chapters. And for this reason functionalism – and, in particular, its *relational* conception of consciousness – demands our special attention. A brain state or computer state that has a certain set of input/output relations will count as an instance of the type of consciousness usually associated with those input–output relations. This way of seeing things makes content of secondary importance compared with external relations, defining mental states in terms of their relations to things they are not, and so overlooking their 'inner' or 'qualitative' or introspectible nature.[5] This is brought home by the following consequence of functionalism: since it defines mental states in terms of their causes and effects, it seems to allow the possibility that two mental states could have the same causal relations (and so, in functionalist terms, count as the same mental state) and yet differ in their qualitative content. Indeed, the presence or absence of qualitative content seems to be a minor consideration, as has been pointed out by those critics of functionalism who have raised the 'absent qualia' problem.

OBJECTIONS TO FUNCTIONALISM

The Absent Qualia Argument

Let us express functionalism in the form of a diagram, as it will make this objection easier to grasp. A mental state M is defined by its relations to an input (sensory input, stimulus) I and an output (behaviour, response) O as follows:

$$I \longrightarrow M \longrightarrow O$$

M is whatever has these causal or functional relations. In the theory, I, O and M are all, importantly, types – for example pains. I are types of inputs typically associated with pain, O are types of outputs typically recognised as pain behaviour. In the application of the theory to a particular instance of pain, we shall have to consider the instances of input, mental state and output, i, m and o respectively.

It is possible to imagine a computer or alien-brain state that had the same functional relations as those that, in us, are associated with the experience of pain but which, nonetheless, were not associated with the qualitative experience of pain. Or one could imagine a neural event maintaining the same input–output relations independently of whether it had any actual qualitative, experiential content. In other words an m that had an i as its causal antecedent and an o as its causal descendent, but which was not painful to someone or something. Since this is imaginable, and certainly not self-contradictory, it indicates a possible dissociation between functional states and actual experiences, so that the latter cannot, after all, be identified with the former.

Various answers have been suggested to the 'absent qualia' problem. For example, Paul Churchland[6] has, somewhat hopefully, asserted that sensory qualia will be an *inevitable* accompaniment of any system with a particular functional organisation. In other words, that the problem is unreal and the 'absent qualia' thought experiment is inadmissable. This response however, is unconvincing. Indeed, it seems to miss the point of the objection; which is scarcely surprising since any theory of consciousness that grants a secondary or afterthought status to the qualitative nature of mental states has clearly not grasped its object. For this qualitative nature is the essence of such states. The essence of pain – or of my experience of red – is the qualitative content of the experience and only secondarily relates to its causal ancestors and descendants. To refer to the essence of consciousness upstream and downstream is to cause it to evaporate.

Block's Chinese Crowd Thought-Experiment

Functionalism may be advanced at various levels of abstraction. If we put it in its purest Turing form, where what is in question is not particular causal relations but a type of functional organisation, then it is possible to imagine a situation in which the theory would predict qualia when none is possible. Ned Block[7] has constructed a thought-experiment that suggests arrangements of matter which no one would describe as mental and which would, nevertheless, fulfil the functionalist criteria for mentality. These arrangements of matter would count as functionalist minds but could not be imagined as being associated with qualia, with subjective experiences.

Block imagines a spectacular scenario in which all the members of a nation of a thousand million people (approximately as numerous as the cells in the human brain) are issued with two-way radios that connect them to each other and also to radio satellites which give instructions to an artificial body, a kind of robot. The system of a thousand million people in communication with one another and with satellites amounts to an external 'brain' connected to the artificial body (the robot) by radio. This arrangement simulates the relationship between the brain cells in a human head and their means of communication with one another and with the body and it would appear, for that reason, to fulfil the functionalist criteria for mentality. However, no one would wish to claim that the system of a thousand million people plus radios plus satellite would constitute a large mind or a succession of mental states. Intuitively, it would seem to lack the necessary unity; there would seem to be no basis for synthesis into agglomerate-mind-qualia or agglomerate-mind-thoughts.

What this thought-experiment, which seems to show that functionalism is committed to attributing mentality to certain arrangements of matter that manifestly could not have mentality, indicates is that functionalism is too inclusive; the criteria for defining mentality are too lax; which is precisely what one would expect from a theory that overlooked the essential features of mental contents.

The Inverted Spectrum Argument

If the essence of mental contents lies in their causal relations, then it is possible that two people might have totally different experiences and yet those experiences, by virtue of having the same types of causal relations, would count as belonging to the same functionally-defined types. Supposing, for example, your spectrum is inverted in relation to mine: when I look at red objects, I have what is actually a sensation of green, and when I look at green objects, I have what is actually a sensation of red. You, on the other hand, have the normal sensations of red and green. There is no way in which you can inspect my qualia directly, so that the only way in which you could know about my different way of experiencing colours would be from the different behavioural consequences. Since the spectrum inversion is complete, however, I make the same observational and behavioural discriminations as you do. Our experiences are functionally identical – they would have identical input–output relations – but are experientially totally different. This must suggest that the functional account of experiences – that it doesn't matter what is in the middle as long as the connections are right – does not capture their essence.

Paul and Patricia Churchland[8] have suggested a counter-argument to the inverted qualia objection. They make the remarkable concession that one must distinguish between the individual physical realisations of functional states (which have an intrinsic nature upon which our introspective identification of them depends) and the type-identity of a given mental state, which is not dependent on that intrinsic nature and may vary from instance to instance of the same type of mental state. They then go on to assert that, so long as the mental states have the right causal relations (e.g. sensations of red are caused by things that are normally said to be red) they are indeed red *'whatever their intrinsic character'*! The intrinsic qualia, they say, 'merely serve as salient features that permit quick introspective identification of sensations'.

This is a desperate attempt to maintain the inner emptiness of consciousness and the marginal status of qualia, reducing them to their function, and a rather esoteric one at that. Specific qualia, the Churchlands claim, are not essential to the type-identity of mental states, any more than black-on-orange stripes are essential to the type-identity of tigers. Even assuming that this analogy holds up, it works only because the classification and identification of objects is carried out from the outside and depends on certain externally arrived at, and externally applied, categories. Typing is exterior to the object and if functionalist typing is comparably exterior to mental contents, then it is not surprising that it can be performed independently of the subjective inner experiences that form the true essence of those contents.

Paul Churchland, however, presses his defence of functionalism against the inverted spectrum argument further. He concedes that his 'solution' requires the functionalist to admit the reality of qualia as things distinct from, and logically independent of, functional relations. How can there be room for them in his world picture? He finds room by identifying qualia with the physical properties of whatever physical states instantiate the mental (functional) states that display them. Such a physical state will, typically, be a group or *set* of neuronal firing frequencies. Under such an analysis, however, it seems as if functionalism becomes indistinguishable from a token–token version of the mind–body identity theory. Churchland resists this suggestion by arguing as follows. If the qualitative character of a sensation-of-red is really a spiking frequency of 90 hertz specifically in a certain neural pathway, it might be anticipated that an electromechanical robot in whom quite different pathways are hosting the 90 hertz frequency, would have different qualia. However, if it is the spiking frequency, rather than the medium that carries it, that matters to the mechanisms of discrimination, the robot might experience the same qualia in response to 90 hertz in a copper pathway.

This is, of course, logically possible. But functionalism seems to have dealt with the inverted spectrum problem only at the cost of losing at least part of its own distinctive identity. For if it is, say, the spiking frequency that matters as well as its causal antecedents or consequences, then we have moved away from functionalism; away from the position that it is not the material (or events) out of which the mental content is composed but its input–output relations that count.

Subjective Experiences as Theoretical Entities

If pain is defined in general (type–type) terms as that which has a certain upstream causal relation to a particular type of damaging event and a certain downstream causal relation to a particular type of behaviour (withdrawal, cries, facial expressions), then great problems arise. For a start, it is not possible to delineate the characteristics of pain behaviour. Such behaviour cannot, for example, be defined on the basis of its own physical properties. The facial expressions associated with pain may occur in the absence of pain (as in acting, pretending) or may not occur when someone has pain (stoicism). We can imagine an individual with congenital insensitivity to pain – and such individuals do exist – who experiences no discomfort when subjected to damaging stimuli but who, nonetheless, exhibits pain behaviour to show solidarity with the rest of humanity, to demonstrate that he is like the rest of us and not a freak, etc., or to ensure that he is treated with the same care as the rest of us and is not exposed unnecessarily to damaging stimuli in the future. The input–output relations would meet the functionalist criteria for pain and yet the individual would not have the subjective experience of pain.

This double dissociation between pain and its input–output relations is underlined by the enormous overlap between the facial expressions that occur when someone is in pain and those that occur in the absence of pain. (It is arguable that a facial movement is only a grimace – or a genuine grimace – when it is prompted by actual pain). More generally, it is difficult to classify behaviour into pain behaviour or non-pain behaviour purely on the basis of its physical characteristics. For example, toothache may prompt me to board a number 2 bus which will take me near to a dentist. This act will share many features with the action of boarding a number 2 bus to go to town shopping; indeed, it may have more features in common with this than with other actions related to toothache or other pains. The only means of classifying behaviours to ensure that the classification captures all pain behaviours and excludes non-pain behaviours is by positing the existence of something called pain whose essence is not merely the type of events that elicits it and the types of actions it prompts (or the wider causal consequences it has) but a subjective sensation. Without the latter, there can be no way of organising the observable events – the physical movements – and of dividing them into pain behaviour and non-pain behaviour. The type–type relations posited in functionalism are thus undermined by functionalism itself which removes the only basis for classifying bodily movements into functional types, namely their relation to subjective experience.

The problem arises from the way functionalism defines mental items in terms of their roles. Roles are abstract, theoretical, or even hypothetical entities. To elevate subjective, qualitative, experiences to the status of theoretical entities, to make the most near the most far off, is to invert the true order of things. One thinks of sensations and perceptions, experiences, as the ground floor and theoretical entities (arising out of general laws) as belonging to the upper storeys. This inversion is similar to that discussed in relation to computational theories of mind, in which calculations and other logical operations were placed at the root and heart of experience; or experience was derived from (inescapably abstract) calculations. The inversion is the inevitable result of putting the type before the token, the general before the particular, the possible before the actual, so making the identity of qualia primarily a type identity that is – relatively unimportantly – instantiated in particulars. In reality, of course, it is the token, the actual (which is only secondarily an instance), which is primary. And the token escapes the (generalised) functional net.

The Argument from the Knowledge of the Subjective Quality of Experience

One of the most popular arguments against functionalism, and against all those theories of consciousness that would reduce it to input–output relations in principle observable from outside, emphasises that qualia, or the inner, aspects of consciousness unobservable from without, *do* make a difference. This difference made by the things that escape the functionalist (or physicalist) net is of fundamental importance. To overlook it is to overlook the nature of consciousness. Nagel[9] has famously argued that even if I knew everything there is to know about the nervous system of a bat, I should still not know what it is like to be a bat. However complete our objective scientific knowledge about an organism, we should still not know what it is like to be that organism. We should not know what being that organism, and having that organism's experiences, is like *for* the organism. In other words, third-person scientific knowledge does not take us inside another's first-person (or first-animal) experience. Qualitative experiences, qualia, lie beyond the reach of objective investigation and so elude the net of scientific laws; subjective experience cannot be dissolved into formulae connecting inputs and outputs. Neither the publicly observable events in the nervous system nor their functional relations to publicly observable inputs and outputs can be identified with consciousness which is essentially subjective. Nagel's argument – which is directed equally against functionalism and the logical behaviourism and central state materialism from which it is derived – is rooted in a larger thesis, regarding the irreducibility of subjectivity to objective laws, the non-reduction of the (positional) subjective view to the objective 'view from nowhere'.[10]

Nagel's position has been supported by Jackson,[11] using the following thought experiment. Imagine a utopian superscientist who knows all there is to know about the brain and how it works. Imagine also that he has lived his entire life cut off from colours (for example he is confined to a black-and-white room and receives all his knowledge about the world from a black-and-white television). He does not know what it is like to experience colour. It would appear then that the utopian neuroscientist (1) knows everything there is to know about brain states and their properties; (2) does not know everything there is to know about sensations and their properties. From this it would follow that knowing everything there is to know about brain states and their properties is not the same as knowing all there is to know about sensations and their properties. The actual experience of something is not the same as knowledge of the brain activity corresponding to the experience. Subjective sensation lies somehow beyond the reach of science and, even more, beyond the reach of law-like descriptions of the functional relations between events in the brain.

It has been counter-argued, against Nagel and Jackson, that knowing what it is like to be a bat (or to have a particular sort of subjective experience) is not additional knowledge but having a different sort of aspect on, access to, or angle on, the same knowledge. For example, Churchland:

> The difference between a person who knows all about the visual cortex but has never enjoyed the-sensation-of-red, and a person who knows no science but knows well the-sensation-of-red, may reside not in what is respectively known by each (brainstates by the former, non-physical qualia by the latter), but rather in the different type, or medium or level of representation each has of exactly the same thing: brain states. [12]

Nagel's argument, Churchland claims, points to different types of knowledge, rather than to different types of things known.

This counter-argument is inadmissible because 'levels' are secondary to consciousness, and 'types' and 'media' – especially of representation – can be discriminated only within consciousness. In fact, Churchland's response implies a version of the dual-aspect theory and shares the fundamental fault of that theory as discussed in Chapter 3: that of assuming the notion of viewpoints when one is comparing the physical and mental aspects of the same phenomena. 'Aspects', viewpoints' are concepts that are permitted only within an actual or imagined consciousness. His counter-argument is, anyway, beside the point. For the force of Nagel's case is that the 'knowing what it is like to be a bat' is *not* really a piece of additional (factual) *knowledge*. The point of Nagel's argument is that (subjective) experience lies *outside* (objective) knowledge. In fact Nagel's paper is vulnerable to this misinterpretation because it seems to suggest that first-person experience lies beyond scientific knowledge – as if direct access to such experience would count as an additional piece of knowledge. This is to invert the relationship between first-person experience and third-person knowledge and consequently to present experience as the last citadel to be stormed by advancing knowledge. This is radically misconceived because experience is primary and knowledge is secondary. It is worth while developing this point as it is frequently overlooked – as in Michael Tye's recent critique of Nagel. [13] Tye thinks he can counter the Nagel–Jackson arguments by showing that there are no subjective experiential *facts* which physical information cannot encompass.

Tye invites us to imagine a twenty-third century congenitally blind superscientist Jones who has 'exhaustive knowledge of what goes on in us when we see colours and use colour words'. Jones is about to undergo an operation to give him sight. Won't post-operative Jones know something that pre-operative Jones did not – namely what it is like to have the experience of seeing red, blue, green, etc? Yes, Tye says, post-operative Jones will know what pre-operative Jones could not know: that a particular experience e has a specific phenomenal content which may be rigidly designated 'R'. This is not the same as knowing (in general) what it is like to undergo any experience with content R since this kind of know-ledge can be possessed by persons who hold no belief about the particular experience e – and could, theoretically be available to pre-operative Jones.

By concentrating on token experiences rather than types of experience, Tye claims to strengthen the anti-physicalist force of the Argument from Knowledge. He then attacks this strengthened version of the argument. He concedes that of course Jones *will* learn something about e when he gains his sight – he will discover what e is (phenomenally) like. But there is, Tye maintains, a conceptual distinction between discovering a new fact and discover-ing what a new experience is like. Jones' post-operative revelations fall into the latter category. Since he does not acquire new *facts* as a result of his operation, his case, Tye argues, presents no difficulties for the physicalist; and neither, more generally, does the subjective character of experience.

There is an assumption at work here: that if Jones's post-operative discoveries do not amount to additional facts, are non-factual, then subjective experience does not present a threat to physicalism. Now this is a very peculiar assumption indeed. If we think of 'factual knowledge' as the kind of objective information made available by scientific investigation, then *of course* Jones is not in possession of any new fact as a result of his operation because it is assumed, *ex hypothesi*, that he already knows all that there is (factually) to know about sight pre-operatively. The scarcely sur-prising discovery that Jones does not learn any new facts is damaging for the case against physicalism only if the arguments from the subjective qualities of experience are interpreted as arguments about *factual knowledge*. But they are crucially *not* about such knowledge – and therein lies their whole point.

That anti-physicalism does *not* require the subjective quality of experience to be itself a new set of facts is something Tye and many others who have argued against Nagel seem not to grasp. Tye cannot, however, be held solely to blame for this. For Nagel's own paper asserts that his 'realism about the subjective domain implies a belief in the existence of *facts* beyond the reach of human concepts' (italics mine). These are facts that embody a particular point of view. Nagel's argument, further developed in *The View from Nowhere* (see note 10), is that scientific facts are precisely those facts which are not rooted in, or contingent upon, a particular point of view. Science, or objective knowledge, approximates to 'a view from nowhere'. I feel uneasy about Nagel's use of the word 'fact' in relation to the subjective character of experience and it may have been at least in part responsible for Tye's thinking that Nagel's argument can be answered by showing that, if post-operative Jones discovers no new facts, then subjective experience does not present a threat to physicalism.

Behind Tye's misunderstanding of Nagel – and perhaps even in Nagel's own position – is a deeper misunderstanding betrayed in an inversion of the relationships between subjective experience and objective factual knowledge. The nature of this inversion may be shown by an even more ambitious thought experiment. Let us postulate a twenty-sixth century super-superscientist who is not only blind but also deaf, numb, anosmic and lacking proprioception and taste – in other words totally sense-less. Can we imagine that, despite these disabilities, it would be possible for him to have exhaustive factual knowledge of what his fellows with normal senses know so that when sense experience is made possible for him by a spectacular neurosurgical coup he learns nothing new? Of course not; for he would have no means of gaining pre-operative access to scientific, or indeed any, knowledge; his colleagues would have been unable to communicate with him. This illustrates a more general point about the relations between subjective experience and knowledge.

While it is possible to conceive of an individual or organism having experiences in the absence of factual knowledge (enjoying 'brute' or 'low grade' awareness), it is not possible to conceive of that individual or organism being knowledgeable in the absence of any sense experiences whatsoever. The impossibility of my twenty-sixth century super-superscientist is an indirect reminder of the obvious fact that sense experience is a *precondition* of factual knowledge. This gets overlooked in single-sense thought experiments – such as Tye's involving the blind superscientist – where the defective sense may be bypassed, from the point of view of factual knowledge, by those that are intact. Such single-sense thought experiments give the misleading impression that subjective experience is something merely tacked on to, or at least additional to, factual knowledge.

And this is perhaps how Tye interprets the argument behind Nagel's original example – the subjective experience of a bat – since Nagel's paper deals with a particular, though to his mind exemplary, area of knowledge/experience. When we are dealing with specific areas of the outside world, knowledge may indeed precede experience. There are many cases – perhaps they are in the majority – where we *know* of something before we *experience* it. But the fact that we often know of things before we have sensory experience of them does not alter the overall priorities of factual knowledge and sense experience. Whether or not objective knowledge is a relative latecomer in consciousness is uncertain; but what is certain is that it can be conceived of as emerging only against the background, and out of, necessarily pre-existing sense experience. That is why my sense-less twenty-sixth century super-super-scientist, exhaustively knowledgeable about a world to which he has no access through sense experience, is unimaginable.

Tye's demonstration that 'a person who knows what it is like to undergo a characteristic experience of seeing red does not thereby know any further fact than a person who has all the relevant physical information' actually *supports* the anti-physicalist case by reminding us that the subjective quality of experience is not something that is tacked on to knowledge, as a supplementary store of facts; it is not an additional piece of knowledge. To someone who already knows everything, the *experience* of what is known cannot count as more *knowledge*. But this only shows that experience is not the same as objective or factual knowledge – which is precisely what the argument from the subjective qualities of experience is all about. Or should be about.

It is important, however, not to fall into the mistake of thinking that subjective experience is merely something that goes beyond or in some mystical way 'transcends' factual knowledge. Of course subjective experience may seem to have this character when we are thinking of our knowledge of a particular entity, such as a bat, which has experiences of its own. We appear to be able to advance upon its subjective experiences, with our increasingly precise and detailed objective knowledge about its nervous system, as if by successive approximations; moving towards, but never actually reaching, the asymptote of 'complete knowledge' in whose tightly drawn net subjective experience can then be captured. It was this view that Nagel opposed with his assertion that, however exhaustive our knowledge, we would never arrive at the subjective experience of the object of our knowledge.

But an anti-physicalist who starts from the idea of the subjective quality of experience as something that eludes knowledge has already conceded too much to the physicalist – by *localising* subjective experience, so that it is either 'out there' (as in the case of the bat) or a mere missing ingredient (as in the case of the blind or deaf super-scientists). Subjective experience then begins to look like a further territory (perhaps the last territory) to be captured by, for or in objective knowledge. But this is to see things upside down; for sense experience is prior to knowledge; it is the ground out of which knowledge grows. The idea of the subjective quality of experience either as something that at present lies beyond objective knowledge or something that can be captured in it is totally misleading. Although Nagel is right against Tye – there *is* more to experience than can be captured in objective science – both are wrong in seeing experience as merely going 'beyond' knowledge. Experience is not merely 'knowledge plus'. Nagel's argument – which is about the ineliminability of the phenomenal experience, of the subjective viewpoint – is misunderstood if it is seen as an argument that subjective experience is additional or something tacked on to knowledge.

The fundamental error – that of inverting the relations between knowledge and subjective experience (and between secondary general truth and primary particular experience) – is widely subscribed to in both physicalist and anti-physicalist camps. Behind the arguments about whether or not subjective experience could become a domain of objective scientific knowledge – so that 'experiencing *e*' becomes 'knowing what *e* is phenomenally like' and the latter passes imperceptibly into 'factual knowledge of *e*-like experiences' – is the idea that objective factual knowledge encloses, encompasses, subjective experience. Precisely the reverse is true. By making us aware of this, Tye has performed the unwitting service of showing the real basis, and hence bringing out the true strength, of the anti-physicalist case.

The Logico-Causal Waltz

Another insufficiently noticed problem with functionalism is the rather too easy way it moves between causal and logical relations. Consider Fodor:

> The basic concept [underlying the cognitive scientist's account of intentionality] is simple but striking. Assume that there are such things as mental symbols (mental representations) and that mental symbols have semantic properties. On this view having a belief involves being related to a mental symbol, and the belief inherits its semantic properties from the mental symbol that figures in the relation. Mental processes (thinking, perceiving learning, and so on) involve causal interactions among relational states such as having a belief. The semantic properties of the words and sentences we utter are in turn inherited from the semantic properties of the mental states that language expresses.
>
> Associating the semantic properties of mental states with those of mental symbols is fully compatible with the computer metaphor, because it is natural to think of the computer as a mechanism that manipulates symbols. A computer is a causal chain of computer events and the links in the chain are operations on semantically interpreted formulas in a machine code.
>
> The current idea is that the semantic properties of a mental representation are determined by aspects of its functional role. In other words, a sufficient condition for having semantic properties can be specified in causal terms. [14]

Although the sequence of events unfolding in a computer has both causal and logical connectedness – a series of gates opening in response to inputs and producing an output is both a causal and a logical sequence – the two types of connectedness are not identical. Indeed, that they do not belong to the same level is central to functionalism and is the ground upon which it distinguishes, and distances, itself from central-state materialism and the mind–body identity theory. It is clear that causal relations are embedded in individual embodiments and their properties are likewise defined. Logical relations *per se* are not thus embedded and refer to the abstract or general patterns of events. Logical relations between symbols do not stand in causal relation to one another: symbols do not causally interact. An algorithm is not a set of causal inter-actions; it does not take place; it does not occur at a particular place in space and at a particular point in time. By merging the concepts of causal and logical connectedness, functionalism undermines its own rationale. Moreover, the assumption that the embodiment of the right kind of logic will also have the right causal connections seems safe only so long as one fuses logical and causal connectivity.

Roger Penrose has pointed out[15] that the relation between causal determinism and computability (algorithmic behaviour) is not clear-cut. He refers to mathematical results which indicate that a non-computable evolution can arise even with very simple classical-type deterministic systems. Significantly, he concludes that deterministic behaviour does not imply algorithmic, that is computable, behaviour. It is not therefore a foregone conclusion that a flow of events, causally connected in the way that functionalism describes, is necessarily computable; even less can we assume that the causal connectedness of events in a physical system and the logical connectedness of the steps in a program may be assimilated to one another.

In this connection, it is worth noticing the ambiguous status of causation in functionalism. McGinn,[16] identifies the attractiveness of functionalism as residing in the manner in which it lifts the basis of mind from physico-chemical events of a certain type (which, after all, may occur outside of the brain without associated consciousness) to 'certain higher-order properties of the brain, namely the (supposedly) more abstract *causal* properties possessed by physico-chemical states of the brain' (see note 12). Such talk of causal *properties* (and even more of causal *roles*) has the purpose of raising the object of discussion not only above specific physico-chemical events but above specific causes. We are back with dispositions, with abstractions, far removed from individual spatio-temporally located occurrent events. We are back, in short, with notions which, being derived from minds, are very suitable for building minds with!

THE FUNDAMENTAL FLAWS OF FUNCTIONALISM

Functionalism fails to grasp that mind is most importantly a point of arrival, where one sort of journeying ends, rather than a through way. It is a 'here' and the basis of 'here'. And functionalism also fails to understand the consequences of its refusal to recognise the status of mind: much of its customary terminology loses its legitimacy. For the very use of terms such as 'input' and 'output', 'receptor' and 'effector', 'afferent' and 'efferent', implies an acceptance of the mind (or of some central topos) as a point of arrival. As has already been pointed out (in Chapter 3), physicalist theorists are not entitled to use such terms; for, denying themselves mind understood as a point of view, they have no point of reference to determine where one passes over to the other; where, for example, inputs become outputs. Once consciousness is emptied of content, once it has ceased to be a point of arrival, 'input' and 'output' have the status of residual anthropomorphisms. We cannot, for example, apply them to computers considered in isolation from the individuals that make use of them, outside of the field of a consciousness. They are thus inadmissible in a theory such as functionalism that dissolves consciousness into relations, and which does not admit the qualia as terminus, as a turn-round point. Mind could not be reduced to inputs and outputs because the distinction between them presupposes mind; they are relative terms, relations perceived by mind, and make sense only in relation to a viewpoint.

This failure to grasp mind, or consciousness, as a point of arrival and departure, as a terminus and origin, is connected with another fundamental failure of functionalism: it denies, or overlooks, the primacy, the centrality, the all-pervading nature, of subjective experience, quite separate from its role in promoting action (or reaction). We have only to think how much of human life is spent seeking out experiences for their own sake – independently of our physiological needs (recreation, holidays, sunbathing, art, sexual adventures, eating, drinking, reading, and talking for pleasure, etc.).

The emptying of consciousness is not unique to explicitly functionalist accounts of it, where inputs and outputs are seen as parts of a logico-causal chain. It is equally evident in those computational theories where the emphasis is on logical, rather than causal, relations. We have already examined the defects in the idea that the mind is based on a neural processor and that processing is essentially similar to number/logic/sentence crunching. This idea, too, empties consciousness. Suppose that consciousness really did consist of 'information handling' and that the latter were simply a sequence of states logically linking an input with an output. Consider, as an example of such a sequence, the process of calculation, this being the most characteristic operation of a computer. Calculation consists essentially of the manipulation of numerical symbols according to certain rules. These symbols, as we have discussed, in themselves mean nothing: they are quantities without quality. They do not, without further interpretation, even have the quality of being 'large' or 'small'. Such calculative procedures (if one is entitled in the absence of consciousness to speak of them as calculations, which is highly dubious) may well be useful for controlling say muscular movement by a process of 'dead reckoning' but hardly answer to the nature of experience. The reduction of consciousness to information handling quickly leads to its being emptied if 'information' is understood in the sense in which it is used in computer-talk.

The curious idea that mind consists only of mindless computations or the application of algorithms, or that mind is mindful only in its output, its products, is, as already suggested in the previous chapter, a by-product of a great movement of thought in western consciousness: the attempted digitisation of consciousness is the latest phase in the project of mathematising nature. The mathematisation of consciousness, of the mathematiser, so that consciousness itself becomes a set of digits, is however, doomed. For digits are empty, not substantial. Although this was touched on in the previous chapter, I should like to examine it further, for it is central to the theme of the emptying of consciousness.

Lashley, in his celebrated paper 'The Problem of Serial Order in Behaviour',[17] which marks his loss of faith in behaviourism, nevertheless reiterates his belief that the final goal of the sciences is to express all phenomena in terms of certain fundamental equations derived from physics and chemistry. This is the central tenet of physicalism. It is, however, a curious belief. For equations do not assert or describe or depict material reality. They merely describe the quantitative relations between possibilities captured in the general form of variables. They are, in short, empty. Indeed, the more general they are, the more they approach pure emptiness. And the same is true when consciousness is reduced to the operations of a universal Turing machine. When it is suggested that 'the activities that constitute conscious intelligence are all *computational procedures* of some kind or other', so that 'what is important for mentality is not the matter of which the creature is made, but the structure of the internal activities which that matter sustains',[18] we are left with a curious conception of mind and a somewhat unclear one. Is mind a structure? An abstract of the functional organisation of the brain, its set of programs, its software? Or is it the abstract function of that functional organisation?

The Explicit Animal

The computational descriptions of something as concrete as the experience of seeing highlight these problems. For cognitive scientists such as Johnson-Laird, it will be recalled, vision 'is rather like finding value of x in the equation $5 = x + y'$. It boils down to sums. Now, of course, there is an interpretive and calculative element behind vision but this cannot be all there is. The final form of vision may be influenced by calculation. But it is not itself the process of calculation. Or is the visual field a calculative field? Similarly, David Marr put *inference* at the heart of perception; but what does the inference infer *to*? Is a visual field a set of conclusions? A solid sphere of conclusion?[19]

In conclusion, functionalism, like other input–output accounts of consciousness, empties it. Consciousness gets defined in terms of, and drains into, that which it is not: unconscious processes. The general principle that the external relations of events do not capture their essence cannot be magically suspended for mental events, however scientifically convenient this would be.

6

Man, the Explicit Animal

Man need not be degraded to a machine by being denied to be a ghost in a machine. He might, after all, be a sort of animal, namely, a higher mammal. There has yet to be ventured the hazardous leap to the hypothesis that perhaps he is man.

Gilbert Ryle[1]

INTRODUCTION: DEFINING MAN OR REMEMBERING WHAT WE ARE

I have described how consciousness has been emptied by much modern thought. The purpose of the present chapter is to begin the process of restoring human consciousness; by drawing attention to its *difference* and its *all-pervasiveness*, to prepare for the positive characterisation of consciousness that I shall attempt in the next chapter. For reasons I shall discuss in that chapter, consciousness is rather tricky stuff to get hold of and even more to display. In order to succeed in convincing anyone of its substantive reality, one must proceed by indirection and 'come at' consciousness via that which it is not. One such approach is to show what *human* consciousness amounts to by contrasting the creatures that possess such consciousness with those that do not. And this is the strategy of the present chapter: to compare man with the animals; or (since man is neither machine nor angel) with the *other* animals.[2] It is necessary to emphasise at the outset that I am not denying that other, non-human, animals are conscious; only underlining the unique degree to which consciousness is developed in humans. That, however successful philosophers and others may think they have been in reducing animals to the status of soft machines, of automata driven by the wetware of a nervous system, this apparent success cannot be transferred to humans.[3]

MAN, THE SELF-DEFINING ANIMAL

The human species, it seems, has a predilection for pithy descriptions of itself. The history of written thought is marked by the species' repeated attempts to seize hold of itself in a handful of words – as if to enable it to hold itself up to the light; or to catch sight of itself as from a great distance; or to strain towards a self-recognition so cold it may pass for objectivity. The comparison with other animals is its favoured way of getting at its own nature; or at its distance from Nature and from simpler natures. We get to know ourselves through our differences from things which are different from us but not so different as to make comparison unilluminating. Animals seem to be our nearest ontological kin; and so their natures seem to hold up a mirror to our own. Animals are (to use Levi-Strauss's term) *bonnes a penser* – things that are good for thinking about ourselves with;[4] they are (according to Foucault) that Other through which we can encounter the Same which is ourselves.[5]

And so man has repeatedly defined himself as a kind of animal – but one with special qualities; or, since those special qualities are not to be found anywhere else in the animal kingdom, as an animal who is not, in certain important respects, an animal at all: an animal at an irreducible distance from animality. Animal but not animal; a very special kind of animal: this is the perspective from which the present chapter is written.

Man has called himself (among other things): the rational animal; the moral animal; the consciously choosing animal; the deliberately evil animal; the political animal; the toolmaking animal; the historical animal; the commodity-making animal; the economical animal; the foreseeing animal; the promising animal; the death-knowing animal; the art-making or aesthetic animal; the explaining animal; the cause-bearing animal; the classifying animal; the measuring animal; the counting animal; the metaphor-making animal; the talking animal; the laughing animal; the religious animal; the spiritual animal; the metaphysical animal; the wondering animal . . . Man, it seems, is the self-predicating animal.

Some of these definitions are obviously far too specific, far too narrow, to capture all that importantly distinguishes man from other animals. Others seem too close to the kind of self-admiring evaluation that invites cynical scorn: defining man as 'the rational animal' or 'the moral animal' elicits shallow mockery or profound, sorrowing dissent. Moreover none of the definitions gets to the bottom of things – to the primordial difference between man and other animals; indeed, between man and all other forms of matter. The epithets pick out striking characteristics that seem or seemed (to certain men) to distinguish men from their ontologically closest neighbours; but they do not pin down what it is that lies behind or encompasses these differences. As definitions, they may answer to a focal surprise but not to the rounded and total astonishment that should mark our profoundest encounters with ourselves. The primary argument of this chapter is that these epithets identify only secondary or symptomatic differences and that there is a more fundamental difference from which they are all derived.

Even so, I shall begin by examining some of these distinctive characteristics, for they each illuminate one facet of this fundamental difference between man and the rest. Before doing so, I must discuss three sorts of objection that any attempt to arrive at a definition of human nature by contrasting ourselves with animals may provoke:

OBJECTIONS TO ANIMAL–HUMAN COMPARISONS

Comparisons are Based on Distorted Accounts of Both Animal and Human Natures

Midgley[6] demonstrates how most man–animal comparisons have been rigged in man's favour. Animals are observed unsympathetically, especially where they are a threat to ourselves or to our livelihood (crops, livestock); or uncomprehendingly, so that the true subtlety of their behaviour is overlooked, misunderstood or denied; or in hostile and alien settings (zoos, laboratories) and contexts (the farmyard, the hunting-field) where the animal's opportunities for innovative and complex behavioural expression are severely curtailed. Human beings, by contrast, have been observed over the widest possible range of settings by comprehending and sympathetic observers disposed to place the most favourable interpretation upon their behaviour. 'Human beings are judged by their ideal performance, animals by their actual one' (p. 210); 'Theorists consider animals as they are, and human beings as they should be' (p. 277).

There is Unlikely to be a Single Characteristic that Differentiates Humans from Other Animals

This, again, is powerfully argued by Midgley who suggests that the search for such a characteristic derives

> from the old tradition of defining things by genus and differentia; that is by naming first the class to which each thing belongs, and then the characteristic which marks it out from other members of that class. This rather hopeful scheme is supposed to enable us to find a formula stating the essence of each thing. (p. 203)

She gives several reasons why the search for the human differential essence is misconceived.

Her first reason is that 'we cannot expect that things not made by man will necessarily have an essence that we can grasp and a single characteristic essence we can see the point of'. If essence is to be reduced to function, this is certainly the case; but I cannot otherwise see why it should not be possible to identify and specify the distinctive features of a non-artefactual or natural kind. After all, we have no difficulty in specifying defining physical features of animal species.

Her second point is more telling (though not, I think, insuperable): the search for a human essence is vitiated by an oversimple attitude which cannot appreciate that qualities may be *more* or *less* – more or less essential to the species concerned, more or less possessed of it. It cannot, in short, recognise degrees. This all-or-none tendency is strikingly evinced in the historical tradition of completely denying souls, consciousness, 'true' language, moral understanding and various other supposedly distinctively human characteristics to animals. Midgley prefers to think of animals as, depending on the species, having consciousness to a greater or lesser degree; communicating at different levels; being endowed with a nascent morality appropriate to their way of life; having the roots of a soul; and so on. She is against the idea of an absolute break between animals and man; against the yes–no and in favour of the graded.

Finally, she objects that most of the features identified as man's unique and characteristic excellence are too focal and specific – an objection with which I would agree. Distinguishing characteristics are more likely to be *structural* properties, 'affecting the whole organisation of the life of the species': instead of a single distinguishing mark for man, we look rather for a knot of general structural properties' (p. 253). She instances the case of conceptual thought in man and also suggests that 'language might form part of such a knot, instead of being an isolated miracle'. Moreover, such properties need not be exclusive to the species in question; merely possessed by them to a unique degree. The engineering capacity of beavers is not in itself unique – other animals share some of its features; it is unique only in the degree and kind of its development.

Humans Differ From Other Animals Precisely in Virtue of Having *No* Fixed Nature

This position, which Midgley also discusses, has two versions. The first, particularly associated with behaviourist psychologists, sociologists and political thinkers of an historicist persuasion, is that man has no universal, innate essence. The individual is a blank sheet upon which experience – learning, social conditioning – writes. Such characteristics as man has will therefore be experience-dependent and, since experience is mediated via society whose character is historically determined, will be socially and historically – in short culturally – determined.

The suggestion that a formless blob could be shaped into a man by other formless blobs is intrinsically implausible; moreover, it goes against an increasing quantity of empirical evidence which seems to indicate that not only are there certain species universals of faculties such as language and in the functioning of the central nervous system (for example the properties of central neurones) but also in gestures, facial expressions and behavioural traits.

The second version of the denial of an intrinsic human nature is most widely associated with the existentialist philosophers, in particular Sartre. The appeal to one's nature – either as a species inheritance or as the set of fixed properties one has congenitally – to explain or to excuse one's behaviour is to succumb to, or to choose, bad faith. Existentialist philosophers therefore deny the idea of a human essence. Every moment is a moment of self-creation, of self-definition. To be, in the way that humans are, means to choose what one is; and that includes choosing to acknowledge the freedom one has to choose oneself. Man is condemned to be free. The self is not an inert given but the product of a continuous choice based in turn upon an original act of synthesis that assumes a world as 'my' world and shapes it accordingly. Even the constraints that seem to limit or foreclose choice are a manifestation of freedom; for the facticity of the world has the status of a constraint only in relation to freely chosen projects.

The existentialist view of unconstrained freedom – so that the human soul is not so much a *tabula rasa* as a pure writing without paper or ink – died partly as a result of Sartre's failed attempts to reconcile his existentialism with his recognition of the reality of political oppression and unfreedom; and partly as a result of a changing fashion and the rise of structuralism that placed *the system*, of which the individual was a small part, at the centre of things rather than his utterly transparent and yet mysteriously potent and substantive self or 'for-itself'. Nevertheless any attempt to get at man's species-essence must take account of the fact that, to a unique degree, man has defined, and is continuing to re-define, himself.

There are problems, then, confronting anyone who would wish to identify distinctively human characteristics setting off man from other animals:

(a)   the danger of taking a partial (in both senses of the word) view of animals and an equally partial view of ourselves;
(b)   the requirement that the chosen characteristic be a structural, rather than a focal, surface, feature;
(c)   the need to take account of the fact that man, to a unique degree perhaps, is self-defining and self-transforming.

I do not believe that these problems are insuperable and, despite them, I am not discouraged from attempting to arrive at a sharpened image of ourselves as conscious beings through identifying a root contrast between us and other animals. As Jane Goodall points out,

[it] is only through real understanding of the ways in which chimpanzees and men show similarities of behaviour that we can reflect, with meaning, on the ways in which men and chimpanzees *differ*. And only then can we really begin to appreciate, in a biological and spiritual manner, the full extent of man's uniqueness.[7]

As Kipling might have put it: What do they know of humans who only humans know? The point is to be aware of the pitfalls in establishing differences. There are both moral and intellectual dangers.

The moral dangers are more easily dealt with.[8] The very process of emphasising that man is qualitatively different from other animals may seem to encourage an even more contemptuous and contemptible attitude towards them than is presently the norm. It should not do so; whatever differences reflection may reveal between man and animals, it should not diminish the latter. Only bad philosophy can reduce animals to machines – machinomorphic descriptions of animals are no more acceptable than anthropomorphic ones or animalomorphic or machinomorphic descriptions of humans – or to deny their capacity for suffering. It is prejudice, and unenlightened apparent self-interest, rather than contemplation of the actual differences between man and animals, that motivate denial of the consciousness of animals and diminish the importance of their suffering or of the crime of inflicting unnecessary pain upon them. This has other, even greater dangers: a crude, simplifying conception of non-human animals (seeing their behaviour as a series of narrowly defined responses to narrowly defined stimuli) encourages a similar denaturing view of human beings. The terminology used to debase other animals is readily transferable to man. It is unlikely that a crude behaviourist approach to man would have maintained its hold on a generation of psychologists without first establishing itself in the field of animal psychology.

I have already discussed the intellectual dangers. In trying to reach my own defining or distinguishing characteristic of man I shall be mindful of criticisms of previous attempts to identify what lies at the root of the difference(s) between man and his ontological cousins. Whatever this feature is, it cannot be simple; it may be present to differing degrees in other animals (or rather underlie things that are present to differing degrees); it must be structural; and it must encompass man's unique capacity for self-definition and self-transformation, the fact that it seems to lie in his nature to evolve further and further away from Nature, or from the state of nature. At the very least, it should be based on fact and observation rather than prejudice and special pleading or a misconceived, panic-stricken desire to preserve human dignity by distancing man from the animals.

I shall move towards my own characterisation of the human essence indirectly, via a discussion of some of the classical definitions of man. This oblique approach is not as perverse as it may sound, or merely an attempt to build up suspense before I pull the rabbit out of the hat. The underlying logic is that the feature I wish to propose lies at the root of the defining features suggested by others. The latter are consequences or symptoms.

SOME HUMAN SELF-DEFINITIONS

The Rational Animal

This is the most celebrated definition of man, traditionally attributed to Aristotle, though, as Midgley points out, Aristotle himself did not give this definition. Behind it is recognition of man as a creature whose behaviour is explicitly linked with its specific goals or larger purposes. 'I did this because . . .' Human acts are propelled by reasons rather than being brought about merely through material causes operating on organ systems or being driven by unquestioned instincts. Behaviour is defended on general grounds, even universalised. Moreover, the form of actions is modified by general considerations concerning the most effective way of bringing about desired outcomes. Means and ends are explicitly identified and the method of connecting them crystallised in method. General methods are established for extending knowledge and power, for passing from ignorance and uncertainty to knowledge and control; and for deriving the future from the past.

This definition has become the target of much shallow derision. So much for 'man, the rational animal', people will say, after having seen newsreel pictures of a massacre or, on a smaller scale, having watched a political argument degenerate into a punch-up. The fact that people sometimes, or often, behave in ways that are at odds with their best interests, or that of humanity as a whole, in no way reduces the extraordinary domination of reason in human life. Even the conduct of all-out war – that paradigm of unreason – requires the deployment of immensely complex reasoning (think of the logistical problems of getting the troops to the places where they are to slaughter one another, of keeping them fit enough and sufficiently well fed to make sure they are on top slaughtering form, and so on).[9]

Reason itself seems, moreover, to be rooted in something even deeper than itself. As Midgley points out, rationality is not merely a matter of cleverness, but also of integration, the latter meaning 'having a character, acting as a whole, having a firm and effective priority system' (p. 262). Nor is it a question of an abstract logic, a series of syllogisms, operating in, and directing, human behaviour, rather as the simple laws of physics operate in, and direct, the movements of material objects. Logic is only the skeleton of understanding, of realisation and recognition, and is no more identical with them than axes or dimensions are identical with experienced space. Reason is not an external force acting, as if from without, as a control upon passions, an alien presence within the soul. For reason is not primarily abstract ratiocination: its primary home is among the passions, the emotions; it is these latter that give reason the substrate upon which it can work, the soil from which it can arise. Reason and passion are united in *motivation*; in the practical reasoning that makes purposeful action possible.

Reason then is not an isolated faculty – it is rooted in so much else, it pervades so much of what we are, it is a fundamental attitude of the human psyche. Nor is it a single faculty, but a nexus of faculties: practicality; sensibleness; reasonableness; abstract reason using general laws, symbols and calculations; and, finally, its own skeleton, logic. And these are not monometric, arranged on a single scale.

What is special about reasoning in man is the extent to which it *can* be made explicit; that it can be uprooted from the practical needs of the moment to such a degree that the question of its integration with other faculties is raised and that it may seem at times to be (in Midgley's words) regarded as a colonising force. Man, uniquely, has identified reason as a *faculty*; has made reason conscious of itself; talks of general principles and identifies the rules of inference; even produces accounts, albeit conflicting, of logic, its skeleton. Man often specifically discriminates between behaviour he describes as being in accordance with reason and that which he thinks is unreasonable – and gives reasons for doing so.

In short, man reasons about reason; and reasons about his reasoning about reason; and so on. None of this kind of activity is observed in animals. And it is not a minor, second order, development: the distances between an animal seemingly reasoning about how to escape from a trap in which it is caught and the hunter reasoning about how to set better traps (in the light of what has been observed about the animal's usual patterns of behaviour) are enormous. And there are further enormous distances between the hunter's reasoning and, say, Aristotle reasoning about the essence of reason and the rules of inference. And they illustrate the extent to which reason in man is not implicit, not entirely embedded in individual situations. Human reason rises above individual situations – in general laws and principles and rules of inference – in order to deal better with them. It is *explicit*.

The variousness of human reason – it encompasses the sensibleness embedded in practical activity and arguments conducted in symbolic logic about the adequacy of Fregean logic – stems from its explicitness. Explicitness permits a proliferation of the forms of reason beyond its narrow identification with, say, logic or mathematical reasoning, or with degrees of reasonableness in behaviour that could be arranged monometrically on a single scale.

The Economic Animal

For Marx, man is fundamentally a producing animal:

> Men can be distinguished from animals by consciousness, by religion or anything else you like. They themselves begin to distinguish themselves from animals as soon as they begin to *produce* their means of subsistence, a step which is conditioned by their physical organisation. By producing their means of subsistence, men are indirectly producing their actual material life.
>
> This mode of production must not be considered simply as being the production of the physical existence of the individuals. Rather it is a definite form of activity of these individuals, a definite *mode of life* on their part. As individuals express their life, so they are. What they are, therefore, coincides with their production, both with *what* they produce and *how* they produce.[10]

These are striking thoughts; but they do not seem to get to the heart of the matter which lies in the unique *relation* of humans to their productivity. For it is out of this relation to, and attitude towards and awareness of, productivity, that *homo economicus* and much of human history have emerged. At the root of this distinctively human relation to productivity is an explicit awareness of the connection between needs and the objects that will satisfy them. This is the *sine qua non* of the transformation of objects of need (or objects that will satisfy need) into commodities.

Let us go back to the beginning, to the gathering and storing of naturally occurring foods. We can regard this as the most elementary form of productivity. Although the materials gathered (nuts, fruit, etc.) are not produced in the sense of being processed, the activity of gathering can be plausibly treated as a primitive form of labour and its results as products. What makes this count as 'labour' (while grazing does not) is the clear temporal separation between the process of obtaining the object of need and the actual satisfaction of the needs. The storing animal is concerned with the satisfaction of *future* needs. This does not, however, make non-human animals into producers in the way that humans are. Man is distinguished from other animals by the degree to which the future of need, implicit in the storing of food, is explicit. Human need has an *explicit* future tense: I want this now, but I will also need (more of) this in the future. Moreover, items of need are not only stored up for the future; they have the explicit character of commodities that will serve *any* comparable need; not only my future needs but those of any other creature who has a similar need.

At the heart of the transformation of objects of need into commodities (and so of the emergence of *homo economicus*), then, is the clear separation of the object of need from the moment of its satisfaction, and, increasingly, of the object of need from the experienced need itself and from the individual who experiences it. In the case of hunting and gathering, the need-related activity is not clearly separated from a need-driven one. With storage, we have the beginning of a separation of the two and the recognition of the future tense of need.

This becomes more fully explicit with the emergence of farming whose complex activities manifestly relate to future, rather than present, needs. The things needed to maintain life are grown (rather than merely found growing); are herded and tended, (as opposed merely to being bumped into or chased after). The sheep being tended will not serve the present hunger experienced by the shepherd. The future tense of need is yet more explicit in agriculture (as opposed to animal husbandry) where man genuinely does 'produce the means of his own subsistence'. He not only stores the objects of need but is in a large part responsible for their existence: gathering and storage are only a small part of an overall picture of complex need-related activities that will serve not present but future needs. Agriculture marks the full transformation of need-related activity into *labour* and the objects of need that result from that activity into *produce*.[11]

Agricultural man is thus at a decisive distance from animals – even from those animals such as squirrels whose instinctual storage of food seems to imply an inchoate recognition of the future tense of need, of needs distinct from actual sensations associated with need. The scene is now set for further major transformations in the field of need-related activity. *Labour* in the service of future rather than present needs dominates existence; and the objects of need acquire a life and status of their own. They are ripe to evolve into *commodities*. This latter change – which will open the way towards a collective life based largely upon cooperative manufacture – will be closely connected with the changing context of labour. In agricultural communities, it will become obvious that many people working together will better serve the needs of all than each working individually for himself.

The first collective will, one may surmise, base itself upon the natural occurring collective of the family. Within that unit, one individual will dominate over others: the women and children will work not only with, but also for, the father. As larger collectives form, so the scene will be set for the hierarchical differentiation into those for whom work is done and those who do the work, those who own the means of production and those who have only their labour to sell, into bosses and workers. The occasional war and the capture of slaves will expedite the emergence of this idea. The early collectives will also provide the context in which different talents can emerge: the strong, the shrewd, the skilful will come to the fore in different situations, in different crises. Upon this naturally occurring differentiation will be based a future division of labour – a horizontal differentiation in addition to the vertical one already mentioned. Finally, the collective will make explicit something that is implicit in mere loosely cooperative activity: the collectivisation of need.

The hunger faced by the collective as a result of the failure of their collective activity in a poor harvest is an explicitly collective hunger. The emergence of such a hunger marks a giant step in the socialisation of initially physiological needs and their liberation from the uncommunicated experience of the individual body. The equivalence of need – my hunger is the same as your hunger, as any hunger – has, through the provision of general, collective solutions, led to the objectification and generalisation of need. This is reinforced by the increasing interdependence of individuals upon one another; even in an inhuman slave camp, the masters have to recognise the reality and equivalence of the needs of the slaves in order that the slaves shall remain alive and productive. The collectivisation of need as (acknowledged) *scarcity*, described by Sartre as 'the fundamental but contingent relation of man to Nature'[12] is a most remarkable distancing of man from animality, from the organic state in which it is, of course, rooted. Scarcity is felt need projected from the physiological to the social plane, from the hypothalamus to the public domain. And out of this recognition of others' needs, of how others share the needs that one has oneself, out of this universalisation of one's own needs, many other things develop.

The transformation of the objects of need into *commodities* and the collectivisation of need into *scarcity* set the scene for the next step: the emergence of the explicit notion of the *value* of the object of need. This value will become increasingly uprooted from its primary source in experienced need; it will cease to be measured by the intensity with which the object appeals to the appetites. Traditionally, the explicit value of an object of need is thought to have been first quantified in terms of other objects serving other needs. The value of a sheep could be expressed in terms of the number of bushels of corn to which it was thought to be equivalent, in terms of its exchange value. And then exchange value itself underwent a gradual transition into, or was superseded by, *price*. As strangers met strangers and needs multiplied – for utensils as well as corn, for utility goods such as clothes as well as meat, for instruments of labour such as ploughs as well as for the products of labour, for luxuries such as jewellery as well as salt – it became impossible to quantify the exchange value of objects of need in terms of other objects of need. Currencies were developed as the universal measure of value – or at least as the universal bearer of exchange value – and increasingly money reflected *market value* rather than an *intrinsic value* that could be measured in the stomach or on the pulse, in hours or days free of physiological need.

With the transformation of objects of need into commodities and the displacement of exchange value by market value and prices,[13] labour was less frequently rewarded by a share of the products of the labour. These were anyway frequently too specialised to satisfy all the needs of the labourer. More often, labour was rewarded with the means of purchasing the fruits of others' labour. The common crop of those who laboured was money, the passport to all objects of need. With the further differentiation of labour, it was possible to be rewarded for activities which were only remotely connected with meeting physiological need. The early service industries – the priesthood, medicine, professional soldiering and so on – emerged.

The above sketch is not intended as a factual account of the early steps of human economic history nor even a rational reconstruction of the embryology of *homo economicus*. It is simply a device for drawing attention to, and annotating, the huge distances that separate perfectly ordinary human need-related activity from the need-driven behaviour of even the highest animals. Cash payment for non-productive activity within the service industries stands at an extraordinary distance from animal servicing of physiological need. Salaried man is at the far end of a vast journey, of an astounding distancing of need from itself resulting in the increasing liberation of need from its organic origin and from implicitness. Although I have described the components of this journey as if they followed naturally from one another, there is in fact neither logical nor mechanical necessity driving the species down this track. The story I have outlined is one of continuous progression into the unprecedented and the underivable. Why *should* one species, uniquely among the many millions of others, toil to satisfy needs that he will have in several years' time? Why should man be the only site in the planet where the fruits of labour are transformed into commodities? Why should he, alone among all the others, inhabit a world of wages and prices? Why should man alone be able to degrade the life of his conspecifics into a condition for living-for-others in which he is (to use Marx's phrase), 'personified labour-time'? Why should man, uniquely among the animals, be able to place such vast distances between himself and his needs so that he is able to serve them with such awesome efficiency? How did he get such insight into his needs, how did he get to know himself thus?

To suggest that human economic institutions have their origins in instinctual, animal behaviour is to deepen, not to reduce, the mystery and to make the gulf between man and animals more, not less, unfathomable, as I shall discuss presently.

The Moral Animal

We have already noted how human – and indeed much animal – behaviour is moved at least in part by reason rather than merely being 'energised' by drives or, at a lower level of organisation, driven by reflex mechanisms primed to respond stereotypically to stereotyped aspects of external events or objects. Of course, there are certain universal characteristics and stereotypical features of human behaviour, as there are of animal behaviour. But the universality and stereotyping is not as tight-meshed as in the case of animals; and, moreover, humans, unlike animals, recognise the universality. The behaving human's knowledge of what he is doing is pitched at a certain level of generality. Activity is related to explicit purpose, to explicit outcomes. The effects of behaviour are also explicitly available to the behaver; and this explicitness encompasses not only those effects that relate to the desired goal but the incidental effects on other humans, the equivalence of whose needs (similar content, equal importance) is recognised in principle, even if it is neither felt on the pulse nor acted on in practice. The respect for others which this presupposes is itself based upon a capacity to generalise oneself – to appreciate that, fundamentally, 'he' is like 'me' and has an existence that goes beyond his interactions with me. It is rooted in an intuition that those who enter my world themselves have worlds that I enter.

This explicit generality – which generalises not only the actions but also the actor and others upon whom the actions impinges – is the foundation of a distinctly human morality. If physiological need and instinctual drives energise behaviour, explicit generality, itself not derivable from physiological need or drives, makes it possible for behaviour to be shaped, mediated, even driven, by social pressures expressed in and transmitted through moral precepts and formal codes. These extend and elaborate the recognition, at the root of morality, of the other as equivalent to oneself.

Other things arise out of this. The moral animal feels the need for recognition. Recognition is, as Hegel emphasised, a fundamental human need, essential to a self-conscious and rational creature seeing himself as living in a coherent world with other creatures like himself. The moral animal can pass judgement on his own or another's behaviour, and his need for recognition (and so for the approval of others) can make such judgements – or even the possibility of them – influential in shaping behaviour. Most important from the point of view of the distinctively human morality, man can experience strong emotions about behaviour that does not directly impinge on himself. The development of emotions separate from simple occasioning events enables them to grow in complexity. This may be why man, the uniquely moral animal, is also uniquely the consciously evil animal – as a product, perhaps, of an unsatisfied need for recognition and the thwarting of attempts to acquire it.

To suggest that humans are unique among the animals in having a fully developed morality – in the sense of an explicit codified morality – is to run the danger of seeming to claim that humans are uniquely well behaved. Nothing could, of course,be further from the truth. Midgley marshalls sufficient evidence to suggest to a dispassionate observer that man is uniquely ill-behaved. No other animals destroys its conspecifics on such a mass scale; no other animal routinely tortures, unjustly imprisons and tyrannises over other animals; and so on. Man seems unique in the extent of his conscious evil. Midgley's argument that the wickedness of beasts is a projection of humans' sense of their own wickedness is persuasive: once the gods had been redefined as good and divine possession could no longer be blamed for human atrocities, the burden of guilt had to be made bearable by blaming the crimes on something else. The Beast Within, or beastly possession, provided the necessary scapegoat. Swinburne's claim that 'men . . . have an awareness of goodness and moral obligation lacking in animals'[14] begins to seem rather odd. Surely, after Auschwitz . . . But to react in this way is a sign that one has misunderstood the argument that is being advanced. The essential point is that human morality (and immorality) is qualitatively different from the constraints that regulate other animals' dealings with their conspecifics.

Just how easy it is to underestimate this difference is illustrated by Midgley's suggestion that human morality is derived from a rather weak but genuine instinctive inhibition against killing his own species, an inhibition very similar to that which controls the behaviour of other species. She then adds that 'Conceptual thought formalizes and extends what instinct started' (p. 41). This would seem fine if it did not seem to imply that the role of conceptual thought in developing a specifically human morality were a comparatively minor one – a question of giving final shape to something whose essential content has already been fixed; *merely* a question of formalisation and of extension. To see the difference between human morality and the instinctive constraints that regulate animal's behaviour towards their conspecifics in this way is to bypass the great mystery of human morality and to overlook a gulf between man and animals; to leap over, or diminish the huge gap between, say, the operation of instinctive inhibition on the one hand and reading or writing a treatise on comparative morality on the other. It misses an essential difference between humanity (and inhumanity) and animality (and beastliness) in a fundamental area of life.

One way of reminding oneself of the size of this difference is to think of the transitions from tropisms to ethological traits; from ethological traits to customs; from customs to statutes; and from statutes to contracts. Man has undertaken the greatest part of the journey from ethological traits to contracts in isolation.

The Political Animal

Both humans and animals form groups. The simplest groups are spatial aggregations but in both man and animals, groups may take the form of complex social formations rather than mere spatial aggregations. In some animals, for example ants, the complexity is stereotyped, role differences being reflected in bodily structure; in others, such as many birds (e.g. geese, jackdaws), carnivores (wolves and wild dogs), elephants, whales and dolphins, and the higher primates, complexity of social grouping is based on rather open instincts and there is considerable room for improvisation. Leaving aside these differences in styles of grouping, we can say that most animals form groups and that these groups are social. They are not, however, political; and this is a crucial distinction between human and animal groupings. Man is, uniquely, a political animal.

What is meant by 'political'? Let me try to elucidate the term in its widest sense by looking at certain features of human groupings. The collectivisation of need into scarcity is related to the explicit recognition of common interests. Many animals act in a cooperative fashion but this is highly stereotyped and is not based on, nor does it require, this recognition of common interests, a conscious pact. It occurs but is not affirmed: social behaviour has evolved biologically rather than being based in an historical social contract. In contrast, human groupings, which extend outside of natural groupings – such as those based on kinship or geographical accidents – are, and need to be, explicit. They cannot depend on natural inertia to maintain them. They will, for example, typically be reinforced by insignia underlining belonging; by oaths of loyalty and other explicit bonding procedures. Hence clans gathered under totems, teams, clubs, professional organisations, nations. Group identity is *asserted*; and this will emphasise the threat represented to common group interests in the context of scarcity (a permanent possibility of human life) by the interests of other groupings. Groupings will therefore be not only internally cooperative but externally adversarial. They will have the appearance of concentrations of power opposed to other concentrations of power.

Although there is a hostile relationship between conspecific animal groups, the reason for that hostility is not explicit. That is why what I have said so far is only the beginning of the political story. Despite the benefits of cooperation, and though groupings are founded on the basis of an explicit equivalence of 'your' need and 'my' need, the individual human's interest cannot be totally absorbed into the common interest. In consequence, there will always be the possibility of conflict. This is especially likely as groups are functional or beneficial only with respect to certain needs or certain aspects of their satisfaction. Two individuals may cooperate in the collective cultivation of a field but will be in conflict when competing for the attentions of a particular woman. A group – and the power structure within a group – may have legitimacy with respect only to particular goals.

In order to maintain the stability of the group even when cooperation is not clearly of benefit, power will have to be invested in an individual, or group of individuals, to whose authority the group as a whole submits. This will be necessary to ensure that individuals conform to group needs even at the cost of their own temporary disadvantage. Indeed, the stabilisation of the group and the emergence of a hierarchy, and a ruling class, will create a sub-population of permanently disadvantaged individuals; or individuals who put more into the group than they get from it. There will, moreover, be a tendency to extend the legitimate power of the authority to areas other than those in which it maintains the coherence of the group in cooperative activity. Sub-groups will work together to maintain that illegitimately extended power; the power structure within the group, embodied in certain acknowledged hierarchies, will become self-legitimating, with the mobilisation of religious, moral and rationalising and material forces.

This, at least, is one of the most popular explanatory paradigms of political philosophy. At any rate, it sets the scene for power struggles between sub-groups which will have all the character of the external conflicts between one group and another. Factions will emerge, expressing the feelings of disaffected individuals that the power of the Authority is alien to them. Such factions, expressing collective grievances, a complex sense of rights and duties and obligations, are central to politics. They are totally absent from animal group in-fighting, at the very least because animals do not have the means to express complex grievances, even less to turn them into slogans, manifestoes and political parties.

In arguing for the uniquely political nature of human groupings, it is not necessary to deny the complex reality of animal ensembles – either of the transient groupings of creatures that may hunt in packs or more permanent groupings maintained for less narrowly defined ends, including companionship. As Midgley points out, several groups of animals

> have independently 'invented' fairly advanced forms of social life. They are, that is, not 'anonymous herds' whose members stay together and take no notice of one another. They can *do* things together, help and look after one another to some extent, and have individual friendships. (p. 335)

At the root of many animal groups is 'attachment; a bond of affection constantly fed and maintained by friendly attentions' (p. 338). Peacemaking is an important feature of animal social life: 'The positive social bond consists of friendly gestures that arise from the need to consider an existing possibility of aggression'. Group stability is maintained by a dominance hierarchy which is far from tyrannical; indeed,

> rank is very closely linked with the behaviour typical of parent and child. Those of lower rank defer to those they respect in the same way that they did to their own parents, and where conflict looms, one participant has often only to make infantile gestures to appease the other, who responds with parental ones. (pp. 335–6)

The complexity of animal groups, then, is not in question; and, as in the case of humans, animal groups answer to a collective need that is inchoately collectivised. Animal groups too may acquire a strengthened solidarity in response to the threats posed by other groupings, either within or outside of the index group. The groups, however, are not explicit in the sense of being liable to develop anything like a constitution, a codified law or a myth of their own origin and legitimacy. There are no formal rights, duties or obligations and no appeal to them or rhetoric of them. Such codified, explicit laws, laid down in permanent documents, enable human groupings to be formed and maintained which are not defined or limited by spatial cohabitation: between individuals who have never met one another; between large numbers of individuals who could never, because of their numbers, encounter one another; and across continents and centuries. The manner in which I can be treated by the group corresponding to Great Britain has been decisively influenced by the signing of the Magna Carta. Such are political groupings; and in this very important and wide-ranging sense, animal groupings are not political groupings at all. Man is, uniquely, a political animal.

The Historical Animal

All species change with time but the vast majority of these changes are mediated through species-wide alterations in bodily structure and composition, themselves a reflection of changes in the genetic blueprint. The human animal changes at an astonishing rate and, in contrast with other animals, most of these changes are mediated by changes in collective knowledge and skills, themselves embodied in rapidly evolving artefacts and in the huge accumulations of knowledge housed outside of the body. The quickening pace of change is beautifully summarised by Maynard Smith:

> About 400 million years ago the first aquatic vertebrates evolved; at least two million years ago man's ancestors first chipped stones to make simple tools. Less than ten thousand years ago, in the neolithic revolution, animals and plants were first domesticated. If a film, greatly speeded up, were to be made of vertebrate evolution, to run for a total of two hours, tool-making man would appear only in the last minute. If another two-hour film were made of the history of tool-making man, the domestication of animals and plants would be shown only during the last half-minute, and the period between the invention of the steam engine and the discovery of atomic energy would be only one second.[15]

With the emergence of *homo sapiens*, it would seem that history has broken free of evolution. As Maynard Smith (p. 312) observes, 'we can be fairly confident that the "nature" (i.e. genetically determined capacities) of human beings has not greatly changed since the neolithic revolution, since 7,000 years is too short a period for major evolutionary changes'; yet during this time the life of human beings has changed out of all recognition. Moreover, especially since we have started planning for our remote descendents as well as for ourselves and our contemporaries, the human species advances towards its own future with its eyes at least partly open.

Of course, individual organisms can adapt to changed circumstances and some of these behavioural adaptations can be transmitted directly without the mediation of genetic change. Tits learn how to open milk bottles, macaque monkeys acquire the habit of washing their sweet potatoes before they eat them. These new behaviour patterns are culturally transmitted from generation to generation; their emergence is an historical and not an evolutionary event. But in all animals apart from man, they contribute in only a minor way to species change; they are merely sporadic events. In the vast majority of cases, advances are transmitted to future generations by cultural and not by genetic means. Maynard Smith again:

> There is no need to wait for the genetic assimilation of a new adaptive advance made by an individual. Such advances are transmitted to future generations by cultural and not by genetic means; children do not inherit a 'racial memory'; they learn what their parents teach them. . . . It is this change from genetic to cultural transmission which determines the differences between evolutionary and historical processes, and is responsible for the greater rapidity of the latter. (p. 313)

In animals, by contrast, 'instead of one historical event leading directly to another, as in human history, . . . each such event has been followed by long periods of genetic evolution' (p. 314).

The opposition between Nature and History has been an important rallying point for political and social theorists – especially self-styled progressives and conservatives. Marxists and other left-wing thinkers are irritated by writers who attribute the Order of (Human) things to the work of Nature, when it is, in their opinion, clearly historically derived; for this eternises the way things are and consequently obstructs changes that would benefit society as a whole. The appeal to Nature – and consequently to unchange-ability – is, they argue, very much in the interest of those who are benefiting from the status quo. Conservatives not only naturalise the social order but also the individual's position in it: our 'proper stations' correspond to our own intrinsic properties, rather than being the product of conflict and historical accident and stabilised by self-legitimating activity of the privileged. An aristocrat, the naturalising, essentialist, conservative argument goes, is intrinsi-cally aristocratic; his point of origin confers certain properties upon him that befit him for his high station. The opposite viewpoint, espoused by those of a progressive and melioristic turn of mind, is that, far from there being a fixed individual and general human nature, human nature is culturally or historically determined and will vary from culture to culture. Likewise, an individual's nature is culturally determined or conditioned by his own history, by the social experience to which he has been exposed since birth.

One could reconcile the warring viewpoints of the 'naturalists' and the 'culturalists' or the 'naturalists' and the 'historicists' by saying that it is human nature to be historically determined and to encounter nature mediated by culture. This is not, however, to deny the innate or the genetic element in human nature. Although humanity has changed out of all recognition independently of any change in the human genome, that genome is still central to what we are. We are not determined by, say, our physiology but we are embedded in it; it is the ground upon which we stand, the natural pitch upon which we play our cultural games, the coordinates with respect to which our history unfolds. And this is true at the psychological level as well. There is a legitimate analogy between the jealousy one animal may feel towards another that has secured a large piece of meat and the jealousy one individual may feel towards another because he can afford to go to an expensive restaurant. The two situations are analogous, yes; but there is an enormous distance between them, a distance I marked out in the *homo economicus* section.

To fail to see this distance – and more generally to fail to notice the extent to which evolving culture, rather than fixed nature, determines the content of human lives – is to overlook a profound difference between man and animals. As history unfolds, we do not lose our roots in nature – our embodied state ensures that we remain a piece of nature – but we diverge more and more from other pieces of nature. Man is a living creature whose evolution has forked off from the general evolutionary process. His environment is increasingly a man-made one and his preoccupations distinctively human.

Since we are talking about Culture and Nature, a word or two about Structural Anthropology may be in order here. Consider Levi-Strauss's meta-myth about cooking.[16] Man discovered that food could be transformed from its natural state, while still retaining its edibility and nutritional value; this, according to Levi-Strauss, was a crucial moment in the establishment of an explicitly human culture set off against Nature. The functionalist explanation of cooking can be set aside: the food probably didn't taste any better cooked (the preference for cooked over raw food is acquired) and the microbiological advantage of cooking was probably not evident at the time that cooking entered the human scene. No, behind the preference for the cooked over the raw was a desire to set oneself off from nature: Man, the Cooking Animal, reaffirms his difference from, and superiority to, the beasts and asserts his distinctive species being. From this initial difference unravelled a thousand distinctions and distances from the other beasts and the world of nature in general.

This somewhat flippant account of the thesis of *The Raw and the Cooked* is offered only because it provides another example of a tendency to overlook, by rather taking for granted, an extraordinary property of human beings: their ability to *elaborate* differences and out of them create enormous multi-dimensional distances. The cooking story is not sufficient to account for the origin of culture or of the culture–nature divide; for what it leaves unexplained is the propensity *to make so much out of a difference*. This propensity is an *ability*; it is possible only because, for humans, differences are explicitly appreciated, so that their implications can be elaborated. Animals and men are different; but the 'we are different from them' is different for animals than for man; we are conscious of, and make much of, this difference. Without *this* difference – this different attitude to difference – no amount of happy or astounding accidents could account for the emergence of a vast proliferating culture increasingly separating man from other pieces of nature.

The Technological Animal

*men make tools, and so can change their environment to suit themselves
instead of evolving new, genetically determined adaptations to new
environments.*[17]

Man, according to Benjamin Franklin, is The Toolmaking Animal.
In a sense this definition begins too far along the road taken by
organisms in manipulating their own environment to ensure
survival, to bring out the full strangeness of man. To see what he
is, you have to step back a little further.

Begin at the beginning. Think of a simple multicellular organism
moving, by virtue of a tropism, in the direction of an area of
different pH in the fluid medium in which it happens to be. The
purpose of this behaviour is to keep it in an environment most
favourable to survival, i.e. in an environment least likely to
overthrow the polyphasic dynamic equilibrium that describes the
conditions under which the organism counts as being alive. The
organism is unaware of its need to move towards the more
favourable environment, cannot anticipate what may happen to
change its environment and has no strategy to cope with changes
in pH outside of those which it can correct by tropism-driven
swimming. In contrast, a human animal recognises a vast number
of the conditions necessary for its life and comfort and is constantly
taking steps to ensure that not only present but also future comfort
and safety is ensured. The maintenance of, or the bringing about
of, conditions directly, indirectly or remotely related to pleasure,
comfort and survival, is the constant preoccupation of the human
animal. It is tempting to claim that, in this respect, man is no
different from many other animals. But there are important differences that can be highlighted by using the tropism-driven primitive organism as a zero point to measure how far man has travelled
into self-consciousness – and, indeed, to make the road along
which he has travelled visible.

Human survival-related activity takes the form of solving problems
by means of artefacts using *methods, rules and techniques*. The
solutions sought involve the application of principles, conceived at
different levels of generality, to particular circumstances. Under-
neath all man's problem-solving is this intuition of *a general
principle with particular application*. The here-and-now is always an
instance. The development of enduring artefacts with certain

general properties designed to enable them to deal with whole classes of problem-situations exemplifies this extraordinary, inexplicable intuition apparently denied to other animals.

Man is the tool-making animal, *homo sapiens* is *homo faber*; whereas at best certain animals may be tool-finding animals. Animal tools are neither manufactured, nor are they preserved and stored against future uses on future occasions. The early human artefacts were extensions of the body, and modelled on the body's powers, to magnify those powers. With the advent of the wheel, the search for technical solutions to the problems of living was liberated from the implicit and severely limiting metaphor of the body. Technology woke into itself and tools began their long evolution to the kind of gadgets we now take for granted: artefacts designed in accordance with abstract solutions provided for generalised problems. The means to satisfy needs became quite separate from the activity of the needing body or even the form of that activity.

The development of distinctively human tools has been associated with an increasingly clear appreciation of both the nature of need and of the relationships between the events that will bring about their satisfaction. Tools are the most powerful possible testimony to the self-knowledge of human need. It is in technology that, above all, the explicitness of the human condition to humans is made apparent. Technology demands explicitness; it is explicitness embodied. This is vividly illustrated when the satisfaction of a need is reduced to a path between two explicitly defined states and that path is redescribed in the form of a computer program. (This is not to say that the computer is itself explicit. Rather, it embodies explicitness. Just as the sounds of language are not themselves meaning, but the embodiments of meaning that are 'cashed' elsewhere. The explicitness is in the technologist not the technology.)

The fact that in the early stages of tool production, the underlying principles were not made fully explicit is illustrated by the extraordinary constancy of the size (some 9 inches) and shape of hand axes over 100 000 years across several continents. As Maynard Smith points out, 'this wide distribution in space and time of a particular type of tool implies a process of meticulous copying for many generations' (Maynard Smith, p. 315). The value of 'try it and see' and the search for the underlying principles, which lie at the root of modern technological advance was not recognised until the Renaissance whose exemplary – indeed emblematic – figure was Leonardo da Vinci. This late entry of the fully-developed experimental method is a tribute to the egregious character of the method. In Maynard's Smith's two-hour film of tool-making man, 'try it and see' has been around only for between two and three seconds.

The difference between the tools used by animals – stones for throwing at enemies, sticks for getting at food that would otherwise be out of reach – and those used by man are not merely differences of degree. That man makes his own tools; that those tools are not mere extensions of his body or modelled on his body; that he stores tools for future use; that the tools have been designed with reference to stated general principles; that they may be enormously complex (as in the case of the robots used in car manufacture) – these are all symptoms of a fundamental underlying difference. To suggest that a chimpanzee picking up a rock to scare off an intruder is in the same business as an individual calculating the necessary quantities of radioactive material to make an atomic bomb, determining the size of the explosion it would cause, pondering how big an explosion would be necessary to demoralise the enemy sufficiently to make it surrender, thinking about the dangers presented to his own side by failing to meet certain storage conditions, is to stretch credulity to the limit.[18]

The Classifying Animal

There is a (somewhat tendentious) sense in which all animals classify the contents of those parts of the world they come into contact with. A primitive multi-cellular organism that moves towards a life-sustaining type of substance and away from another, life-threatening one – for example, the flatworm moving towards food and away from strong light – could be described as *behaviourally* classifying the contents of the world into 'good' things and 'bad' things. But these 'behavioural classifications' are only implicit and really exist only in the organism – man – that observes and describes the organism's behaviour. Any labels we give to the two types of item have specific content only in so far as the labels belong to a much wider system of classification – namely the system of language – the use of which it would be absurd to attribute to a primitive organism.[19] To suggest that such an organism has the concepts 'good' and 'bad' – with the meanings these terms have for us, with the work they do for us – would be no less implausible than to suggest that it has the concepts 'Good for me' and 'Bad for me'; or 'Liable to improve my chances of survival' and 'Liable to cause me harm'; and so on.

The claim that man is uniquely 'the classifying animal' is easy to sustain when the only rivals are primitive multi-cellular organisms. It is less easy to sustain when one considers the higher animals. In order to do this it is necessary to look more carefully at the nature of classification.

First of all, true classification deals in universals. The classes corresponding to terms – 'dog', 'green', etc. – are infinite and open-ended and encompass a whole universe of possible instances. Secondly, it is systematic: classification does not operate through a heap of isolated terms. The terms are closely interrelated; they belong to sets ('green', 'blue', etc.); they have logical relations to one another (synonyms, hyponyms, admissible combinations, appropriateness of application); and they are comprehensive, in the sense that they cover all possibilities in a defined range. Thirdly (and this follows from the first two points), classification cannot be embodied in, or reduced to or dissolved in, discriminant behaviour directed towards the classified objects, but involves the use of symbols specific to the purpose. These symbols will be explicitly symbols: they will not be mistaken for the things classified; they will stand off from the world whose contents are being classified.

Only man is a classifier in this sense. For only he is explicitly – that is to say separately – aware of the labels of the classes into which things are classified and is able to distinguish the classes from the things classified. In human consciousness, the classes, and their labels, have a separate existence. Generality has a home of its own. And because of this, objects can not only be classified but, since the classes are distinguished from their members, *re*-classified. The real nature of human classification – as opposed to any animal analogue based on discriminant behaviour or upon signalling – is revealed in the fact that man is the re-classifying animal. Unlike creatures 'classifying' objects by discriminant behaviour, man does not assimilate the objects entirely into the categories to which they are assigned. The objects remain distinct from their classes; and so they are available for indefinite re-classification.

Nothing could be in more complete contrast to this than the 'behavioural classification' thought to be implicit in, for example, the response of a robin to a red patch painted on to a brown background. The robin attacks objects that conform to this pattern and it is argued that the robin has effectively placed such objects in a general class – that of 'rival robins' or 'enemies'. The fact that we cannot confidently say what that class is, or that the class will vary in accordance with how *we* describe the robin's behaviour, should make it clear that, so far as the robin is concerned, no such class exists. Stimulus generalisation, such that an organism will exhibit a conditioned response not only to the conditioning stimuli but to other stimuli which share with it certain characteristics, has also been taken to be an animal equivalent of classification. The animal, it is argued, by behaving towards a range of similar stimuli as if they were the same, is effectively classifying those stimuli together. Unfortunately, this would seem to base classification on *failures* behaviourally to discriminate between similar stimuli. And it would follow from this that all entities which elicit the same behaviour are being classified together. This would suggest that animals have access to very abstract categories indeed, such as 'air', 'enemies' and even 'walkables', 'barkabilia', 'space', etc.

All true classification is explicit; that is, the class label is distinct from the class members. In behavioural 'classification', the label does not exist except in the mind of the spectator – the human being – observing the behaviour.

The Talking Animal

The feature most commonly invoked in attempts to pinpoint the differences between man and other animals is, of course, man's possession of language and discussion of classification brings us naturally to this. Much of the debate revolves around whether man is unique in having language (in other words whether the other animals, that assuredly have communication systems, really have language at all) or whether his uniqueness resides only in certain features of his language.[20]

It is important not to get side-tracked into secondary issues. My own position is that human language has certain fundamental differences from all other animal communication systems (or rather one fundamental difference from which many others follow; or a fundamental difference which determines the entire character of human language). Whether we should conclude from this that only humans have 'true language' is a mere matter of definition and therefore of little interest.

So in what sense is human language unique? One has first of all to consider its scope and consequences. Language ranges over the entire experienced universe, penetrating every aspect of reality at every level – at the level of the atom, of the cell, of the leaf, of the tree, of the forest, of the nation, of the planet, of the galaxy. And language has a multitude of types of levels. For example, I can talk about what you did; about your feelings about what you did; about my theory about your feelings about what you did; about your attitude to my theory about what you did; about my feelings about your attitude to my theory; and so on. Talk, moreover, is not confined to the actual. Our ability to refer to that which is absent is only the beginning; we can refer not only to the absent actual but also to the absent possible (and language has given birth to vast, proliferating worlds of the possible that enormously outnumber and out-size the unimaginably large actual one); and to the impossible. To quote George Steiner, '*Anything* can be said and, in consequence written, about *anything*':

> Only language knows no conceptual, no projective finality. We are at liberty to say anything, to say what we will about anything, about everything and nothing (the latter a particularly striking and metaphysically intriguing licence). No deep-lying grammatical constraint, if any such can indeed be shown to obtain, abrogates the anarchic ubiquity of possible discourse . . . Language need halt at no frontier, not even, in respect of conceptual and narrative constructs, at that of death . . . Inside grammar, future tenses, optatives, conditionals are the formal articulation of the conceptual and imaginative phenomenality of the unbounded.[21]

The possibilities of language are unconfined by the physiological constraints that limit other human activities. As Steiner has said elsewhere, 'Man has talked himself free of organic constraint'.[22]

So much for the scope of human language. What of its consequences? These are so enormous that it is impossible to see them whole: language is the air in which our minds breathe, the very space in which our consciousness is deployed. There is, consequently, no place outside of language from which we can see it. As a result, some thinkers have focused on relatively small, though telling, consequences of man's being the talking animal. Nietzsche and Marcel,[23] for example, were sufficiently struck by one linguistic activity peculiar to man – that of promising – to see it as a defining characteristic. Man was 'the promising animal'. What excited them was the fact that promising – and, more particularly, the keeping of promises – involved the individual in committing his own future. This in turn presupposed an explicit sense of one's own future and a belief in one's own continuity. If I promise to do something (or sign a contract, or undertake certain responsibilities), I bind at least part of my future self. I am working on the assumption that my future self will feel itself to be bound by my present self, that it will recognise it as the same as *its*-self. Promising makes the future and the extension of a unified self over time, explicit. It is, however, but one aspect of language-mediated explicitness, albeit an important and exemplary one.

One could think of virtually every aspect of civilisation, and of humanity as opposed to animality, as a consequence of the curious gift of language. But placing language at the root of all that divides man from the rest of the animal kingdom and opposes civilisation to nature will be unilluminating unless we consider the phenomenon itself and try to identify what it is about language that accounts for its scope and momentous consequences.

Every attempt to pinpoint features unique to human language seem doomed to refutation by counter-examples. Let us consider some such attempts:

1. *Human language refers to that which is absent.*
Whereas animal cries usually refer to (or, strictly, are triggered by) present dangers, prey, etc., human talk is not so restricted.

Counter-example: the bee's dance, referring to pollen supply which is absent in the sense of being outside of the current sensory field of both the sender and recipient of the message. Of course such absence is a restricted absence. The dance could not refer to a future, or a remotely past, or a never-existing supply of pollen. Even so, reference to the absent does not seem to be a sharply distinguishing feature of human language as opposed to animal communication systems.

2. *Human language uses arbitrary, conventional, rather than natural signs.*
Counter-example: again the bee's dance. The elements of the dance bear no natural relation to the things they signify. There is, for example, no physical similarity between the waggle dance and the locations it is used to signify.

3. *Human language has a complex syntax not evident in animal signalling systems.*

Counter-example: yet again, the bee's dance. One could regard the different components of the dance and the relationships between them as being analogous to different parts of speech and their syntactical ordering. Certainly, there are rules of combination that seem essential to the message. Grammar, however, is very much in the eye of the beholder. It is possible to describe animal languages in terms of complex rules that, under the most objective definitions of grammar, seem grammatical – just as one can describe animal beliefs, etc., in propositional terms.

The point is that to look for specific distinguishing features between human language and animal communication systems is misconceived. It will be obvious, of course, that whatever features are considered, they will be developed to an unimaginably greater degree in human language. But this will not capture the fundamental difference between human and animal language. For one can always redescribe animal communication systems in terms that make them seem like human language; as if, for example, they were based on a system of arbitrary signs organised grammatically and capable of having reference to absent as well as present objects, to particulars as well as generalities. It will be more fruitful to ask ourselves why human language has its unique capacity for development.

Let us consider arbitrariness. This, according to Saussure, is the 'primordial' fact of language; and yet it is a feature arguably shared by the signs used in non-human communication. The arbitrary sign is not a mere index, causally related to that which it signifies, as clouds are to rain. Nor is it an icon, signifying 'naturally' in virtue of replicating some aspect of the significate. Arbitrariness thus sets off the sign, separating it from a causal net or a mere mirroring of reality. The arbitrary sign is an explicit sign; it could not be mistaken for the significate, or an effect or consequence or symptom of the significate, or another instance of it. Arbitrary signs are signs that wear their status – the fact that they are signs – as signs on their sleeves. And yet man is the only animal who has appreciated this and exploited its possible consequences. If the sign is uprooted from the significate, it may not only be able to signify a present significate or one that is absent but actual; it may also be used to signify the possible (but non-existent) and the impossible. Signifying, moreover, may not only be uprooted from the significate but also from the context in which the significate is usually signified. It may, finally, be uprooted from the natural processes of signifying: from utterance. These developments seem inevitable; but their inevitability is an effect of hindsight and their non-inevitability can be inferred from the fact that no other animal has used its communication system in the way that humans have. The consequences are momentous.

The most important consequence results from the separation of the processes of signifying from the act of signification, from utterance. This is the emergence of writing – often, though dangerously, thought of as: the storage of communication outside of the moment of its being communicated; the storage of information outside of the body; or the transformation of communication-events into enduring objects. With writing, the transmission and preservation of knowledge no longer depends on the frailty of the human body and, in particular the limitations of memory and attention. It is on writing, and on comparable systems of written communication, more than on anything else, that the divergence of human history from bodily evolution, and the astonishingly rapid cultural evolution from physiological change, have depended. Without writing, the process by which accumulated knowledge and expertise is handed down from one generation to the next – so that each generation is the beneficiary of the experience and collective genius of all who have gone before – would not have been possible.

The most important and most distinctive features of human language are consequences of its having the explicit status of being a language. The uniqueness of human language is that it is a communication system that knows what it is. Humans are not alone in having a language composed of arbitrary signs; but they are alone in seeing that arbitrariness and exploiting the possibilities that flow from it. Of course other animals may sometimes play with signs. They may, for example, produce warning cries in the spirit of fun and mischief, suggesting that they have some dim sense of the status of signs as signs. But that sense is at best nascent and transient and never unfolds even to the extent that would justify one in thinking that the animal was explicitly aware that its signs were a way of bringing about a belief in another animal – a belief based on the second animal's recognition of the intention of the first. In contrast, the sense of the other person trying to say something is elementary in humans. It is part of the basic structure of ordinary communication. The entry into human language (as opposed to the acquisition of mere competence in signalling) involves recognition of signs as signs. Understanding mediated through arbitrary signs has to be based on an appreciation that the signs are signs. Speech, because it has to be understood in order to have its effects, can fail to have those effects. Signs operating through the causal mechanisms of natural association cannot fail in this way.[24]

The distinctive nature of human language is not, then, based in the objectively demonstrable complexities of the system. Any system can be redescribed in such a way as to seem enormously complex; it can have complexities and sophistications foisted upon it. So we can, if we like, find grammars and parts of speech and propositions in the language of bees. But the proof of the pudding is in the eating and, if the bee language has these properties, the bees do remarkably little with them. They certainly haven't used them to improve pollen-finding over the millenia in which they have been using their language. Whereas man, if he does indeed have only the same means at his disposal as bees, has made much, much more of them. He has (to borrow von Humboldt's phrase) 'made infinite use of finite means'. This is because in using language we are conscious of language itself; when we speak, we are explicitly aware of what we are doing or trying to do. It is this that has enabled us to do almost anything with our language – to the point where discourse has developed an unlimited complexity.

The most telling sign of this consciousness – that language is language, that signs are signs – is the all-pervasive presence of meta-language. This is evident from the earliest years. Tiny children relish the sound of words in parallel with appreciating their meaning. They play with language as well as use it. Punning, rhyming, etc. are early, not late, forms of linguistic behaviour. And the meta-linguistic dimension remains a major presence in human discourse. We quote what other people say; and so do toddlers ('Man said "No!" to doggy'). We imitate (and mock) how they say it, we ask for the meaning of words. We are taught the grammar and general characteristics of language. We do exercises to improve our powers of self-expression or to modify our accents or our tone of voice. We are aware of how others may be differently aware from ourselves of certain features in our own speech. We learn others' languages and dialects. And so on, through the innumerable layers of consciousness and self-consciousness of talk and writing and talk about talk and talk about writing and writing about writing and writing about talk about writing. Meta-linguistic awareness reaches from the top to the bottom of language. Man may not be uniquely the talking animal; but he is uniquely the meta-linguistic animal.

At the highest level, we should note that he is the only animal who is astonished by his language, is intrigued by it and has theories about it. His is the only species that communicates theories of communication. *Homo linguisticus* may be a small sub-population of *homo sapiens* but he is a symptomatic one. He is, of course, a sub-species of *homo theoreticus* (if the macaronic may be forgiven), a character whom we shall discuss presently.

Am I arguing that man is, after all, The Talking (or meta-talking) Animal? Is it language, then, that lies at the bottom of everything, of all the differences between humanity and animality? No. The uniqueness of human language, and in particular of its meta-linguistic dimension, is itself only a symptom of a deeper difference; of the uniqueness of man the explicit animal. What language does is to make explicitness itself explicit: in language, the sense of material objects, for example, is embodied in events – words – that are independent of those things (I have developed this point of view in more detail elsewhere.[25]) Language makes explicit sense itself explicit: it lifts it off the specific material objects in which for non-human animals it is entirely embedded or embodied and for human animals is primarily embedded or embodied. The arbitrariness of linguistic signs distances them from that which they signify.[26]

The Sense-making Animal

We have only glimpses of how other animals see the world whereas we have first-hand knowledge of how humans (or at least ourselves and those we know or know of) see the world. It is easy, therefore, to exaggerate the differences between man and animals; in particular, to overlook the faculties animals share with, but are unable communicate to, us. How much idea does a dog watching me type this chapter have of what I am doing or thinking? Probably more than he could tell me. Even allowing for this lack of access to the inner life of animals, however, it seems as if men have impulses that take them far beyond the animal world; at the root of these impulses seems to be the desire to make general sense of things.

For Lichtenberg, man was 'the cause-bearing animal'. This is striking but too narrow to capture man's great theorising impulse. Theorising has two major sources: the practical need to make things go better, to meet one's needs more effectively (goal-orientated theorising); and impractical wonder. The second of these sources is often overlooked because, in the mythology of early man (i.e. the myths we late men have about our ancestors) the technical and the theological seem to converge. The role of the theologian, we are told, was to determine the attitudes and wishes of the gods and to promote those ritual behaviours which would make them favourable to man and his purposes. A Rain Dance is both a recognition of Higher Beings and a practical technique for bringing about that desired end. Nevertheless, the sense that there are Higher Beings is based upon an ultimately impractical wonder, whose supremely impractical expression is the intuition that this life and this world are only a small part of what there is and one that, moreover, may not be all that important.

This theorising or, more generally, *sense-making* instinct carries man through specific solutions to specific problems to the greater problems. Man is an explaining and explanation-seeking animal. The faculty has several components: the impulse to classify and generalise; the need to control the world in accordance with the purposes and goals related to need; and a feeling that there are further purposes operating in, and more powerful controls operating on, the world. The intuition that there are gods and that there are laws of nature have the same ultimate source; and they converge in the concept of necessity, fate, destiny or The Law. Their continuing close relationship is dramatically demonstrated in the way in which, according to Whitehead, the Principle of the Uniformity of Nature derived from the unification of the gods into One God in Christian culture.[27] The quest of the explaining animal is a protracted one and carries him a long way: it begins with the casual classification of experience had in the open field of everyday life and advances towards the testing of explicitly formulated hypotheses under controlled conditions. He starts out from the attempt to make low-grade practical predictions, and so sharpen expectancy to particular expectations, and advances to the search for laws of the widest scope. In the course of his journey from the one to the other, man woke out of his status as a creature simply finding the most convenient and efficient and safest ways round the world and started seeing the world as a theatre for investigations.

A crucial step was the intuition of, and consequently the search for, *general* solutions; his seeing that a particular problem is but an instance of a whole class of similar problems and that the right sort of solution to the problem would be a solution to a whole class of problems.

Man, then, is to a unique degree a sense-making animal. And the kind of sense he makes, or tries to make, of himself and of the world he finds himself in, is unique. Granted, all animals make some kind of sense of the world. They 'sus out' the ecological niche in which they find themselves. And they try, in some cases, to extend that sense by exploratory and even experimental behaviour. But their need for sense is satisfied, even saturated, by outcomes that satisfy physiological need. Art, science, philosophy and religion, are all manifestations, to a greater or lesser degree, of a hunger for more, or more complete, sense, activated by a feeling that the deliverances of experience are an incomplete account of what there is, what it and they mean.[28]

And so man is an art-making animal, creating artefacts that serve no clear practical purpose; creating images of himself – in words, in pictures – in order to know himself better; creating images of the world, to impose order on felt chaos; 'cultivating the emotions for their own sake' (Whitehead) to escape the insufficiency of ordinary experience. The peculiar character of art and what it implies about human distinctiveness is often not fully appreciated. In her discussion of behaviour suggestive of dancing observed by Jane Goodall in chimpanzees, Mary Midgley suggests that this 'throws a sharp and sudden light on the origin of human sport and dancing'. 'Naturally', she adds, 'this sort of thing is not just what goes on at the Bolshoi Ballet. But it does something to indicate on what bush, growing out of what soil, ballet is a flower'.[29] We have only to consider what distances separate the guileless brief ritual of the chimpanzees (seen by Jane Goodall only three times in ten years of observation) from the complex and self-conscious procedures of ballet to doubt this claim. If the chimpanzees had a Rain Dance correspondent, then I might start considering this claim as plausible. Midgley's suggestion, discussed earlier in relation to human morality, that 'Conceptual thought formalizes and extends what instinct started' is, as I expressed then, to encapsulate the entire miracle in an aside and so overlook it.

Man is also the scientific animal, driven by a sense that the sense of the world is incomplete though it may be completable – in, for example, discoverable laws of nature. And he is the metaphysical animal, a wondering animal, whose sense of the incompleteness of the sense of the world is less focused, more hungry, and drives his attempts to reach a vision that unifies the scattered occasions of experience. He is the religious or spiritual animal whose sense that the sense of the world is incompletable – because life terminates in death and we are finite beings set down in infinity – leads him to postulate a Supreme Being or a Next World beyond this world where the sense of this world and of himself is completed. He is the death-discovering animal; and, uniquely aware that his own existence is not securely grounded, he transforms his abstract, unfocused fears, his awareness of the continual possibility of suffering, into the image of One Who will answer all fears, who can control all suffering; and turns death from a terminus into a gateway and 'the world' (itself a concept produced by very high-level synthetic activity of consciousness) into '*this* world', a limited whole, set off against a Next World. Physical, moral, existential and spiritual uncertainty converge in the dream of a benign all-powerful Being; or the rival dream of a benign all-powerful science that will permit complete control over the universe and bring an end to death, suffering and all that conflicts with human desires.

Man, driven by an active, *cultivated* uncertainty, uniquely comes face to face with the irremediably incomplete intelligibility of the world and the inexplicability of the fact that the world is intelligible at all. Here, at the boundaries of sense, in his astonishment at the senseless fact that the world makes partial sense, the sense-making animal is at an infinite distance from all other creatures.

SPELLING OUT THE DISTANCES

We could summarise most of what has been said so far in a sentence: *Man knows what he is doing*. To assert this, however, is not adequate to our purpose of making consciousness so *visible* that it cannot be denied, eliminated, assimilated into the properties of matter, or simply overlooked, as in the theories we have examined in previous chapters. For this purpose, it has been essential to unpack the various ways in which human consciousness is elaborated and to show the great spaces that have opened up between man and other forms of matter, including his closest ontological cousins, the non-human animals. Those great spaces still remain even when it is conceded that human consciousness is deeply interpenetrated by unconsciousness (or 'the Unconscious') and that most animals have some degree of consciousness, that they seem to have some notion of what they are doing. Nevertheless, the twin claims that the heart of human consciousness is occupied by various forms of the Unconscious (the Id, the political Unconscious, the linguistic Unconscious, etc.) and that animal consciousness is very similar to the human variety, act like a pincer movement making the distinctive miracle of human consciousness more difficult to see. For this reason, in order to secure the ground that has been gained so far, it is worth, at the risk of some repetition, adopting a different approach to the task of making human consciousness visible and undeniable and of demonstrating the many different ways in which we have to modify, or distance ourselves from, the concept of animality in order to arrive at that of humanity.

Let us therefore imagine a thought experiment in which someone tries to derive man as we know him from that of 'other' animals. In the course of that derivation, a succession of transformations or displacements would be required, a multitude of huge gaps would have to be crossed. Some exemplary gaps are seen in the table that follows.

Animals	*Man*
instinctive behaviour	rational action
appetite-driven activity	behaviour according to a written code
corporeal evolution	historical development
spatial herding	self-legitimating grouping
object-needing	commodity wanting
need-driven behaviour	salaried labour
extensions to bodies	complex autonomous machines
responses to changing reality	behaviour planned in response to complex, predictive accounts of actual and possible reality
tropisms	systems of classification and re-classification
reacting to stimuli	seeking out ways of finding new and more complex pleasures.

The same point is made in the second table through more specific instances:

Some Exemplary Distances Between Man and Animals

	Typical instance	
Observed Parameter	Animals	Man
Feeding behaviour	Hunt for food Chase prey	Plan a restaurant meal Choose a cheaper main course that will not financially embarrass host
Grouping behaviour	Form spatial herd	Identify with group who have similar interest in stamp collecting
Species development	Change bodily form	Legislate over nutrition, education, etc.
Object of need	Prey	Sufficient income to pay mortgage
Tools	Stick	Machine to assist the manufacture of surgical instruments
Response to unknown event, object	Startle	Classification, explanation, metaphor
Learning	Undergo operant conditioning	Organise babysitter so that can attend next year's course of evening classes

I shall presently argue that all that is distinctive about man may be gathered up in the fact that he is *the explicit animal*. In preparation for that conclusion, let me tease out some of the dimensions of human explicitness as they relate to the fundamental categories of needs, means, communication, time, sense, and sense of self. This will involve going over some ground already covered but those readers who are already convinced of the point I have been endeavouring to make may wish to regard the next few pages less as an analysis of a difference than as a celebration of a mystery.

Needs

For man, uniquely among the animals, the objects of need are transformed into commodities whose value is quantified not physiologically (with the subjective dimension of intensity of appetite) but in monetary terms. Need-related activity takes the form of labour: access to the objects of need is indirect, via activity that is usually quite unrelated to them (for example, a doctor tends more sick people in order to pay off his gambling debts; a bricklayer works overtime to fund his interest in philately). In addition, needs are measured not by their moment-to-moment felt intensity but in terms of predicted requirements over time. There is stockpiling and storekeeping; and not only at an individual but at a collective level.

Means

In the simplest case, an animal satisfies a need by moving towards or chasing after its object. When, as in man, needs are made explicit to the needer, pursuit of their satisfaction involves increasingly complex, increasingly indirect, increasingly conscious means. The means and the needs they serve become generalised: the means take the form of a general solution. Modern technology is the culmination of such explicitness. Without explicitness, technology would not have been liberated from the model of the body-as-means; wheels would not have displaced legs; electrical or electronic solutions replaced mechanical ones. Once means are made explicit, their refinement is not constrained by accidental features of the first, the 'natural' solutions. Fire can be supplanted by light bulbs and radiators. Technology is means that know themselves, connecting explicit goals to present states by the application of general principles; it is therefore free to evolve by internal growth, by self-refinement.

Communication

Man consciously deploys signs to convey propositional sense. He recognises his signs for what they are: signs. He quotes, and reflects on, what has been said. Within his sign system, he distinguishes the possible from the actual and can separately assert possibilities and actualities. He distinguishes also the particular and the general (without a complex sign system, neither the particular nor the general has explicit existence).[30] He is able to assert that something (a predicate) is true of something (a subject): he can dismantle and reassemble the world in thought. He can refer to what is the case and so transform material reality into the truth conditions of statements. At the level of object language, he consciously classifies and re-classifies; and at the level of meta-language he uses, plays with and mentions signs. And in writing he stores his signs not only outside of his own body but also – and here the extreme case would be the reference library – outside of the situations and occasions in which they might signify. All of these extraordinary developments depend upon the explicit recognition of signs as signs.

Time

Man not only ages, and suffers time as duration, but also divides time up and measures it. An individual consciously projects himself into a future related to the present and consciously reflects on the past in which he distinguishes the general past from his own past and that of others. He binds himself to the future and to the past by taking on commitments and by acknowledging responsibility for certain past events. Commitment to the future may sometimes be quite detailed, as in a timetable that reaches for months ahead. He knows his own age (and so is positioned in his life), and his own probable span and his own certain finitude. He is aware that his life is a temporal process among other temporal processes that will out-endure him and have been present before him. He situates his own time, his lifespan, in History which out-spans his own history.

Sense

The world does not merely impose its patterns on man. He identifies patterns and transforms them into laws which he uses to refine expectancy and to increase the power he has in ordering his affairs. He induces, abducts, conjectures, infers. Expectation is refined into, and by, reasons and hypotheses. Man's expectations are so refined that he is able to experience higher level surprises that are far remote from mere startle responses: he can be astonished at unexpected patterns in a cloud chamber. He has strategies for finding explanations, adopts discovery procedures. He is capable of the active uncertainty of thought and cultivates doubt in order to deepen his understanding. Behind all of this is a sense that the world makes sense, even a partially unified sense. This intuition is itself most explicit in science with its assumptions of uniformity and its regulative idea of a unified explanation of all things. Underlying this is a further intuition that the fact that the world makes sense itself is quite inexplicable, indeed senseless – an intuition that brings science to the edge of religion.

Sense of Self

Man entertains complex ideas of who or what he is. He sees himself as different from or similar to other individuals, groups, types or species. He locates himself with respect to colleagues, friends, relatives, teams, clubs, nations, historical predecessors. He contrasts himself with or derives his self-image from other entities – things, animals, people. He locates himself on a thousand maps of varying scope. He proposes horizon after horizon against which he cuts a silhouette. He finds himself in society, in history, and in an intuited schema that transcends society and history.

CONCLUSION: MAN, THE EXPLICIT ANIMAL

Philosophy, Wittgenstein once remarked, 'consists of assembling reminders for a purpose'.[31] I quote this in defence of my method of proceeding in this chapter and the devotion of many pages to describing features of ourselves with which we are all familiar. I do not apologise for stating the obvious at such length because it is precisely the obvious that gets taken for granted and consequently overlooked when we consider our own nature and compare ourselves with the other species inhabiting this planet. In consequence, although we take this for granted in our behaviour towards, and the way we think about, non-human animals in our everyday life, we seem to forget when we philosophise upon our own nature that we are utterly and absolutely different from them. It would be absurd to deny that we have much in common with other animals: we, too, have physiological needs and also share some of their socialising instincts. Nevertheless, all of these things have been utterly transformed in us *because they are explicit in us*.

In emphasising our distinctiveness from the other animals, I am not trying to downgrade them, to suggest that they are unconscious automata, that they lack purposes or intentions or even lasting character traits. Even less, as I have already made clear, would I wish to suggest that they are incapable of suffering, and so to justify our treating them badly or to diminish our responsibility for treating them worse than is necessary for our own survival. We do not have to downgrade animals to back up our claim to uniqueness. We simply have to hold on to an undistorted view of ourselves. Such a view inescapably reveals us as an animal whose distances from other animals is many-dimensional, whose cultural divergence from the rest of nature is infinitely elaborated.

I am not, of course, denying that we are in very important senses natural; that we have natural needs; or that culture is rooted in nature. Nor am I trying to suggest that in us intelligence has wholly replaced instinct (a position that Midgley forcibly and convincingly refutes). Our needs are, in many places, analogous to those which we discern in animals: for food, shelter, affection and so on. But, although the general framework of instinct has not been supplanted, the instincts themselves have been utterly transformed. Yes, there is a distant analogy between the nesting behaviour of a chaffinch and my purchase of a house; but the closer we look at the details of my behaviour (for example, the row I have with the solicitor about the time the conveyancing is taking; or my guilt over a decision to postpone filling in yet another form because I am feeling lazy) the more remote the analogy seems. We often say of a woman who decorates a bedroom just before she goes into labour that she is 'nest-building'; but the decision as to whether to have one coat of paint or two and the discussion as to whether to buy the paint from B&Q or Texas shows just how far the analogy, even in this particularly compelling case, can go: not very far. Of course, our culture must have some kind of givens – physiological needs, for example – to work on. However, in so far as there is a distinctive human nature, it is institutional and conventional rather than, say, physiological; or, rather, it is one in which the expression of the physiological has been transformed by institutions, customs, conventions rituals and statutes. And this transformation is the result ultimately not of the emergence of a collective human unconscious – Society, History, Oedipal forces or whatever – but of the operation of consciousness, of explicitness, and their free play within the ordinary behaviour of individuals.

The passage from natural needs and drives to human institutions and patterns of behaviour – let us say from mating to marriage, from mating calls to love letters – is predicated upon an infinitely developable explicitness. The lover who writes a carefully calculated letter to put himself in the best possible light is not merely enacting a variant of a bird singing a stereotyped song. *He knows what he is doing*[32] – is awake to his goal, his methods and to the object of his attention – in a way whose difference is a matter not merely of degree but of kind. This wakefulness is one that is continually waking up to itself, reflecting on itself, seeing what it is, what it wants. We have no evidence that it is shared by the singing blackbird.

Even in such 'beastly' areas as sexual behaviour (according to Kant, 'Sexuality exposes one to the danger of equality with the beasts'), human beings operate at an immense distance from animals. To refer to behaviour that surrounds mating in both humans and animals by the same terms (e.g. 'courtship rituals') is at least as misleading as it is illuminating; as liable to lead to a serious distortion of both human and animal behaviour as it is to show up valid analogies.

As I have suggested, the greater part of the contents of this chapter should be superfluous since the reminders it assembles are sufficiently obvious; nevertheless, it is necessary to state, and to reiterate, these things because they are forgotten by many philosophers thinking about human consciousness. The fact that human beings share many properties with animals – for example bodies that run on very similar principles – has led to our assimilating animality to humanity rather too easily, to regarding man as some kind of (admittedly rather special) animal. Of course, we are more like animals than we are like machines or angels; but we are not 'just', 'at bottom', animals or unimportantly different from the other animals. All of the characterisations I have discussed above – the rational animal, the moral animal, the sense-making animal, etc. – capture only single dimensions of the multidimensional distance between man and the animals. To assert this infinitely complex difference by adding a single predicate to 'animal' – to see man as an animal with a particular faculty – is to close the gap, or to make shallow the unbridgeable gulf, that lies between humanity and animality. For these predicates, these isolated faculties, are all *symptoms* – of man's utter otherness from animality. The unbridgeableness of the distance is owed to explicitness, itself the very essence of human consciousness, which permits indefinite autonomous development. Explicitness turns difference into a multidimensional infinity.

It must be emphasised that when I characterise man as 'the explicit animal', I am not talking of just another faculty. Midgley has demonstrated the vacuousness of single faculty accounts of man. The main weakness of such accounts that it is impossible to think of a faculty that one could not *read into* the behaviour of other animals, no feature that could not plausibly be claimed to be echoed in some animal or other.[33] Even leaving one's spraint on the ground could be taken, by someone desperate to assert the continuity between man and animals, as a primitive form of writing. And other faculties, that animals do not possess, such as that of drawing up timetables, seem too specific to mark our difference from the beasts. Explicitness, or the power of making explicit, is deeper and wider than any mere faculty, such as reason; or, if it is to be thought of as a faculty at all, we may think of it as that faculty in virtue of which our faculties – which indeed may be analogous in their embryonic forms to animal faculties – may develop to an extraordinary degree. Or as 'the faculty-making faculty'.

The power of making explicit seems to answer the requirement for a 'mark of man' that would not fall foul of the criticisms I outlined at the beginning of this chapter. The problems in identifying distinctively human characteristics setting off man from other animals included: the danger of a partial view of animals and an equally partial view of ourselves; the need for the chosen characteristic to be a structural, rather than a focal, surface, feature – one that affected the whole organisation of the life of the species rather than being just 'an isolated miracle'; and the need to take account of the fact that man, to a unique degree perhaps, is self-defining and self-transforming. The characterisation of man as 'the explicit animal' seems to meet these problems and requirements.

The definition also, I think, helps us to deal with the question of the relationship between animal faculties and human ones. Is the difference between human language and animal communication systems simply one of degree of complexity? Is animal intelligence similar to but simply less well-developed than human intelligence? Are the ape dances described by Jane Goodall embryonic or primitive versions of the Bolshoi ballet? In other words, is man just a creature who has travelled along the same road as other animals but has simply gone much further? Are animal and human achievements points along the same axis? Are we dealing with differences of degree or of kind? The answer is that we are dealing with enormous differences of degree that have been made possible by a different route of development of the faculties – which are, therefore, in a sense, of a different kind. Human faculties have achieved their present advanced state by different means – by progressive and successive application of the power of making explicit. As a result of this, their development has been so extraordinary that they have evolved into things of different kinds. In their mode of development and, less convincingly perhaps, in the destinations they have so far reached, they are different in kind. We may think of the power of making explicit as the faculty that permits faculties that have animal origins to be transformed to the point where their relationship to animal faculties is purely notional or even metaphorical. Consider the ape rain dance and the Bolshoi ballet. The complex booking system, the notices in the newspaper, the competitiveness between career ballerinas – these are all secondary developments, yes; but they symptomatise what happened to dancing once it entered the life of the explicit animal.

My vision of the relationship between human and animal faculties may be captured by imagining the animals fighting their way through a wilderness near to the beginning of a motorway that humans are travelling along at sixty miles an hour. The animals may move in the wilderness parallel to that motorway for a few yards but cannot drive on it. With a few exceptions, each generation of animals, moreover, begins at the same point in the wilderness as the last and there is no cumulative progress – not even painfully slow progress – except in so far as the animal's body changes over vast periods of time. The power of making explicit, the explicitness inherent in human consciousness, is what makes motorway travel possible for humans and lack of it that denies animals such travel. The analogies between human and animal faculties deceive us into thinking that we and they are travelling along the same road, that they are on the same road as us, only further back. In fact, animals are not even on the road; only at a location corresponding to a point just beyond the beginning of the road. Thus the relation between animal tool-using and human technology; or between animal communication and human language.

My method of delineating the differences between man and animals has been to take certain characteristics and show how they have unfolded in human life; or how many folds, how much complexity and elaboration, they have acquired. My description has no pretence to being an historical or genetic account of the evolution of human faculties and institutions. It is merely a way of showing how far we are from the animals, and not a way of describing, even less explaining, the road we have taken in getting from animality to humanity. My ultimate purpose is to show how remote we are from automata or machines; to underline the unique extent to which we know what we are doing. (If tomorrow someone were to show me that animals did, after all, have as complex and elaborated and self-conscious a consciousness as ours – so that, for example, there were animal analogues for human learning techniques such as organising babysitters so that one can go to an evening class – I would not be too upset, though I would be *very* surprised. I would simply transfer some of the distances I am currently assigning to the gap between man and animals to that between man and machines. The distance between man and machines would remain undiminished. The *size* of consciousness, and the importance of deliberate conscious behaviour and of the mediations of consciousness, would still be as great).

My account of the difference between man and animals leaves the relationship between them deeply puzzling and the transition from the one to the other almost inexplicable. It may be argued that this is the result of the techniques of analysis I have used. Is it not possible that each step in the unfolding of *homo economicus*, for example, seems to be underivable from the starting conditions, and the overall trajectory unprecedented, only because I have taken faculties in isolation? That in other words, *homo economicus* would seem less of 'an isolated miracle' (to use Midgley's phrase) if the evolution of human language were considered at the same time. That we can understand the development of the parts only if we understand the development of the whole. To understand the whole without understanding the parts seems to be a tall order, though I am sympathetic to this. It is my position, after all, that all of these developments do have a single precondition and motor: the power of explicitness. The particular trajectories I have traced, however, do not distort explicitness or exaggerate its mysteriousness; they merely uncover its multifarious working and show its mysteriousness.

I am not, of course, denying the evolutionary explanation of the origin of the human *body*: morphologically, physiologically, biochemically, neurobiologically, etc. it is clear that that body has evolved from the bodies of non-human predecessors. I have no doubt that, in this sense, the primates are our immediate ancestors. But the emergence of explicitness – which created the gulf between man and the other animals – does not seem to fit into this story about bodies.

Ought I to apologise for this failure to accommodate the explicitness story into the evolution-of-bodies story? Not at all. It is better to have an unsolved problem than a false solution. We have grown accustomed to the idea that human development takes place outside of the evolutionary process. We shall have to accustom ourselves to the related idea that the origin of this capacity to evolve outside of the genome also fails to fit into the evolutionary scheme. In his essay 'Truth and Lie in the Extra-Moral Sense'[34] Nietzsche suggested, with masterly sarcasm, that man was a clever animal who simply 'invented knowledge'. This is an absurd suggestion but it is about the best explanation we have so far of this curious state of affairs whereby man, uniquely, enjoys a capacity to make explicit that can unfold without limit.

The power of explicitness seems to be *sui generis*, underivable. And for this reason it shares with consciousness an inability to fit into the evolutionary scheme. This correspondence is not surprising; for explicitness is the essence of human consciousness. And it is to consciousness that we must now return. The ultimate purpose of the present discussion of the difference between man and the other animals has not been to downgrade animals but to protect man from the downgrading that begins with seeing him as 'only an animal'. Those who animalise man use this as a first step to machinising him; for they downgrade animals as well and tend to reduce them to the status of machines. They dislike seeing the obvious and recognising that, unlike machines, animals have purposes, intentions and affections and in many instances, as Midgley repeatedly emphasises, enduring character traits that organise their behaviour over long periods of time and across many settings. In short, those who are practised in the art of overlooking the obvious traits of human beings will be past-masters when it comes to overlooking the obvious characteristics of animals. The perverse skill necessary to reduce humans to animals will take the reduction of animals to machines in its stride. By drawing attention to the distances between man and animals, I have hoped to make the visible impossible not to notice. Once the nature of man as the explicit animal is grasped and explicitness is understood as the essence of consciousness, it becomes much more difficult to overlook the all-encompassing nature of con-sciousness, to eliminate, marginalise or underplay its role in behaviour, to reduce it to a focal property of a creature similar in essential respects to non-conscious entities such as lower animals and machines – so that the difference between an event's happening and something being done is minimalised or denied. The purpose of this 'assembly of reminders', then, has been to draw attention to the inadequacy of current popular views about consciousness; to enable us to approach with the requisite critical spirit the recent attempts we have discussed in this book to explain, or explain away, or to downgrade, or to denature, consciousness. The importance of my claim that man has a fundamentally different type of consciousness from the animals is that it provides a further layer of defence against the temptation to see humans, or human consciousness, as machine-like.

7

Recovering Consciousness

> ... the million-petalled flower
> Of being here.
>
> Philip Larkin

INTRODUCTION: MECHANISING MAN

My central thesis is that human beings are most importantly conscious, intelligent, deliberate creatures. They are inescapably this and to a unique degree. Of course, they have properties in common with other sorts of entities, animate and inanimate, but they are fundamentally different from them. In so far as he is an animal at all, man is an explicit animal and this capacity for making explicit cannot be assimilated to the properties either of machines or of biological systems as they are usually understood.

Explicitness – without which little of what is human in us could be described, never mind accounted for in any coherent way – is not merely the latest stage, the icing on the cake, the top layer of other, everyday, faculties. It permeates the ground floor of the humblest human activity. Even tasks that could conceivably be automated are often carried out consciously and, indeed, self-consciously. If the assimilation of humanity to animality is perverse, the assimilation of humanity to materialist machinality is even more so. For some writers, physicalist reductionism presents an appalling vision of an essentially machine world.[1] For others the reduction of mental life to physical events among which qualia and the subjective quality of experience live a marginal, dubious existence, seems to take away the scent and flavour of ordinary existence. I sympathise with both attitudes; but they seem to miss the essential point: that the machinisation of consciousness, or the replacement of consciousness by mechanism and the reduction of the person to an animal-machine, with a concomitant refusal to

210

acknowledge the true nature of consciousness and its central place in our lives, is to deny our essential nature.

In the version of consciousness served up by functionalist philosophers, causal theorists, cognitive psychologists and others, it seems as if the mechanisms thought to underlie its production invade consciousness itself, so that it becomes indistinguishable from them. Consciousness dissolves into the causal net, the computational process, or whatever. The thinking brain becomes an automation, and thought itself a series of mechanical events. Even where the role of consciousness in seemingly deliberate action is acknowledged, consciousness itself is somehow mechanised. (Even so, the machinising of conscious human beings, and of consciousness, which pervades cognitive psychology, is often presented as a benign, tender-minded successor to the more tough-minded hard-line physicalist behaviourism.) Take, for example, the following syllogism from Johnson-Laird:[2]

> Human beings are animals (Darwin)
> Animals are machines (Descartes)
> Therefore: Human beings are machines (La Mettrie).

He describes this as a 'mechanomorphic' syllogism. And certainly the tendency of most current approaches to consciousness – whether by biologists or by psychologists – is best described as 'mechanomorphic' or 'mechanising'.

The project of displacing consciousness by mechanism and/or mechanising consciousness itself has depended, as we have seen, upon strategic deployment of crucially ambiguous key terms such as 'memory', 'information', 'language', 'code', and 'signal'. These terms have been lifted from our ordinary discourse about human beings and human life and applied, as helpful metaphors, to machines. They are then reapplied to humans. They have, that is to say, a foot in both camps – that of the ordinary description of human beings in everyday terms and that of the description of the functions and capabilities of machines – and thus act as mediators between discourses appropriate to humans and to machines and dissolving the barriers between them. The terminology first anthropomorphises machines and this makes it possible to machinise humans. Or man and animals are described in such a way as to machinise them while animals and machines are described in such a way as to anthropomorphise them. The resulting conception of man is of a creature half-way between man and machine – a mechanical animal, perhaps.

DELIBERATENESS, AUTOMATICITY AND CONSCIOUSNESS

The connotations of 'mechanical' are complex. They include 'occurring in the absence of consciousness' or 'not requiring deliberate intention'. But 'mechanical' also implies 'law-like' or, more specifically, having a law-like relation to antecedent conditions. A mechanism does not require the intervention of consciousness or deliberate effort precisely because it occurs in conformity with universal, physical, laws. The outcome, or outputs, of mechanism *happen, rather than are brought about*. Moreover, unlike the result of a voluntary action, the outcome of a mechanism is guaranteed – always assuming that nothing new occurs to perturb the system.

The relationship in ordinary behaviour between consciousness and deliberateness on the one hand and automaticity on the other is not easily captured. For a start, the boundary separating the automatic from the deliberate is blurred by the complex intercutting between deliberateness and automaticity. All deliberate behaviour is made up of combinations of automatic – innate or acquired – elements. I am deliberately walking across the road to avoid you, yes; but this deliberate action is composed of ambulatory events rooted in unconditioned and conditioned reflexes, innate physiological complexes and learned sequences. These events are, of course, tailored to the particular circumstances in which I find myself and the tailoring depends upon my being conscious of my surroundings. As I cross the road, I adjust my step to take account of the depth of the kerb, I avoid the dog dirt in the gutter and I wait until a car has gone by. Such occasion-specific adjustments cannot be programmed in advance, because every occasion is different; and yet they are also rooted in automatic mechanisms. At a higher level, it is obvious that, during the course of any act that is prolonged more than a few seconds, I switch between deliberately paying attention to the act and entrusting the continuation of the act to an automatic pilot. This switching back and forth is particularly striking (and particularly puzzling) in the case of prolonged activities such as driving. One may drive several miles along a motorway without deliberately 'enacting driving', with the higher reaches of one's consciousness apparently given over to the music on the car radio, to the object one is reaching for in one's pocket, to the person one is going to meet at the end of the journey, to yesterday's insult, etc. etc. Despite this, one is available to act immediately to avoid an obstacle totally unforeseen in the journey's 'action script'. In other words, driving can become deliberate at a moment's notice. This switch to deliberateness is not itself deliberate: it happens automatically.[3]

The switching between deliberateness and automaticity and the interweaving of deliberate and automatic elements in actions seem to invite a modification of the simplistic view of deliberate willed behaviour as the (continuous) expression of conscious intentions. This view of voluntary behaviour seems also to be threatened by the somewhat tenuous relation between the actual content of the action and that of the intention behind it. I have discussed this elsewhere[4] – but one or two points are worth reiterating here.

For a start, the intention will always be framed at a higher level of generality than the action itself. Suppose I am on the beach throwing stones into the sea. The intention behind my actions specifies only a search for stones-in-general. It does not specify the particular stones, with their very particular locations and their very particular properties, that I actually pick up to throw. In this, as in other instances of voluntary actions realising preconceived intentions (the very paradigms of voluntary actions), the action that realises the intention will exceed in specificity, and so will have details unenvisaged in, the intention. Compared with any actual action, all intentions are relatively non-specific. Intentions, even for simple actions, are, as it were, riddled with unsaturated variables; compared with the actions driven, licensed, authorised by them, they are vague in the extreme. If this is true of a simple action such as picking up a stone to throw it into the sea, how much more true is it of complex actions, such as taking a train to London. The number of details necessarily left open by the intention – or the amount of unspecified material entrained in the prolonged sequence of actions that fulfils the intention – is enormous. (Think of all the things that happen during a train journey; all the sub-routines filling out the two- or three-hour ride.) Our most deliberate behaviour is porous to the unscheduled.

The role of conscious deliberation, even in actions that are conceived at the most conscious level and go precisely according to plan, seems therefore to be quite severely circumscribed. There are two further constraints. The first, less important from the point of view of the present discussion, is that the agenda even for free action is determined from without: most of our actions are *re-actions* to circumstances and events we have not brought about. I choose to greet you but do not choose that you should suddenly come into the room at that moment to be greeted. I choose to duck to avoid a football but do not choose that there should be a ball requiring me to avoid it. Most of the events driving most of the actions in our lives are unscheduled. A second, more important constraint on the freedom and deliberateness of voluntary action arise from the fact that the fulfilment of an intention will always depend upon an element of luck. Indeed the interpenetration of luck, chance and agency is very complex.[5]

The complexity of the relationship between consciousness and deliberate behaviour has not entirely escaped the attention of neuroscientists. Part of this complexity may be captured by the distinction, emphasised in recent cognitive neuroscience, between two different forms of knowledge, one subserving the acquisition and retention of new skills (procedural knowledge) and the other concerned with factual information (declarative knowledge). It has been suggested that these two forms of knowledge (which corres-pond roughly to Ryle's 'knowing how' and 'knowing that'; or to habit memory versus occurrent or episodic memory) are subserved by anatomically distinct systems in the brain.[6] Some of the evi-dence for this derives from observations made on amnesia patients that I briefly referred to in Chapter 2.

Amnesia is characterised by profound deficits in the establish-ment of new memories and in the retrieval of certain older memories laid down before the onset of amnesia. There is now good evidence, however, that important forms of memory and learning are preserved in amnesia; for example, amnesic patients can learn new skills – pattern analysing skills, sensory-motor skills and cognitive skills. These new skills are learned and remembered *despite complete memory loss for both the general and specific details associated with the original learning trials.* On the basis of these and other observations, neuroscientists accept that knowledge exists in at least two forms: declarative knowledge or memory with record, relating to the acquisition of specific facts, data or personal experi-ence; and procedural knowledge, or memory without record, concerned with the development of new sensory-motor or cogni-tive skills. Declarative knowledge appears to be vulnerable to damage in the medial temporal cortex and diencephalon, and procedural memory to damage in the basal ganglia and their afferent projections to the frontal cortex.

This conceptual – and apparently anatomically based – distinction between two sorts of memory underlines the complex relationship between consciousness, conscious deliberation, intention and actual behaviour. It underlines how much of our (visible or motor) behaviour is deeply rooted in unconscious or automatic mechanisms. We could not behave at all without many things happening automatically in us; and even the deliberate, 'higher level', occasion-specific, tailor-made aspects of behaviour are only intermittently lit by consciousness. This was evident to ordinary self-observation long before the evidence from recent neuropsychology that complex, higher order, procedures are controlled by procedural 'memories without record', memories that are quite distinct from factual, episodic, 'memories with record'.

It is important, however, not to draw the wrong inference from this: that a memoryless, unselfconscious (indeed unconscious) automaton has us totally in its grip. For the distinction between the two kinds of memory emphasises the distinctive character and the objective reality of *both* kinds: impersonal, third-person, procedural, habit memory; and personal, first-person, declarative, occurrent memory. It limits the scope of, but does not eliminate, or overthrow the centrality of, a self-possessed consciousness acting in accordance with 'memories with record'; or, indeed, of a self-consciousness that continues uninterrupted for much of our lives.[7]

The fact that so much can, and has to, be achieved through mechanism, or ultimately handed over to it, does not, then, diminish the importance of consciousness or give grounds for eliminating it from our discussion of humanity. What it does diminish is the explanatory value of evolutionary theories of consciousness, as was discussed in Chapter 2: if so much can be achieved through mechanism, what additional survival capability does consciousness confer? Mechanism seems to serve most purposes very well; and consciousness would seem to have little to offer by way of making mechanism go with a swing. The obvious fact that consciousness is predicated upon, interacts with, is rooted in, mechanism and that our behaviour is in part a deliberate exploitation of mechanism, certainly raises the problem of defining, and understanding, the place of consciousness amid (intra-corporeal and extra-corporeal) mechanism.

This as yet hardly attempted problem will prove insoluble if one begins with mechanism, or tries to derive consciousness from mechanism – as in those accounts that assimilate conscious behaviour and consciousness itself to fixed input–output relations of a computer, whose programs act in a certain predetermined way on the material presented to it, and the equally fixed effects of certain causes acting on a stable system. Such accounts find qualia an embarrassment and so try to eliminate them: light, for example, may produce behavioural responses through photosensitive receptors but the qualitative experience of brightness is superfluous.

The displacement of consciousness by mechanism, or the attempt to reduce consciousness to mechanism, is invariably unsuccessful. Consciousness, banished from the places where it manifestly is, has a habit of reappearing in places where it has no right to be. I spoke in Chapter 4 of 'the return of the repressed'. After the discussion in Chapter 7, this could be rechristened 'the fallacy of misplaced explicitness'. It is well illustrated in Johnson-Laird's shrewd criticism of the 'production system' view of the architecture of the mind.

Production systems are ways of generating and executing hierarchical plans that will take the organism from an initial state to a goal by means of a sequence of rule-governed operations. Production-system accounts of memory, learning and the retrieval of knowledge prior to using it in functional behaviour, assume that the processes governing learning depend on symbolic rules. 'The significance of a particular symbol in a production system depends entirely on the rules in which it occurs.' Moreover:

> these rules have to be spelt out with an explicit structure within the system. You might think it rather odd that such rules, which are so easily paraphrased in English, lie beneath the surface of your mental life. If you could lift the lid off the mind and peer in, would you really find sets of principles laid out like an Act of Parliament . . . ?[8]

This worry partly explains the attraction of parallel distributed processing models which seem to model how the mind might learn, etc. With the most elementary architecture and, more importantly, without having the faintest idea what it is doing or, even, that it is doing it.[9]

EXHIBITING CONSCIOUSNESS

The assertion that human life is essentially conscious and explicit and governed by a consciousness that seems to have no upper limit of self-reference and self-awareness will seem obvious to the point of banality to anyone not bewitched by some biological or computational, in short mechanical, model of man. Nevertheless it is contrary to the prevailing intellectual trends; and it is certainly a minority view among philosophers, psychologists and many other groups of scientists and non-scientists. The apparent banality, and even emptiness, of my thesis is not, however, surprising; for it represents a point of view that is difficult to demonstrate, even less to support with formal proof; for it lies beyond, or beneath, formal proof. One is therefore left baldly asserting it, as someone restating the self-evident, so that one becomes party to a rather unsatisfactory intellectual activity whose paradigm instances are Dr Johnson's 'refutation' of Berkeleian idealism by kicking a stone or G. E. Moore's 'proof' of the existence of an external world by holding up his two hands. Worse than this, the thesis is not only difficult to prove; it is actually rather elusive: one cannot give surface and body to it beyond the intellectually rather uninteresting – and seemingly naive and reactionary – statement of the obvious. The difficult of getting hold of the thesis is not accidental: it is connected with its essential tendency and this we should address first.

Hjelmslev's often quoted assertion that language is precisely that which gets overlooked could be applied with even greater justification to consciousness. The reasons for the overlooking are comparable. Language gets overlooked – so that, for example its role in structuring the world is underestimated[10] – simply because it is present in all discourses about the world. And something rather similar is true of consciousness. That of which we are conscious occludes, displaces, deletes, draws attention away from, consciousness itself. It is as if the places that consciousness might occupy are already occupied by the objects of consciousness, so that consciousness has no home of its own. We seem able to describe the contents of consciousness only by means of strained descriptions of our experiences; for example, instead of saying 'I am seeing a flower', I say 'I am having the sensation of seeing a flower'.

I suspect it was this, or something like it, that led Sartre in *Being and Nothingness*[11] to present consciousness as essentially negative, a Nothingness that arises in the plenitude of Being so that Being is for-itself rather than merely in-itself. It is simply that which is other than its object, creating the mutual otherness of itself and the object which it posits as being before, or present to, it.

> The being of consciousness does not coincide with itself in full equivalence . . . consciousness – the for-itself – is a being which is not what it is and which is what it is not. (pp. 74, 79)

This goes beyond Hume's vision of 'the mind's great propensity to spread itself on external objects, and to conjoin with them any internal impressions they occasion'.[12] Mind, according to Sartre, does not merely mate with the external world; it is in the nature of consciousness to be 'sacrificed' to its intentional objects – and hence to be invisible and insubstantial.

If consciousness were nothing or Nothingness (which doesn't seem a lot more than nothing), philosophers of mind, cognitive psychologists and others could be forgiven for overlooking it. And such forgiveness comes more readily when one recalls the results of trying to furnish consciousness with contents of its own, independent of its intentional objects. For example, the Kantian 'I am' or 'I think' which are supposed to accompany all our thoughts or indeed all our moments of consciousness. The absurdity of this is readily identified: the ground – or ground floor – of self-presence does not speak in English, let alone address itself in English (or French if the consciousness is that of a Frenchman), telling itself what it is or what it is doing. Consciousness could not make itself more conscious, or arrive at self-consciousness, by an unremitting reiterative mutter.

Another way of characterising consciousness is to describe it as a representation of the world: the contents of consciousness are in some sense a picture or model of its objects. This account serves two purposes: to explain both what consciousness is but also how it works. The long history of the representational theory of consciousness goes back at least as far as Socrates' belief that perception was pictures in the soul and Aristotle's idea that perception consisted of receiving 'the form of sensible objects without their matter'.[13] The notion of 'pictures in the soul' needed updating when consciousness was conceived in terms of brain activity. A popular updating has been that of an isomorphism between the cortical activity and the perceived object.

According to Kohler,[14] the cortical projection is similar in form to the retinal image, which is characterised by cortical electrical currents corresponding to these contours. Along with many other twentieth-century physiologists and philosophers, Kohler assumed not only a one–one (or at least a one–many) correspondence of mental states to neurophysiological process-patterns but also an isomorphism of the patterns in the phenomenal fields with the simultaneous patterns of neural processes in various areas of the brain. Such are the modern pictures in the soul. There are yet more sophisticated versions of the representational conception of consciousness associated with cognitive psychology and computational theories of the mind. These, however, are beside our present purpose as the representations are usually thought of as mainly unconscious or, if conscious in the conventional sense, only unimportantly so.

The fundamental problem with making consciousness a kind of picture was well expressed by Helmholtz, who espoused a causal theory of perception. Since 'our apperceptions and ideas are *effects* wrought on our nervous system by the objects that are thus apprehended and conceived' any picture would depend 'both on the nature of what causes the effect and on that of the person on whom the effect is produced'.[15] Since both parties will have contributed to this interaction, the picture, if there be such, cannot look like the object. 'Idea and thing conceived belong to two entirely different worlds'. And so, nearly a hundred years before Kohler, Helmholtz dismissed the idea that the perceived object was isomorphically represented in the brain of the perceiver. Moreover, pictures wouldn't constitute perceptions:

> Now I ask, what similarity can be imagined between the process in the brain that is concomitant with the idea of the table and the table itself? Is the form of the table supposed to be outlined by electric currents? And when the person with the idea has the idea that he is walking around the table, must the person then be outlined by electric currents? . . . And granted that a keen imagination is not frightened away by these and similar hypotheses, such an electrical reproduction of the table in the brain would be simply another bodily object to be perceived, but no idea of the table. (pp. 188–9)

In other words, representational theories of consciousness run into the homunculus problem; and where the pictures in the soul or representations are thought to be painted in nervous impulses, the theories inherit all the problems of the neurophysiological theories of perception. The latter are as unhelpful when we are trying to give consciousness a substance as when we are trying to understand perception.

It is difficult, then, to characterise consciousness in a positive way, in a way that distinguishes it from that which it is conscious of, without falling into the trap of giving it an absurdly specific content. I tried in Chapter 6 to make human consciousness visible by, as it were, coming upon it from a great distance, by comparing humans with animals. (This is not to imply, as I emphasised, that animals are unconscious; only that animal consciousness is crucially less well developed: it lacks the property of endlessly unfolding explicitness, of an unlimited self-reflexiveness.) One could develop this approach by starting further back, from inanimate objects, and characterise man as a peculiar form of matter; indeed as that form of matter which, among other things, uniquely appears strange to itself and as requiring explanation. But even this move may not reveal consciousness fully, as it were from outside of itself. For 'matter', though all-encompassing and extending beyond humans, consciousness and life, is also the referent of a *concept*, created by man and given discrete, bounded, referable-to existence, in language. As such, matter seems to be posterior to language and so tainted with consciousness, even highest-order consciousness. There is, that is to say, a seemingly irreducible ambiguity at the heart of 'matter': although it is conceived, by definition, as the primordial pre-human given, it is, in so far as it is conceived, a sophisticated concept. It is both that from which all that exists is derived, the ground floor of existence; and yet also that which emerges in its own identity only on the pens and tongues of sophisticated individuals. We may illustrate this Escher staircase as follows:

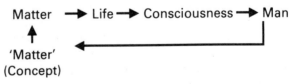

Let me therefore try another approach; for without some sort of positive account of human consciousness, my criticisms of modern theories of it will seem to lack definite point. It is perhaps easier to *show* what human consciousness is than to *say* what it is, though the showing will not make sense without a good deal of saying. Consider this diagram:

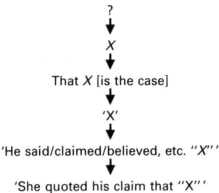

The question mark stands for my unwillingness to commit myself as to what the world contains in the absence of consciousness. Everything below this point in the diagram presupposes consciousness: differentiation into specific, potentially nameable objects (e.g. X); those objects becoming parts of states of affairs that are (explicitly) the case; those states of affairs being explicitly made explicit in verbal descriptions and in assertions to the effect that they are the case; this explicitness being itself made explicit in someone's reporting that someone else said/believed/claimed that it was the case; explicitness being further developed in someone's quoting someone else's assertion that that someone had said that it was the case; and so on, unfolding down an infinite series of meta-statements and meta-states. This progressive explicitness, and not some specific content on all fours with other contents of the world, is what consciousness consists of.

If human consciousness lacks a 'ring-fenced' content of its own, or if its content has a tendency to dissolve into the object of which it is conscious, this is because consciousness *is* that in virtue of which there are explicit 'contents of'. Its own contents are the result of this 'content-making'. Thus consciousness is neither freighted with autonomous material, with new things, novel material, it introduces to the world; nor is it contentless, empty, in the sense that many modern theories require. It makes that which it is not into its own contents, in the process of making them explicit. Explicitness is anterior to, descriptively supersedes – and so seems to fuse – both the afferent and efferent limbs of the perceptual circuit; the afferent causation and the efferent about-ness or intentionality.

To clarify the nature of explicitness and the creation of content, another diagram may be helpful:

. .	. — .	' — '	etc.
X	That X [is the case]	'X'	
(a)	(b)	(c)	

The relationship between the two dots exists in (a) but is only implicit. It is explicitly perceived in (b); the dash expresses what is both a content of consciousness and a feature of the world. This content is expressed, formulated, etc. in (c). Between (b) and (c) the relationship itself acquires an autonomous existence: the explicitness in (b) itself becomes explicit in (c). The way is open to an infinity of levels, or layers, of explicitness.

Although I have illustrated consciousness, and its essential nature in explicitness, through the example of a *relationship* between objects, the principle applies (though it is less easy to exhibit) to consciousness of the properties of objects; and to qualia, which are contents both of consciousness and of objects. (Qualia are properties of objects *qua* contents of consciousness, or contents of consciousness *qua* properties of objects. Neither description is privileged over the other: the emergence of objective properties and of subjective contents are merely different aspects of explicitness and so are logically neither prior nor posterior to one another).

One might encapsulate the nature of consciousness even more succinctly: consciousness is the universal boundless 'that', as in 'That X is the case'.[16] To characterise consciousness in terms of explicitness is also to explain its elusiveness. For in trying to describe consciousness in general one is making it explicit; trying, in other words to get at the heart of consciousness from within consciousness itself. It is not possible to make consciousness visible by pointing to it from the outside because the act of pointing, of making explicit, is inside consciousness. Likewise, consciousness is strictly inexpressible because expressions, and expressions of expressions, are part of it. In short, it is difficult to say in detail what consciousness is because one cannot make explicitness explicit from outside of explicitness. To try to describe consciousness is to attempt to make explicitness explicit – in language that is itself the explicit sense of things made explicit.[17]

Understood as explicitness, consciousness is irreducible, inexplicable, underivable. For it has no primary location – either in the objects of consciousness or as a state of 'standing otherness' to its objects. Consciousness is not a thing; but it is not nothing, either; rather it is the condition of there being explicit things. (Explicitness cannot be thought of as caused, at the very least because causation and causal relations are between entities – events, objects, states of affairs – that have been made explicit. Explicitness is prior to causal relations.) But once one tries to foist specific properties, distinctive qualities, a place of its own, upon consciousness, all sorts of absurdities are possible. It is ripe to be traduced – to be considered as a process or a product; as, for example, the output of a machine, the machine in this case being the brain. To try to fit consciousness into the scheme of things as revealed to consciousness, to place it on all fours with the things it is conscious of, is inevitably doomed; for that scheme of things is posterior to consciousness. As we have seen, one of the most popular ways of giving consciousness 'a local habitation' is to assign it a specific function and to try to understand both its origin and its nature in terms of that function. The absurdities that flow from this have been amply discussed in Chapter 2.

COMPUTERS AND CONSCIOUSNESS REVISITED

There are rather less constricted definitions of consciousness which, though they do not narrow it to a defined function, do reduce it to a more or less defined state. An example is the definition of consciousness as a state of 'conditional readiness'. The attractiveness of such a definition is that it facilitates the computerisation of consciousness. The responsiveness of a computer is conditional: it will respond to certain sorts of inputs but not to others. They have to be of the right sort. Moreover, the computer has to be pre-set to respond. It can respond only to inputs encoded in a certain way; and in order that these trigger search-routines, it has to be primed, so that it can be on the lookout for characters or numerals of a particular sort.

Consciousness is not at all like this. Cognitive psychologists have been over-impressed by the fact that we sometimes tend to see what we expect to see rather than what is actually there and by the fact that we can identify things more quickly if we expect them than if we don't know what to expect. These marginal phenomena should not lead us to lose sight of the obvious: that the readiness of consciousness is both conditional and unconditional, that consciousness is both ready and unready. We are particularly quick to sense what we expect (conditional readiness) but we are also open to what we are totally unprepared for. The continuum of conscious experience contains the expected and the unexpected; the expected frame with the unexpected detail (the Chinese man I encounter on my journey in to work, the dust on the road). The experienced actual is composed of a billion details that are different from the sketch of anticipation, even when anticipation is unusually detailed. Memory and learning prepare us only partially for the moment-to-moment reality of experience.

This extraordinary facet of consciousness is discussed, perhaps without his fully realising what he is doing, by Dennett in his essay on 'The Frame Problem of AI'.[18] Dennett considers the knowledge one has, and needs, in order to accomplish even very trivial tasks. This knowledge is implicit as are the rules according to which I carry out my actions. When I plan to get myself a snack from the fridge, I hardly need to formulate the rule 'If the beer is in the glass, it cannot be in the bottle' or 'When the beer has been emptied into the glass, the pouring action should cease'. Not only are everyday actions hedged about with thousands of implicit rules for action, they are also shaped by thousands of rules for non-action, or rules for determining actions that must be avoided or conditions for discontinuing the action. Artificial intelligence (AI) forces banal information and banal rules to the surface because 'the tasks set by AI start at zero: the computer to be programmed to simulate the agent . . . initially knows nothing at all "about the world"'. This ignorance is very disabling indeed: for not only are there vast numbers of rules to be known ('if X is the case, then do Y') but these rules have enormous lists of conditions attached to them. For example, the rule of the type 'if X is the case, then do Y' has a *ceteris paribus* condition attached to it; and specifying what other things have to be equal for the rule to apply is an enormous undertaking. The list of conditions, indeed, may be interminable. The frame problem arises because the automaton's program has to have this knowledge installed into it. Nothing is obvious to the automaton; nothing can be taken for granted because the automaton doesn't understand the world and has no intuitions or sense of the extension or extensibility of the general rules necessary to shape its activity into behaviour simulating the infinite flexibility and adaptability of recognisably human behaviour. AI workers trying to simulate conscious beings are faced with an explosion of rules necessary to define the appropriate application of rules (or constraints on the application of rules, the conditions under which the rules apply) to prevent problems arising out of a program's application to the real, rough, amorphous world.

The frame problem – the fact that computational devices can operate successfully only within frames of reference that are very highly specified, within a narrow 'world' that has to be installed into them – underlines one of the fundamental differences between complex automata and conscious beings. The frame within which a conscious being operates is infinite, or at least unbounded. The conscious being does not operate only within narrow settings: its field of action and reaction is enormous. It is infinitely hospitable to what, if we were talking of a computer, we would call data. This is evinced in its sensory field which is a continuum of encounterings with relevant and irrelevant objects and events. Preoccupations, particular goals, specific purposes, etc. will favour some of the contents of the sensory field over others; but even the unprivileged, irrelevant ones are still *there*, as a background to, and side by side with, the relevant ones. Consciousness, unlike programmed, rule-governed responsiveness, has an openness, a boundless availability to what, unscheduledly, happens. I am busy writing this – but I hear (that is to say have been available for) – the rather humdrum birdsounds outside in the garden or the creaking of my chair inside the room. If there are boundaries of foreclosure, they are drawn very wide indeed. According to Dennett (p. 144), 'the script or frame approach is an attempt to *pre-solve* the frame problems the particular agent is likely to encounter'. When it comes to human agents, as opposed to artificial ones, the contents of consciousness are signally unscripted; or rather the script of consciousness is only very loosely constrained by anything equivalent to anticipatory installation or initialisation.

The multiplication of rules will not solve the frame problem except for local AI applications that come nowhere near the global scope of consciousness. The explicit rules that may shape consciousness arise out of a background of explicitness; or the soil out of which rules grow, the solution out of which they crystallise, is continuum of explicitness, a field of explicitness. The computer has only discrete countable rules, not this continuum of explicitness, this 'rule mass', this boundless, ruly world.

CONSCIOUSNESS, TRUTH, PURPOSE AND DEIXIS

The continuum of explicitness is not only the condition of the boundless openness of consciousness, its hospitality to the unexpected, the uncategorised, as well as to the expected and the categorised; it is also the condition of the emergence of truth (and falsehood) out of existence. Existence by itself is insufficient to create the categories of truth and falsehood: a pebble is in itself neither true nor false; it simply is. Truth emerges when its existence is transformed into 'that it is the case' and its being the case is asserted. In the absence of explicitness, the existence of the pebble is no more a truth to the effect that 'there is a pebble' than it is a standing falsehood to the effect that 'there is *not* a pebble'.

Truth emerges as a fully-developed category only when *that X [is the case]* is separated from X and given an independent existence; when, that is to say, explicitness itself is made explicit in the form of statements. Truth then takes on the character of a correspondence between statements and that which they purport to be about. Although propositional-form declarative utterances do not contain the whole of the truth (or the whole of falsehood) – we can, after all, have false perceptions or illusions; implicit truth is contained in what is not said (passed over, implied, hinted) as well as in what is said; and gesture, attitude and tone as well as content may convey truth – they do embody the most clear-cut form of truth and present the cleavage between truth and falsehood in a way that can be captured in a truth-conditional analysis. And these forms of truth do bring out most clearly the relationship between existence and truth; between object or state of affairs X and the truth about (and falsehoods about) X.

Truth is neither an inherent property of the material world, nor is it a creation of consciousness. It is the result of the material world being made explicit in consciousness; and of that explicitness being made explicit; and of *that* explicitness being made explicit; and so on. It is as a result of his being the explicit animal that man is the truth-bearing (and the lying, pretending, etc.) animal. He is, furthermore, uniquely the animal for whom the search for the truth (both as an individual quest and as a version of human progress through history) is a plausible version of his destiny.[19]

Consciousness, or explicitness, is also a necessary pre-condition for the emergence of purpose out of process and mechanism. The material world as evisaged in physical science provides no basis for purpose, function, or even, arguably, for discrete mechanisms. (There is mechanism but no discrete mechanisms; for the latter, like 'inputs' and 'outputs', are defined in relation to some envisaged end or goal; their definition requires a point of view). Automata, by definition, lack conscious purposes; if there are no external consciousnesses to transform the events that occur in them into steps towards a goal, they are purpose-free. Only a being that makes the natural order explicit can be credited with having purposes; only such a being will carve aims and objectives out of the unfolding of events. Without explicitness, there can be no 'manipulation' of the natural order, no interventions. A physicalist who talks of the needs, goals and purposes of organisms should convict himself of animomorphism, if not of anthropomorphism.

Without explicitness, then, events and entities do not generate either truth or goals. The most remarkable feature of human consciousness is the possibility of endlessly opening into self- or higher-order- consciousness. We who are conscious know *that* we are and *that we are conscious*, etc. (the knowing *is* the 'that'; the 'that' – knowing – is Being, italicised as it were.) Human consciousness, moreover, is characterised by a distinct sense of being *someone*. I know that I am and that I am *this* (body, person, mind). Such knowledge does not, of course, take the form of constant reminders to myself that I am this. If such reminders were necessary, they would be neither possible nor would they be effective. I could not secure reference to the thing I am, any more than I could discover who I am (in the sense of which existent is me).[20]

Self-consciousness is not merely at the heart of human consciousness; it also provides the most revealing difficulties for many contemporary theories of mind. David Marr, for example, conceived vision as a continuous process of computation which begins with images formed in the retina and culminates in a spatio-temporal world model useful for picking things up and getting about. One would expect that such a conception of vision would manage quite nicely without self-awareness; but he came to the conclusion that even a visually competent robot would have to be controlled by a program that made explicit information about the robot's own position in its visible world. And this admission was against the background of his already having admitted that the computational problem of reconstituting the visual world would be unresolvable without some preconceptions about objects and their appearances. And how would this self-awareness be written into the system? According to Johnson-Laird, 'to be conscious in the sense of self-aware, a computing machine must have an operating system that incorporates a model of itself' (Johnson-Laird, p. 360). This raises many more questions than it answers; for example: What would the model actually model? The hardware as well as the software, including the location of the former? Just the software? In which case, how would that software be modelled? In what language? And how would the model include the model of the software itself? And how would the model indicate that it was a model of the computer itself? How would it ensure self-reference? How would it model, in short, the sense of 'I am this thing' and 'I am here' that pervades ordinary consciousness and self-consciousness?'

I am this and I am here (in the spatial and temporal sense of this place and now): these are intuitions that cannot be derived, or arrived at or recognised on the basis of indirect indications. My being here and now is an absolute given to which all the relativities of space and time relate. The mysterious presupposition of consciousness *that I am this* is primary. Without this presupposition, there is no hereness and thisness. That I am here and now and am *this thing* is no more amenable to proof or demonstration than that I exist. To a system that deals in generalities – a symbol-handling system such as a computer and the mind according to computational theorists – its own existential particularity (the fact that it is a particular embodiment of a program operating in a particular bit of hardware located at a particular point in space and functioning at a particular point in time) lies beyond its reach. A computer program lacks this 'being here-and-now' to make its references other than general. In contrast with the human being which is here *for-itself*, it has no deictic coordinates. The human position or situation is rooted in the intuition of particularity while the computer is, strictly, situationless in this sense. It does not have either what I might call 'the sentiment of actuality' or the existential deictic tautology. By contrast, human consciousness begins from particularity. It is deictic through and through.[21]

The non-derivability of deixis (that I am *this*) is evident also in occurrent memory, with the essential and unique relation to the sense of personal identity that is implicit in it. I do not derive my personal identity from reflecting upon my memories. Rather, personal identity – I remember this; this experience is of something that happened to *me* – is presupposed in 'the sense of being there' that is inherent in memory, just as it is in experience. Trying to do without this presupposition gets one immediately into all sorts of circularities concerning the ownership of memories – and experiences. At the root of a genuine first-person memory is an *I was there* corresponding to the *I am here* of experience. In short, the existential deictic tautology.[22]

There is an interesting discussion by McGinn[23] of the relation between deixis, secondary qualities and the subjective sense of being here and now. He deals, specifically, with indexicals:

> Indexicality is often cited as the paradigm of that which a properly objective conception of the world would exclude: the physicist, we are told, refrains from indexical description of the world. The intuitive reason for this exclusion is that the use of indexicals involves treating oneself as somehow a *centre*, as a privileged coordinate; an objective description should not be thus invidious in its depiction of reality – it must be impartial. Indexicals flout this requirement of objective centreless description because they are semantically relative in their interpretation. (pp. 14–15)

McGinn quotes Russell's assertion that 'no egocentric particulars occur in the language of physics. Physics views space-time impartially, as God might be supposed to view it; there is not, as in perception, a region which is especially warm and intimate and bright, surrounded in all directions by growing darkness'. McGinn and Russell here touch on themes that have pervaded this book. The sense of the here and now, of 'I am this', of the centre, of the *actual* – which is the absolute ground floor of human consciousness – has no place in the viewpointless world of physics and cannot be understood in the terms of the physicalist world picture. The brain, understood as a physical system, could not explain this fundamental feature of human consciousness, this *explicit being here and being this* which characterises our existence and is the basis for our sense of responsibility for things and our active concern for ourselves.

The identification of mind or consciousness with the symbol processing activity of the brain takes us even further from an account of consciousness than non-computational physicalist accounts; for it loses not only *the individual's sense of identification with this thing* (me) but also the entire world of particulars and actuals. For computation over symbols, as discussed in Chapter 4, is general, syntactic, referenceless. The computational mind not only has no contact with itself as *this* but with all particulars. Its world is an existentially unsaturated one of general operations and general possibilities: here-less, now-less, particular-less, this-less, me-less. It lacks conscious identity – it does not exist from its own point of view, for it has nothing to establish a point of view – to lay down the co-ordinates of here and now from which all the absolutes of actuality extend.

LANGUAGE AND CONSCIOUSNESS

I have characterised human language as that in virtue of which explicitness is made explicit. It is the main medium of higher-order explicitness and opens the path to the endless elaboration of explicitness: of consciousness of consciousness; and consciousness of consciousness of consciousness; and so on. Language is not, of course, the only medium in which reflexive self-consciousness can unfold; but it is a matrix in which higher-order unfoldings most typically take place; in which, for example, I become most elaborately aware of your awareness of my awareness of me; or I consider the reason you tried to indicate that your handshake was not as sincere as it might have been, given normal behaviour and expectations.[24]

The signs of human language are radically arbitrary. At the most obvious level, they do not look like, sound like, etc. the objects that are signified through them. They are not, that is to say, iconic and their formations do not signify in virtue of replicating a piece of reality. More importantly, they are arbitrary in the sense of being uprooted from their context: they are not causally related to that which they signify. Natural signs such as clouds signify rain because they cause it. Other natural signs may be effects of what they signify: for example a scream may signify pain or fear or danger. Both kinds of signs may be seen as symptomatic or, at least, synecdochic; the sign and the significate are parts of a single whole – a causal process or sequence. Natural signs are embedded in the same context as their significates. Linguistic signs are not.

Attempts to naturalise human language have, consciously or unconsciously, been directed towards undermining or denying this arbitrariness or, alternatively, reading into natural signs properties – grammar, reference, etc. – that are in fact dependent on arbitrariness. At the very crudest level, it has been suggested that the emission of signs is triggered by the objects they signify and that the meaning of the sign is its effect on the recipient. The presence of the object, for example, is communicated from one individual to another as follows:

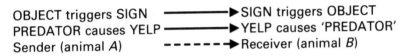

OBJECT triggers SIGN ⟶ SIGN triggers OBJECT
PREDATOR causes YELP ⟶ YELP causes 'PREDATOR'
Sender (animal *A*) ⤏ Receiver (animal *B*)

For example, animal *A* encounters a predator and emits a yelp; animal *B* hears the yelp and behaves as if it had encountered a predator; it, too, runs away. The fact that it runs away is taken to be the cash value of the communication 'There is predator in the vicinity'; it is regarded as the behavioural interpretation of the communication. For the receiver, the sign (the yelp) stands for the object (the predator); it signifies in virtue of stimulating behaviour identical to that which would be triggered by the object itself. Communication between the two animals, therefore, takes place automatically in virtue of a single unbroken causal chain passing through the two organisms. One could take the analogy further – as writers such as Skinner have done – by describing the stimulus producing the yelp as the 'referent' of the yelp: the 'yelp' refers to the predator.

What is wrong with this view of language – a view that bypasses explicitness and consciousness and reduces the transmission of information to the transmission of stimuli by proxies? Pretty well everything, if it is offered as an account of human language. It is wrong empirically and it is, more importantly, wrong conceptually.

First of all, the facts. The production of signs by human beings is not always, or even typically, a triggered response to stimuli; even more rarely are the stimuli the objects signified by the signs. There are a few occasions – as when the sight of fire may trigger the scream 'Fire!' – when the object triggers its name but these are rare. Even on such occasions, the sight of fire may lead to a quite different shout – for example, 'Get the children out!' We more often talk about absent objects or abstract objects. And our talk of (absent or present) objects does not itself consist of emitting the signs corresponding to them: we talk *about* them, predicate things of them; we do not merely enumerate them. Conversation does not consist of yelp-string, yelp-lists. (And there are numerous problems in thinking of yelps and other vocal responses as 'names'.) Moreover, we talk about possible objects and impossible ones as well as actual concrete and abstract ones. The truth is that the occasions and referents of our discourse are extremely complex and it is not even slightly plausible to suggest that our talk-emissions are responses to stimuli. Even the talk of a five-year-old ('When we get home from holidays, I'm going to practice my yo-yo until I'm an expert') could not be subsumed under any kind of stimulus-response model. There is equal implausibility in the attempt to reduce to a behavioural response the recipient's understanding of the communication. We often do not respond outwardly to what is said to us; equally often, our outward response is a further piece of discourse which may or may not be what the sender expected and may, anyway, be only remotely occasioned by what he has said. Finally, the suggestion that we routinely behave towards the sign-stimulus as we would towards the significate is, of course, nonsense. The responses towards signs (and the complexes of signs that constitute ordinary discourse) are as complex as the occasions, and relations to the occasions, that prompt their emission.

So much for the facts that are against stimulus theories of meaning. But what of the conceptual muddle behind them? The fundamental error is that of trying to naturalise linguistic signs, incorporating them into a causal nexus that passes through inanimate objects and organisms alike. This, in turn, results from a failure to understand what lies at the bottom of arbitrariness. Arbitrary signs, to reiterate what was said in the previous chapter, are, precisely because of their arbitrariness, manifestly *signs*. They are visibly signs because they lack all occasion apart from the intention to signify; and this creates the distances from the causal net that have then to be crossed by meaning and reference. True reference is inseparable from the *intention to refer*, just as information cannot be understood, except metaphorically, independently of the intention to inform. My understanding what you are saying depends on my understanding *that you are saying*. I consume your meanings because I understand that it is meaning that you are producing.

Since Grice[25] pointed this out – that being affected by an utterance depends on understanding its meaning and that understanding its meaning in turn depends on understanding the speaker's semantic intention (what he intends you to believe) – the stimulus theory has had little credibility in philosophical circles. Human meaning is an act as well as an influence; there is producer-meaning as well as consumer-meaning. Natural signs may mean things in one sense ('Spots mean measles') but not in another important sense (as when I mean to inform you of something – i.e. to bring about in you a certain belief). Spots may be informative but they are not informants.

Human linguistic meaning – the business of meaning things with words – is an act, not merely a link in a chain of causes and effects passing from an object through a speaker to a receiver. This act requires, utilises arbitrary signs; signs that, being uprooted from a nexus of natural associations, from the chain of causality, display themselves as signs, as human interventions. The appearance of a cloud signifying rain is primarily an event and only secondarily a sign; the arbitrary sign, by contrast, occurs *in order to* signify so signifies its status as a sign. The acquisition of meta-linguistic awareness early in the process of language acquisition and the ubiquity of meta-language in everyday discourse (discussed in the previous chapter) emphasises the way in which linguistic signs are explicitly signs to their users.

Wittgenstein's remarks at the very end of *On Certainty* point up the inadequacy of stimulus theories of meaning. Criticising Descartes' methodological doubt as a starting point for philosophical investigation, he writes as follows:

> I cannot seriously suppose that I am at this moment dreaming. Someone who, dreaming, says 'I am dreaming', even if he speaks audibly in doing so, is no more right than if he said in his dream 'It is raining', while it was in fact raining. Even if his dream were actually connected with the noise of the rain.[26]

The reason I cannot seriously advance the suggestion that I am now dreaming is that, without a fully-conscious communicative intent, any utterance to this effect would be only a set of sounds, a material event but not a true speech act. And it is not possible to be dreaming and at the same time to have a fully-conscious communicative intent. The dreaming man is outside of the conditions essential to communication. A dreamer cannot intend to communicate the fact that he is dreaming without moving outside of his dream state. If, as Novalis says, 'we are close to waking when we dream that we are dreaming',[27] we must needs be wide awake to *assert* that we are dreaming – especially if we assert it in order to initiate a philosophical discussion.

If it so happens that I *am* dreaming when I mutter 'I am dreaming', this coincidence does not make the sounds I produce count as a true statement. Yes, a statement is true when reality coincides with the truth conditions of the statement. But before a vocalisation can be a true statement, it has to be a *statement*; before it can be true, it has to embody a communicative intent. A dreaming man mumbling 'I am dreaming' is no more making a true statement than a dictaphone located inside a corpse playing 'I am dead' is *someone* pronouncing himself dead. Nor would it be so even if the tape were a recording of the ex-man's own voice. Mere coincidence between a series of sounds and the truth conditions of the utterance that would use those sounds is not of itself sufficient to make the sounds a true statement because it is insufficient to make it a *statement*. The communicative intent is crucial and this is most clearly evident where arbitrary signs – signs whose occurrence could not be accounted for by agency-unrelated causes – are deployed.

The final sentence of Wittgenstein's remark – 'Even if his dream were actually connected with the sound of the rain' – is particularly relevant to the present discussion. Statement *S* may seem to be about state of affairs *A* but it is not in fact 'about' anything unless it is motivated by a communicative intent on the part of the speaker. It may have such a communicative intent *ascribed to it by someone other than the speaker* – as when, for example, I, unaware that you are asleep, overhear you mutter 'I am dreaming'; but, under such circumstances, the sounds coming from the speaker's mouth count only as an apparent speech act. Their intentionality is borrowed from a second consciousness – mine – whose interpretive acts release their meaning – a meaning that, curiously, is not meant by the producer; a meaning that, in other words, has a consumer but no producer. The fact that the rain actually caused the vocalisation does not change this state of affairs: it does not make the vocalisation a *statement* to the effect that it is raining.[28]

This should bring out the difference between a sign that signifies through being part of the causal chain – being caused by the object or entity which it signifies, and having the effect of acting proxy for that object or entity – and an arbitrary sign; between a natural and a genuinely linguistic sign. A cloud does not have to be conscious to signify rain; the consciousness necessary for it to count as a sign is provided by the consumer. Natural signs mean things; but the meaning is engendered in the consumer and in the absence of the consumer there is no meaning. Linguistic signs, on the other hand, are *meant* and their interpretation, as Grice has repeatedly emphasised, depends upon seeing that they are meant. As Bennett has put it,[29] the very notion of meaning (of meaning something) depends essentially on intention and belief; and meaning mediated through linguistic signs makes this explicit: my appreciating the meaning of what you are saying depends on my understanding that you are trying to communicate something to me; more specifically, that you are intending to make me believe something. By contrast, a natural sign such as a cloud is not a statement; for example, a standing assertion to the effect that 'it is probably going to rain'. Clouds do not intend the inferences that may be drawn from their presence in the sky. They are not 'about' rain, or the probable occurrence of rain, even though they may cause us to expect rain. It is we, not they, who provide their 'aboutness'. In themselves, they – and other natural signs – are not about anything. The very fact that they rely upon natural association with their significates – similarity of appearance, spatio-temporal association – denies them the distance necessary for fully explicit 'aboutness'; the distance necessary for the intentionality of linguistic signs that forms the basis of the reference they alone can sustain and the truth values only assertions composed of them can carry.

The stimulus theory of meaning incorporates illuminating errors which serve to bring out the true nature of language and its relation to explicitness. The deficiencies of the theory show us what is implicit in the emergence of linguistic meaning. The unnatural sign which creates and maintains, even when it is signifying, its distance from the significate, facilitates the emergence of ever more explicit meanings. It transforms the contents of the world into referents, things of which other things can be predicated. More than any other human faculty, arbitrary sign language elaborates the distances out of which truth about existents can emerge out of existence, so that existence can be transformed into truth and existents become truth conditions. The stimulus theory of meaning, which tries to assimilate meaning, reference and truth into the causal nexus that passes through objects and organisms alike shows us, by its failures, the true miracle and mystery of language.

It is worth emphasising that the truly consistent stimulus-response theories of signs – such as those of Skinner[30] – are ultimately physicalist rather than biological. They deal in causal, rather than specifically behavioural, chains. To assimilate meaning to stimulus or to response, and both of these to parts of a causal chain to be understood ultimately in physicalist terms as 'energy transfers', is to undermine their status as 'meaning', 'stimulus' and 'response'. Skinner, in particular, seems to want to have the world of meaning, of language, and of human beings anthropomorphically, while eating reality in exclusively physicalist terms. Physicalism does not strictly allow 'meaning', 'stimulus' and 'response'. The stimulus theory of meaning has physicalism as its final goal; and yet, if that goal were achieved, 'meaning' would be an inadmissible category. The theory, like the causal theory of perception, assumes a world picture it is trying to demolish.

LANGUAGE, PERCEPTION AND CAUSATION

The analogies between the causal theory of linguistic meaning and the causal theory of perception will be sufficiently evident.[31] They share a common endeavour to reduce 'aboutness' to causal relations – or to show that aboutness can be explained, or explained away, in terms of causal relations. According to the causal theory of meaning, the *meanings* and the material *occasions* of our utterances are identical; or they are determined by the very same items that cause them. In Skinner's words, the referents of what we say control our saying it. The analogy may be shown diagrammatically:

Perception

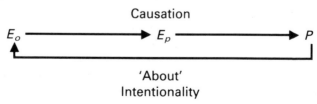

Language

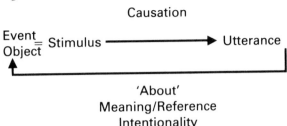

Causation

'About'
Meaning/Reference
Intentionality

In both cases, the properties of the afferent limb are supposed to account for the properties of the efferent limb; or what happens in the afferent limb is supposed to explain what is achieved in the efferent limb. There is it would seem, a hierarchy of explanatory requirement, such that physical causation doesn't require explanation (so that it can provide the ground upon which explanation can stand) while intentionality does; or that, while we are trying to explain intentionality, we can take causation for granted as if it were self-explanatory.

The reduction of linguistic signs to responses (of the producer) and stimuli (for the consumer) – which embeds them in the chain of natural causes and effects – tantamounts to delinguifying language. The cognitive psychologists' ploy of redescribing consciousness as a succession of symbols would seem to be the opposite error of 'linguifying non-linguistic phenomena. The two errors come together in the notion that the mental symbols are the causal chains that pass through the brain, as in Colin McGinn's counter-argument to Searle.

Searle, it will be recalled, argued that the computational theory of mind reduced it to a machine that had syntax but no semantics. Against this, McGinn claims that the symbols manipulated by the cerebral computer do indeed have a semantic content, even though, of course, this cannot be derived from their rules of combination, from the syntax. They come from their causal origin: 'Internal manipulations don't determine reference, but causal relations to the environment might'.[32]

The reduction of consciousness to a train of 'causal symbols' traduces consciousness in two opposite ways: it suppresses the way in which consciousness is offset from the causal chain (so that consciousness makes the causal chains explicit and exploits them in deliberate action); and it overlooks the here-and-now nature of consciousness. To deal with the second point: it will be recalled that a major objection to the cognitive scientists' 'symbolising' of consciousness was that symbols were uninterpreted while consciousness was not incomplete in this way. The counter-argument just discussed tries to argue that the causal relations of their symbols *are* their interpretations; that the cerebral computer is not a purely syntactic machine because it derives its semantics from the events that cause it.

I have already given sufficient indication as to why a causally upstream event cannot without further explanation count as the intentional object or referent of perceptions; but perhaps I could add one further reason, relating to the immediacy of consciousness. If consciousness itself is only a symbol of its causes, whence immediacy, and the sense that I am here-and-now, this-is-here, etc.?[33] If a major fault of the syntactic theory of mind is that, by leaving the mental symbols uninterpreted, it leaves perception itself general (and so contravenes the principle of the primacy of the particular), it is an equal fault of the 'causally interpreted' symbol theory of mind to make of it a place of eternal, incompletable mediation that never reaches immediacy.

EXPLICITNESS, INTENTIONALITY AND MATTER

The failure to recognise the primacy of the actual over the possible, the individual over the class (as well as over the class-member distinction) is not the greatest fault of certain contemporary theories of the mind, though it is a crucial one. No, the greatest fault, especially clear in the cases of those theories that try to reduce perception to the effects of objects on the body or nervous system and to assimilate reference to causation – in short of causal theories, whether of perception, or of meaning, or of action – is a failure to allow for the emergence of intentionality, of aboutness, of explicitness. For perception, for verbal reference, for the emergence of agency in a causal world, we need this irreducible explicitness, this distance which may present itself as 'aboutness'. The plenum of the mechanistic world of unconscious matter and unconscious energy lacks 'aboutness'. The sense of this lack is close to the intuition that prompts Marcel to speak of the (human) universe as 'the dehiscence of Being'. We are particularly inclined to postulate such a dehiscence or an 'opening up' if we think of 'what is primordially there' as being unconscious matter. From such a starting point the world of, and available to, knowledge seems to arise out of an encounter, between matter and consciousness, that opens up matter to consciousness as its condition, its adversary and its possession. It is this opening up that the diagram tries to indicate:

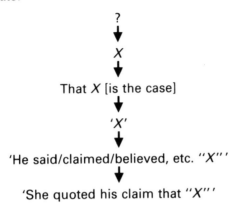

Like the diagrams in the Overture, this should not be thought of as a genetic account of the emergence of consciousness out of matter, of linguistic consciousness out of consciousness, of meta-linguistic consciousness out of a linguistic consciousness etc. Assuming the priority of matter, with consciousness a latecomer developing out of an initially material world, would go against the tendency of this book. The diagram merely indicates distances that would have to be travelled to arrive at the human universe if inanimate matter were the starting point.

Some of the odd ideas about consciousness that are currently in vogue may be traced to a failure to appreciate the global nature of explicitness. This is symptomatised in the tendency to focus on specific, local mental phenomena such as sensations or perceptions or beliefs and to look for the explanation of consciousness in the correlation of these with specific brain activities. To approach the problem this way is to reverse ontological and logical priorities. It is ironical that discrete mental phenomena such as images, occurrent memories, etc., seem like the final challenge for mind–body identity theorists, cognitive psychologists and neurobiologists; as if, once these are solved, the mystery of consciousness will be cracked. For concentrating on isolated mental phenomena is a crucial step towards the misrepresentation of consciousness and preparing it

for reduction to focal brain activity. And by localising consciousness, one prepares the way for the kind of view that 'since
consciousness is a special thing, it must have a special mechanism
of its own' and ideas such as Dennett's belief that the mind 'is our
way of experiencing the machinery of the brain'. Consciousness, it
cannot be too strongly emphasised, is not focal in the way that the
things of which we are conscious are.

The views advanced in the last diagram should not, however, be
construed as a form of idealism. That which is made explicit is not
itself entirely the product of the process of making-explicit. This is
presumably obvious enough. There are constraints, originating
outside of consciousness, upon the contents of consciousness. The
contrast between my thoughts, feelings and sensations and the
objects before me must be retained. What is wrong with idealism is
that it assimilates the object to the subject and so outrages the
fundamental intuition that I am not the object and the object is not
me; that when I see the table, the table is fundamentally other than
me and fundamentally other than my seeing it. This otherness of
the object could not be derived from perception; rather, it is itself a
fundamental intuition or presupposition of perception. As to what
is fundamental, that I shall discuss shortly.

RECONSIDERING MATTER

The rejection of materialist accounts of consciousness raises questions about the status of neurophysiology and cognitive science.
What is neurophysiology discovering? What, moreover, do
common-sense observations about the way consciousness is contingent upon certain states of the brain tell us about its nature? We
cannot reasonably deny that consciousness seems to depend upon
the function of mechanisms that are themselves not conscious,
indeed are automatic. We cannot put the whole of science and the
common sense (natural) standpoint in brackets. I have no wish to
be obscurantist or to turn my back on, or to deny, the enormous
advances in understanding that have come from computers and
neurophysiology. To reject the achievements of neuroscience
would be to walk away from much of what is most exciting about
late-twentieth-century inquiry. But this means that we are faced
with new problems: that of making sense of these sciences and of
their relationship to our subjective experience; and of trying to

understand how sciences that are misconceived at a philosophical or metaphysical level can make substantive progress towards what seems like the truth. To try to deal with the problem of reconciling the position of this book with accepting the validity of science and common sense by suggesting that they represent two different incommensurate areas of discourse or even of knowledge is not merely to be boring but, indeed, to cut across the intuition – and excitement (the excitement necessary to drive philosophy) – that there is some kind of unified explanation of the heterogeneous phenomena of the world.

Could it not be that the mind–body problem as it is addressed by many current researchers in physiology and cognitive science is misconceived? By this I do not mean to imply that there is no problem of understanding the relationship of the mind to the body, or to the brain; only that the favoured contemporary approaches seem to overlook the all-encompassing nature of mind and, more importantly, to take matter for granted. Real advances in the scientific understanding of consciousness may depend on our importing into cognitive psychology and epistemology some of the sophistication that marks modern physical conceptions of matter.

The assumption behind many contemporary attempts to understand mind in materialist terms is that mind is somehow explained if it is reduced to the properties of certain formations of matter. Does such a reduction *explain* anything? It gives us no hint as to why a tiny minority of formations of matter should be conscious while the vast majority are not. So, although the reduction of mind to the properties of matter would eliminate the mind–matter problem by abolishing the gap between mind and matter, it would not greatly advance our understanding of mind. It would simply incorporate the problem of mind into the mystery of matter. Moreover, contemporary physicalism takes matter itself rather for granted, as if it were either not at all mysterious or so comparatively unmysterious that its mysteries might be ignored. The physicalist or materialist position assumes, at any rate, that matter is a self-evident basis upon which mind can be built. It assumes, that is to say, not only the logical and ontological primacy, but also the conceptual transparency, of matter.

In fact the concept of matter is deeply puzzling and, as idealist philosophers have long argued, riddled with contradiction and difficult to conceive of coherently independently of mind. Modern physics has, of course, only made matter more complex and difficult to grasp and has both widened and narrowed the gulf between matter-in-itself and our perceptions; or, since physics, too, is ultimately based on perceptions, between scientific perceptions of matter and our everyday perception of material things. Some thinkers, aware that materialism contributes nothing to explaining why certain formations of matter such as the brain should be conscious when others are not, have appealed to the new physics and the new properties it has discovered in matter to account for the emergence of consciousness.

For example, Phillips (op. cit. – see note 9) refers to the work of Hopfield who, he claims, 'showed how the dynamics of neural nets could be thought of as analogous to those of large populations of simple elements with non-linear interactions, such as disordered magnetic spins'. Hopfield 'used the techniques developed for analysing the dynamics of magnetic spins to show how such populations could provide fast, robust, and capacious memories'. I have already discussed Penrose's suggestion that quantum correlations which may occur over a wide distance (i.e. a concordance of behaviour that seems to be inexplicable purely by chance) might 'play a role in conscious thought-modes':

> Perhaps it is not too fanciful to suggest that quantum correlations could be playing an operative role over large regions of the brain. Might there be any relation between 'a state of awareness' and a highly coherent quantum state in the brain? Is the 'oneness' or 'globality' that seems to be a feature of consciousness connected with this?[34]

The trouble with theories that try to explain consciousness by appealing to properties evident in matter in large – and so seem to cross the matter–mind barrier while still remaining within physicalist science – is it that they signally fail to explain why consciousness should be confined, in the way it seems to be, to very few formations of matter. Arguments whose tendency is to make matter more mind-like are liable to rebound: if the essentials required for consciousness are available in 'simple elements', why aren't these simple elements conscious – assuming that modern physics does not license panpsychism. Why, so far as we know, is only one form of matter (man) fully conscious? As for quantum coherence, this, according to Penrose, has to date been observed only in systems that are not thought to be conscious. It doesn't therefore seem to constitute the special conditions that cause, or permit the emergence of, consciousness.[35]

Eccles, who has for many years tried to reconcile the physicalism implicit in his physiological investigations with his dualist ontology, turns to the ideas of Henry Margenau for a way out of his dilemma.[36] Certainly, Margenau's version of matter is sufficiently attenuated to make it promisingly mental. He asserts that some fields, such as the probability fields of quantum physics, carry neither energy nor matter. And he suggests that in very complicated physical systems such as the brain and sense organs 'whose constitutents are small enough to be governed by probabilistic quantum laws',

> the physical organ is always poised for a multitude of possible changes, each with a definite probability; if one change takes place that requires energy, or more or less energy than another, the intricate organ furnishes it automatically. Hence, if there is a mind–body interaction, the mind would not be called upon to furnish energy.[37]

This suggests a possible solution to the problem that haunts a would-be physiological dualism: if the mind itself lacks both mass and energy, and if it operates through a physical system such as the brain, how can it bring anything about without transgressing the law of conservation of mass-energy? The answer, it seems, is that the mind chooses between things that had a predisposition to occur anyway. The energy is already available.

There are many difficulties in the way of accepting this use of modern physics to solve the mind–body problem. First of all, one wonders how real the probabilities are; are they really predispositions or merely frequencies? If the latter, it is difficult to see how they can be selected for or against by a choosing mind. And if they are genuine predispositions, it is difficult to see how they can inhere in matter and yet be discriminated for or against by mind. There is also the obscurity of the claim that the brain is both very complex and yet has constituents that are small enough to be governed by probabilistic laws. Presumably every object is at once very complex – when the many billions of atomic components are considered together as a whole – and very small – when those components are looked at individually. But you can't have your cake macroscopically while you eat it sub-atomically. Indeed, the complexity or simplicity of a system should not cut ice in physics: at a macroscopic level, a pebble is infinitely complex – and very simple. Moreover, what can be done for the brain – description at two levels – can be done for quite brainless objects such as sticks and stones. Margenau, in other words, has not identified features that would distinguish brains from stones and explain why consciousness is so choosy about the material company it keeps. The claim that 'the mind may be regarded as a field in the accepted physical sense of the term' but 'a nonmaterial field . . . [that] does not necessarily have a definite position in space'[38] is, ultimately, obscure. It would be nice to think that it overcame the dualist puzzle referred to above as well as taking on board the Cartesian conception of mind as non-extended and so non-localised. But it does not seem to answer to the power of mind to choose, nor to its being positioned, in the sense of having, or indeed being, a point of view.

Nevertheless, there is considerable merit in the general notion that a modern understanding of the mind–body problem and of mind–matter relationships must take account of modern physics and its conceptions of matter. In particular, it is no longer acceptable to ignore the fact that modern particle physics now recognises the crucial influence of the consciousness of the observer on the observations upon which physical theories depend. The very nature of the sub-atomic world is influenced by the interventions necessary to permit its perception. The ghost that modern neuroscience has evicted even from the human brain has re-entered the world at the sub-atomic level[39] – a fact which makes eliminative materialism, which would reject the notion of the consciousness of human beings, all the more perverse. And it is distinctly odd that the attempted reduction of soft sciences such as psychology to hard science should be being pursued most vigorously when the most fundamental hard science – physics – has become soft-centred. Indeed, it is one of the ironies of the present intellectual scene that it is the physicists, rather than the psychologists and the philosophers who are the guardians of the mind. This has been expressed well by David Bohm:

> While we do not wish to suggest that the analogy between electrons and living beings is complete, we do wish to emphasise that it goes far enough to show that physics has really abandoned

its earlier mechanical bias. Its subject matter already, in certain ways, is far more similar to that of biology than it is to that of Newtonian mechanics. It does seem odd, therefore, that just as physics is moving away from mechanism, biology and psychology are moving closer to it.[40]

In their anxiety to be on the side of the scientific angels, philosophical psychologists are increasingly trying to be like physicists. The only trouble is that their physics is out of date; the angels have moved on elsewhere. The ground upon which modern physics rests is not as firm as it seems to those looking from the standpoint of the once-human sciences. This is a message that has been taken on board by some recent writers on the mind–body problem. I have already referred to Roger Penrose. Among professional philosophers, Michael Lockwood has made a serious attempt to bring together quantum and relativistic physics and the philosophy of mind.[41] His fascinating book is not entirely successful, inasmuch as the physics is not integrated into the philosophy. Where there is a direct attempt to bring them closely together – as in the notion that Bose condensations might be the basis of mental states (pp. 256–9) – the physics has to be taken on trust and the quality of philosophical argument drops sharply.

Despite this it seems that Lockwood's instinct is sound: one way of advancing our understanding of the mind–body problem may lie in a critical reappraisal of the conceptions of matter that are deployed when we think about the problem. The physics of the philosophical physicalist is often rather primitive, certainly pre-quantum and most definitely unaware of the implications of complementarity and the work of scientists such as Alain Aspect who has decisively put the ghost back in the atom. At any rate matter should be more puzzling to materialist philosophers; modern physics has shown that our conception of matter is gaseous with mind and, as Robinson's critique of matter has demonstrated,[42] it is not philosophically transparent. It only seems so when we are busy worrying about something else – such as 'life' or 'mind'.

NEUTRAL MONISM AND THE PRIMACY OF PRESENCE

There are two ways of bridging the gap between consciousness and unconscious matter: materialising consciousness (a move whose termini are eliminative materialism and the mind–body identity theory); and mentalising matter (either invoking post-Classical physics or going the whole Berkeleian hog). Both types of ploy lead to difficulties because, by closing the gap, they leave unexplained the very fact that explanation began with: the special nature of conscious beings, their difference from all else. If conscious beings are matter like everything else, how is it that they have the distinctive property of consciousness; if matter contains the essential elements of consciousness, how is it that matter is not universally conscious?

It may be better not to begin with either mind or matter since both starting points lead to insuperable problems as to how the one gains access to, or interacts with, the other. If primacy is granted to material objects, there seems to be no basis for the way one material object becomes present to another, as when I am aware of something. Neither the intrinsic properties of material objects, nor the (causal) interactions between one material object and another (e.g. the nervous system) seems to account for presence. There seems to be nothing within matter as conventionally conceived to explain how material objects become that which is present; to explain the transition from Object X to 'That there is Object X' or 'That Object X is there (here/in front of me/exists, etc.)'.[43] And the problems that result when one begins with mind seem even more acute. Perception, for example, does not justify the belief that there is 'something out there', beyond perception. There is no way of understanding how perception gives us access to material objects which, by definition, transcend it, are other than it. Matter becomes the hypothesis of an hypostatic reality, for which perception provides no evidence, no justification and no explanation.

In short, if one starts either from mind or from matter, there is no basis for the presence of one object to another. Presence, the inter-relation between subject and object, cannot be *derived* from either matter or mind; it must therefore be primary. It is the subject and object, mind and matter that are derived or secondary substances.

This is scarcely a novel suggestion. Its most celebrated exponent is Spinoza, according to whom

everything which exists in the Universe is to be conceived as a modification or particular differentiation of the unique, all-inclusive substance, whose nature is revealed to us solely under the two infinite attributes, Thought and Extension.[44]

The original substance is neither mind nor matter, the latter being an attribute of the original substance rather than primary substance in itself. Such a view must be distinguished from the dual-aspect theory of the mind–body relationship, from property dualism. For the latter regards mind as one of two aspects of certain specialised formations of matter – namely brain processes. It *localises* mind and gives matter logical and ontological priority in a way that is quite contrary to Spinoza's conception which makes *both* matter and mind aspects or attributes of something more fundamental.

In some sense Spinoza anticipated Russell, who espoused an explicit neutral monism in his middle period.[45] Russell denied that there was any irreducible difference between the mental and the physical and attempted to construct both the mental world and the physical world out of components which are themselves neither mental nor physical but neutral. The difference between the physical and the mental is a difference not of the components but in the way they are put together: appearances are grouped in one way to form physical objects and in another to form minds. Existentialist philosophers, too, sometimes seem to be neutral monists, denying that mind and matter are externally related but equally strongly repudiating any suggestion that mind has primacy over matter. In the rebarbative discussions of writers such as Sartre and Heidegger, there seems to be constant vacillation between an idealism that gives the mind (or the for-itself) priority and a more neutral view that starts with 'being-there' (Dasein), presence, or co-presence, as primary.

Despite the problems associated with all versions of neutral monism – not the least of which is the difficulty of characterising the stuff that exists prior to mind and matter and of conceiving any kind of research programme to cast light on this stuff – the insuperable difficulties of both physicalist and idealist monism, and of dualism, justify an attempt to re-examine the possibilities of neutral monism.

The version of neutral monism that I have hinted at gives primacy to presence. This may seem to be paradoxical, *if presence is seen as a relation between two objects – the subject and the object, or the I and the Other – and if that external relation is modelled on the relations between two material objects.* For then I would seem to be arguing the priority of a relation (presence) over the relevant relata. This apparent paradox is based on misunderstanding. If, as I am suggesting, presence may be anterior to (in the sense of being the underived condition of) the emergence of material objects explicitly present to material bodies – the interaction between objects and subjects, as when subjects perceive objects – then we are not to think of presence as a relation between mutually external relata. Presence is a condition of relations, not itself a relation. Presence is prior to *presence to*; prior to the presence of, for example, *A* to *B*.

Presence is the underived, and underivable, condition of the possibility of individual relations, of the presence of one thing to another, of the object–subject interaction. We may think of the relation of presence in this sense to individual presentations (as when I am aware of an object as being present to me) as analogous to the relation between a Kantian form of sensible intuition such as space and specific spatial relations between myself and individual material objects.

I am not very happy with these notions, if only because they remain insufficiently clarified and I have not yet thought through their implications for the classical problems of epistemology. At the very least their airing expresses my conviction that the presence of one object to another cannot be *derived*. Presence cannot be derived from the properties of (essentially unconscious) matter or from the interaction between two mutually external unconscious objects – the nervous system and the object it perceives. Nor cannot it be derived from consciousness (considered as the perceptions of the subject). Presence is in some crucial sense primary or primordial.

The currently popular view that presence is generated by the interaction between the nervous system and the objects it perceives overlooks the fact that perception *requires* presence – the presence of the perceived object. This is unwittingly admitted in the 'constraint' on perception – that we shall perceive *only that which is present to the nervous system* – that is foundational for the causal (neurophysiological) theory of perception. At any given moment, we can selectively observe those things, from among the things that are present to us, that fall within our sensory field. For example, I can change the contents of my perception by moving my eyes. However, there are constraints upon what I can perceive: I can perceive only that which is present to my nervous system; nothing that is not present can be perceived, it can only be hallucinated. The constraint of 'being genuinely present' cannot, as I showed in Chapter 3, be defined independently of normal perception. So it boils down to this: we can perceive only that which we normally perceive; or, more precisely, that which is present to us is limited to that which is present to us.[46]

To recap, any account of perception, of presence, of consciousness that works inwards from the (material) object of perception to the nervous system fails because it must depend on a prior assumption of presence – of the presence of the object to the nervous system. If, on the other hand, you begin with perception and try to work outwards to the object, you cannot reach it: those who begin with perceptions (curiously, unoccasioned by material objects) cannot arrive at the presence of perception-independent objects. The object, and its actual presence, has to be assumed by (in) perception, so that intentionality shall have an authentic (particular, actual) target. The intentionality of ordinary perception assumes (rather than proves or demonstrates or empirically discovers) the Other, the presence of that which it is not; it does not, cannot, establish it.

So presence cannot be generated by either an inwards (object → nervous system → perception) or an outwards (perception → object) movement arising from the interaction between objects. The intrinsic properties of objects don't seem to account for their being present to other objects; and the nervous system does not seem sufficiently different from other objects for it to be able to confer presence on those objects, if they are not self-intimating.

What I called in Chapter 3 'the tautology of presence' is interwoven with the primacy of presence. Presence has to be assured before genuine perception (i.e. perception *tout court*) is possible. Presence is the condition, not the result, of perception. Presence is the condition of presence.

IN CONCLUSION

I am not under the illusion that I have solved the problem of perception by replacing it with the mystery of presence. Even more discouragingly, my position does not suggest a research programme to further our knowledge or our conceptual understanding of consciousness. We are accustomed to the idea that the truth of things may be neither pleasant nor comforting; we are less accustomed to the idea that the truth may be unfruitful. However, when scientistic, as opposed to scientific, theories of the mind are proliferating at the present rate, it may be better to be fruitlessly illusionless for a while than fruitfully advancing deeper into confusion and untruth: 'to live', as Nietzsche says, 'off the acorns and grass of knowledge, for the sake of truth'. Besides, it may be a little early to despair of advancing our understanding: after recovering consciousness it may take us some time to know what to do with it. As Putnam remarks, 'it is only by seeing that the currently fashionable views do not work that we can begin to see what the current tasks of philosophy might really be'.[47]

In the meantime, philosophers who claim to be at one with the hard scientists must recognise that some physicists have now accepted that matter and consciousness are less alien to one another than has been generally thought. But this does not, of course, license the elimination of either in favour of the other. There is as little ground for thinking of consciousness as secondary to matter (as supervening in certain organisations of matter) as for thinking that matter exists only in the field of consciousness or as a construct out of perception. It is for this reason that I have suggested taking a further look at a neutral monism, according to which the fundamental constituents of the world are neither mental – as conceived in a narrow psychological sense – nor material in the physicalist sense.

This may be a happier starting point for our investigations of both matter and mind and the relationships between them. It would be commendably neutral in the sense of recognising that mind and matter are equally incomprehensible. At at the very least, it would not share the common contemporary intellectual vice of trying to reduce, belittle, marginalise or eliminate consciousness. If, in this book, I have succeeded in making consciousness more difficult to overlook, I shall be more than satisfied.

Notes and References

OVERTURE

1. Michael Dummett, *Frege: Philosophy of Language* (London: Duckworth, 1973).
2. I have criticised this hypocrisy – and the misconceptions that lie behind it – in Raymond Tallis, *Words*, Poetry Matters, 6, Winter 1989, pp. 31–8. (First broadcast as a series of talks on BBC Radio 3, 1988.)
3. Raymond Tallis, *In Defence of Realism* (London: Edward Arnold, 1988). See especially Chapter 1.
4. P. N. Johnson-Laird, *The Computer and the Mind* (London: Fontana, 1988).
5. Colin Blakemore and Susan Greenfield (eds), *Mindwaves* (Oxford: Blackwell, 1987).
6. Paul Churchland, *Matter and Consciousness* (Cambridge, Mass.: Bradford Books, 2nd edn, 1988).

CHAPTER 1: LOSING CONSCIOUSNESS

1. Ludwig Wittgenstein, *Philosophical Investigations*. Trans. G. E. M. Anscombe (Oxford: Blackwell, 2nd edn, 1958) p. 232e.
2. U. T. Place's essay ('Is consciousness a brain process?') is collected, along with several important responses to it, in C. V. Borst (ed.) *The Mind/Brain Identity Theory* (London: Macmillan, 1970).
3. Patricia Churchland, *Neurophilosophy* (Cambridge, Mass., MIT Press, 1986); Colin Blakemore and Susan Greenfield (eds) *Mindwaves* (Oxford: Blackwell, 1987).
4. Simon Blackburn, 'Finding Psychology' in Leslie Stevenson, Roger Squires and John Haldane (eds) *Mind, Causation and Action* (Oxford: Blackwell, 1986). I ought perhaps to add that, as has been pointed out to me, Blackburn's view is not accepted by all. Some would question whether, as a matter of empirical fact, the philosophy of mind has routed the philosophy of language. And it has been argued, for example, that the current interest in the theory of semantic content counts as an interest in the theory of mind only under a certain interpretation of the relationship between mind, language and intentionality.
5. Stephen Stich, *From Folk Psychology to Cognitive Science* (London: MIT Press, 1983). The term 'folk psychology' is a crucial one in current debates and is particularly associated with eliminative materialism. Folk psychology is the everyday, commonsense framework within which we normally understand mental states and processes. It, too, is a theory, or group of theories and cannot escape being questioned. It cannot be accepted on the nod. The implication of the pejorative modifier 'folk' is that this framework is a primitive,

unreflective one which will be superseded by a mature, scientific psychology rooted in neuroscience. Such a psychology will do without most, or indeed, all of those things – such as beliefs, thoughts and desires, even consciousness and awareness – that we normally attribute to people and which cause most of the paradoxes and problems that beset the philosophy and science of the mind. These bothersome entities will simply be eliminated.

6.   K. V. Wilkes, for example, has argued this very forcefully in several publications, most recently in ' –, yìshì, duh, um, and consciousness', her contribution to A. J. Marcel and E. Bisiach (eds) *Consciousness in Contemporary Science* (Oxford: Clarendon Press, 1989). She notes that not only is the term 'consciousness' a late entry into the English language and even English philosophical discourse, but also that it has no exact or even approximate equivalents in other languages. (The examples she chooses are ancient Greek, Croatian and Chinese.) She concludes that consciousness is not a natural kind and that much of our contemporary difficulty comes from the unwarranted assumption that there is a single stuff or entity – namely consciousness – under which such disparate things as pains and thoughts about mathematics can be gathered. She may be right; but even if she were, conscious phenomena would not go away. I do not believe that our problems would be diminished if we were to talk about and puzzle over only 'natural kinds' such as pains and thoughts about mathematics. Indeed, our problems, by being divided in this way, would simply be multiplied. Nor do our troubles arise, as Wilkes suggests, by our overstating the importance of consciousness at the expense of unconscious aspects of (to use her preferred term) 'the psyche'. It is difficult to see how one could exaggerate the importance of something that is with us all our waking lives and is even present in some sense in sleep.

7.   K. S. Lashley, 'The problem of serial order in behaviour', in L. P. Jeffress (ed.) *Cerebral Mechanisms in Behaviour: The Hixon Symposium, 1951*, pp. 112–36.

8.   Gilbert Ryle, *The Concept of Mind* (Harmondsworth: Penguin, 1963).

9.   Indeed, in one dominant version of neo-Darwinian thought, (in which the biological and non-biological approaches converge) information can be transmitted outside of artefacts – in DNA itself. On 'Information', see the Appendix to Chapter 3.

10. A tendency strikingly symptomatised in the title of Colin Blakemore's exposition of recent neurophysiology: *Mechanics of the Mind* (Cambridge University Press).

11. I have discussed the post-Saussureans extensively in two recent books: *Not Saussure* (London: Macmillan, 1988) – see especially chapters 5 (on Lacan) and 6 (on Derrida); and *In Defence of Realism* – see especially chapters 4, 5 and 6. A brief acount of the post-Saussurean assault on the centrality of the individual consciousness is in Raymond Tallis, 'A Cure for Theorrhea', *Critical Review*, 1989; 3(1):7–40.

12. Thomas Nagel, *The View from Nowhere* (Oxford University Press, 1986).

13.   Daniel C. Dennett, *The Intentional Stance* (Cambridge, Mass.: Brad-
      ford Books, 1987), p. 5.

CHAPTER 2: BIOLOGISING CONSCIOUSNESS:
I. EVOLUTIONARY THEORIES

1.   Paul Churchland, *Matter and Consciousness* (Cambridge, Mass.: MIT
     Press, rev. edn, 1988), p. 167.
2.   Patricia Churchland, *Neurophilosophy* (Cambridge, Mass.: MIT Press,
     1986), p. 1.
3.   The evolutionary case for, or explanation of, nervous systems and
     the evolutionary explanation of consciousness tend to merge. This is
     because it is assumed that the possession of consciousness requires
     being equipped with a nervous system. The reason behind this
     assumption is that all those entities to which consciousness has
     been attributed do have highly developed nervous systems. There
     is, however, no a priori reason why this should be the case – and
     recognition of this lack of an a priori case is implicit in computational
     models of consciousness and explicit in functionalism, where it is
     assumed that it is the logical form, not the material structure, of a
     system that will determine whether it is conscious or not. Moreover,
     there is no compelling reason – except the desire to slide past the
     inexplicable – for positing a level of complexity beyond which a
     nervous system inevitably breaks into consciousness.
         The tendency to merge the evolutionary case for nervous systems
     and the evolutionary case for consciousness enables many problems
     to be glossed over; in particular, it permits the assumption that
     consciousness is the best solution to the problem of ensuring
     adaptive behaviour (and that that is why it exists) to pass by with-
     out critical examination. But one should separate consideration of
     the advantage of having a nervous system to mediate adaptive
     behaviour from consideration of the advantage of having conscious-
     ness to mediate adaptive behaviour. This becomes extremely
     difficult if one decides in advance that: (a) consciousness is an
     epiphenomenal accident, a spin-off from the evolution of the
     nervous system; and (b), that consciousness is identical with, or the
     result of, certain configurations of neural activity.
4.   Richard Dawkins, *The Blind Watchmaker* (Harmondsworth: Penguin
     Books, 1988).
5.   John Maynard Smith, *The Theory of Evolution* (Harmondsworth:
     Penguin, 3rd edn, 1975), pp. 261–8.
6.   Mary Midgley, *Beast and Man* (London: Methuen), p. 150.
7.   Maynard Smith, op. cit., p. 264.
8.   Philip Johnson-Laird, *The Computer and the Mind* (London: Fontana,
     1988) p. 79.
9.   Johnson-Laird also discusses the example of the unicellular *E. coli*,
     which he describes as 'a Behaviourist's dream'. It seems to behave
     like an intelligent organism because it migrates towards food and

away from poisons, though in fact it manages without any mental life whatsoever. Summarising the work of Koshland and others, Johnson-Laird describes the things that this organism can achieve without internal representations, memory or choice:

> Evolution has solved its navigational problems without providing it with an internal map. The bacterium's flagellae rotate . . . and when they turn in a counter-clockwise direction they propel it forward, whereas when they turn in a clockwise direction they fly apart and cause it to tumble over and over. It has special receptor proteins that can bind a variety of substances (nutrient and toxic) according to the shape of their molecules; and their reception . . . shifts the gear controlling the directions of the flagellae's rotation. If food is detected, they rotate counter-clockwise, so that the organism moves in a straight line. But if no further particles of food are detected, the direction of rotation begins to alternate: the organism moves at random, thereby ensuring that it will probably stumble on to the path of the nutrient stimuli again. It is thus able to home in on a target that is emitting particles of food, much like an aeroplane flying, somewhat erratically, down a radar beam.

So much can be achieved by mindless automatons, it is difficult to know what evolutionary advantage there could be in the emergence of consciousness, as opposed to the further sophistication of automation. (See later in this chapter, for more discussion of this). The fact that organisms that are generally agreed to be mindless can simulate behaviour that would normally lead one to invoke mind, deliberate purpose, etc. to explain is a warning that we should not infer that a *machine* stimulating the behaviour of conscious organisms is itself conscious. (For the arguments arising out of machine – and in particular computer – simulations of complex behaviour, see Chapter 5 of this book).

10.   In her very penetrating discussion of the overall direction of evolution ('Up and Down' in *Beast and Man*), Midgley suggests that the concept of evolutionary advantage is inseparable from our sense of evolution tending towards the production of creatures like ourselves.

> When, however, people began to think about evolution, they made (as commonly happens) no more changes in their way of thinking than they were forced to. They did not scrap the Great Chain of Being. Instead, they unhooked the top end from Heaven and slung it ahead into the future. Its axis now was time. But its associations with value did not vanish. For good reasons and also bad ones, they proved tenacious. (p. 159)

In placing himself (and conscious creatures nearest to himself) at the top of the evolutionary tree – and seeing them as the kind of thing that evolution has been aiming at – man 'has set up a contest in resembling himself and awarded himself the prize'. Once one takes away survival as a criterion for 'fitness', one is left only with anthropomorphism. This connects with this other consideration: the direction evolution has taken, and even explicit adaptation to survival, seems inevitable only if matter, or the evolutionary process, first had living organisms and then us in its sights. It is only when you work backwards from us that the direction taken by evolution seems explicable in Darwinian terms. This suggests that, above a certain level, Darwinism is not an explanation nor even a framework for explanation.

Midgley also points out that 'The scheme of evolutionary thinking ceases to work at all if we insist on sitting on the fence about what we count as an advantage'.

11. John Eccles, quoted in *The Oxford Companion to the Mind* ed. R. L. Gregory (Oxford University Press, 1987), p. 164.

12. Francis Hitching, *The Neck of the Giraffe or Where Darwin Went Wrong* (London: Pan Books, 1982), quoted in Dawkins. One counter-argument to Hitchens that has been suggested to me (by Howard Robinson) is that harmless mutations could be stored without detriment to the organism until they added up to the genetic conditions of consciousness. However, it seems to me unlikely that the correct collocation of mutations *would* hold together without the operation of natural selection to ensure non-random survival.

13. Colin McGinn, *The Character of Mind* (Oxford University Press, 1982). This view has been contested by certain philosophers; for example William Lycan, *Consciousness* (Cambridge, Mass.: MIT Press, 1987):

> there is no spot *either* on the continuum of teleologicalness *or* amid the various levels of nature where it is plainly natural to drive a decisive wedge, where descriptions of nature can be split neatly into a well-behaved, purely structural, purely mechanistic mode and a more abstract and more dubious, intentional and perhaps vitalistic mode . . . for there is too much and too various biology in between. (p. 45)

But would one really expect the decision as to whether an entity or a species is or is not conscious, and whether the events that take place in it are deliberate actions or mechanical events, to be made on the basis of 'natural' distinctions? What is the force of 'natural' here? Our intuitions as to which animals are or are not conscious, which events are or are not conscious, are unreliable and uncertain; our distinctions are woolly. It does not, however, follow from this that the line between consciousness and non-consciousness is also woolly; that consciousness itself can be partial or incomplete; that there are contents of consciousness that are 'not-quite-there' or 'not-quite-not-there' in a way that corresponds to our uncertainty as to whether they are there or not. A primitive consciousness is consciousness that has primitive contents (senses of dark and light, for example) rather than one that has contents that correspond to those of our consciousness but in an attenuated form. The difference between a photosensitive surface and a seeing organism is as absolute irrespective of how primitive are the visual discriminations made by that organism. The metaphysical jump from unconscious matter to consciousness is no less when that consciousness is primitive (or that of a primitive organism) than it is when the consciousness in question is that of a higher organism. (Though, as Chapters 6 and 7 will discuss, the case of *human* consciousness may be a rather special one, even at the metaphysical level.) My argument, perhaps, is that the jump either takes place or it does not; it has no degrees; or there are no degrees that are analogous to the intensity of a physical parameter. And yet it is this analogy that gives the idea of 'degrees of consciousness' its intuitive appeal.

14. Daniel C. Dennett, *The Intentional Stance* (Cambridge, Mass.: Bradford Books, 1987), p. 106.

15. Dawkins's physicalism is not in doubt; for example, *Blind Watchmaker*, p. 5: 'All appearances to the contrary, the only watchmaker in nature is the blind forces of physics'.

But surely, someone might say, machines and other unconscious entities (lower plants, etc.) have environments. Consciousness, therefore, is not required to establish the distinction between organism and environment. This is mistaken. Take the example of a machine. *We* may see it as environed – indeed the environment is that with which it has input and output relations – but its environment does not exist for the machine itself. Its being environed, or its standing in relation to an environment, requires our consciousnesses. We may think of a machine (or an unconscious organism) as intrinsically environed only as a result of transferring our viewpoint to it.

The belief that machines have environments in the way that conscious organisms do is another instance of the 'thinking by transferred epithet' discussed later in this work. If we were not bewitched by such thinking, we would never forget that physicalism is egalitarian; all pieces of matter are equivalent. The organism cannot be foregrounded over the (background) environment; there is nothing to be the *subject* of the story. Indeed, there is no story: we cannot pick a narrative thread (never mind an explicitly evolutionary one) out of the universe viewed with a steady physicalist gaze.

Incidentally, this argument is not meant to support the idealist contention that there are no natural kinds, that species do not exist, except from the point of view of a classifying consciousness. It merely draws attention to the incompatibility between a 'viewpointless' physicalism and a species- or organism-centred account of the universe.

16. Daniel C. Dennett, *The Intentional Stance*, op. cit., p. 109.

17. Ibid., *passim*.

18. Nicholas Humphrey, 'The Inner Eye of Consciousness', in: Colin Blakemore and Susan Greenfield (eds), *Mindwaves* (Oxford: Blackwell, 1987).

It might be thought that Humphrey's theory represents the extreme limit of absurdity. Actually, there *are* even crazier accounts of the origin of consciousness on offer. Consider Julius Jaynes's *The Origins of Consciousness in the Breakdown of the Bicameral Mind* – expounded (with apparent approval) by Daniel Dennett in *Elbow Room* (Oxford University Press, 1984), pp. 38–43; and in 'Why Everyone is a Novelist', *Times Literary Supplement*, 16–22 September, 1988, pp. 1016, 1028–9. Consciousness, according to Jaynes, began when vocalising but unconscious organisms asked questions that no one heard but themselves. In solitude, they heard, or rather overheard, themselves for the first time. In consequence, they became conscious and from this originated the capacity to engage in conscious thought. This seems to put the cart before the horse in a rather spectacular fashion: one would have thought that being conscious was the condition of overhearing oneself rather than the consequence of it. Jaynes's confusion of priorities, however, is not unique; and his theory is strongly reminiscent of Derrida's attribution of the origin of the idea of presence – and so of presence itself – to the self-presence that itself originated from the 'auto-affection' associated with hearing oneself speak. See my *Not Saussure* (London: Macmillan, 1988), chapter 6, esp. pp. 175–81.

19. The 'biologistic' idea of consciousness sometimes reduces it to a 'problem solving device' or to 'a flow of information', neither of which does justice to the nature of consciousness which is that of our 'being there', of co-presence with a world that situates us and which in part owes its unity to us, either as individuals or collectively.

20. Larry Weiskrantz, 'Neuropsychology and the Nature of Consciousness', in Colin Blakemore and Susan Greenfield (eds) *Mindwaves* (Oxford: Blackwell, 1987). Another interpretation of the blindsight cases is that the subjects are not discriminating entirely without consciousness but only that they are discriminating without self-consciousness; that they lack self-consciousness with respect to their discriminations without it being the case that they lack consciousness. This interpretation would not, however, go against the point that I am making here – that ordinary consciousness (which invariably entrains a good deal of the self-consciousness that is conspicuously missing in blindsight subjects) does not seem to be as essential to adaptive behaviour as has been assumed. Its evolutionary significance therefore remains uncertain.

21. There is, of course, a long tradition of thought which sees the development of consciousness as essentially maladaptive. For Schopenhauer, man, the self-conscious animal, is 'the sick animal'. Dostoevsky, in *Notes from the Underground*, saw increasing self-consciousness as a ghastly mistake and the source of much human sorrow, suffering and conflict and one of the roots of evil in human behaviour. In Kleist's famous essay on the *Puppet Theatre*, the transition from the mechanical movements of the puppet to the activity of a self-conscious human being is a fall from grace. Only in the angels, whose powers of self-reflection are infinite, and who are

able to gather themselves up entirely into reflection, is the grace lost in the fall from mechanism restored.

22.   I have discussed the relationship between explicitness and truth in *Not Saussure* (London: Macmillan, 1988 – see Chapter 7) and *In Defence of Realism* (London: Edward Arnold, 1988 – see Chapter 2). This theme also surfaces in Chapter 7 of the present work.

The idea that evolving consciousness gradually becomes more accurate, that it slowly acquires a more complete account of the world, seems almost a projection on to the biological plane of the Whig version of history. (Indeed, one could characterise the theory of evolution as a Whiggish history of matter; or, in its most radically neo-Darwinian forms, as a mixture of Whiggery and Physics). It is as if there were some pre-existing truth to be uncovered and consciousness were getting better and better – at uncovering it.

The fault with this way of thinking is that the truth in question is itself brought into being by consciousness – in two senses. First, in the absence of consciousness there is, according to physicalism, only Matter; the forms and contents of Matter become the content of truth only when Matter confronts consciousness. Secondly, the form and character of truth is at least in part determined by the consciousness for which the details of Matter are truth. Nevertheless, the gradual approximation of consciousness towards truth – either during evolution or within the history of mankind – is intuitively (and, if one is honest, powerfully) attractive.

If we think how little Stone Age man knew, understood or could control, it is difficult to see things otherwise. It is as if living matter, and in particular the species Man, has had gradually to 'rune out' the planet in which it finds itself over many millenia; and that something – the Truth – has been and is being revealed to him as a result of enormous evolutionary or exploratory or intellectual efforts.

Part of the attraction of this conception of the species' evolution towards the truth of the world around them must be due to its resonance with the theological ideas to which most of us were exposed to in earliest childhood. After the Fall, and the expulsion from Paradise, there is the long struggle to return to truth, and the long, weary pilgrimage of mankind trying to rediscover and re-create Paradise on earth. Evolution and History (and Whiggish evolutionary theory and Whiggish historiography) seem to converge in an idea of a fallen creature gradually earning, through suffering, a place in the full light of truth, understanding, control and joy.

CHAPTER 3: BIOLOGISING CONSCIOUSNESS:
II THE CAUSAL THEORY OF PERCEPTION

1.   H. P. Grice, 'The Causal Theory of Perception'. *Proceedings of the Aristotelian Society*, supp. vol. 35 (1961) pp. 121–68. Reprinted in *The*

Philosophy of Perception, ed. G. J. Warnock (Oxford University Press 1967). The extent to which the CTP is simply an analysis of the concept of perception – such that if an experience is to count as a perception of an object, it must have been caused by that object – and the extent to which it is a genuinely empirical theory remains unclear. This is discussed at length by Paul Snowdon and Howard Robinson, *Proceedings of the Aristotelian Society* (in press).

2.   Thomas Hobbes, *Leviathan*, Part I *Of Man*, Chapter I, *Of Sense*. The CTP goes back at least as far as Aristotle (in the *De Anima*), according to whom perceiving an object is the result of being acted upon by it. Objects of perception, acting via a medium of perception, causally affect the perceiver's sensory apparatus. As a result, the apparatus 'receives the form of the object without its matter'; the change in the apparatus *is* perception. It is not clear whether Aristotle's CTP was a materialist theory; but it is the materialist interpretation, and in particular its neurophysiological version, that I shall concentrate on in the present discussion. This explicitly materialist framework of contemporary neurophysiology originated much later than Aristotle.

3.   J. P. Müller, 'Of the peculiar properties of individual nerves'. In: *Selected Readings in the History of Physiology*, compiled by J. F. Fulton (Springfield, Ill.: Charles C. Thomas, 1966) pp. 289–91. This is reiterated by Helmholtz:

> the profound difference between sensations is not at all determined by the kind of external stimulus but by the sensory nerve affected by the sensation. The same agent may produce different sensations when acting on different nerves; while different agents may produce the same sensation when acting on the same nerves. Every sensory nerve when stimulated by the most diverse agents produces only perceptions involving its characteristic quality circle.

Helmholtz on Perception: its Physiology and Development, Translated by R. M. and R. P. Warren (New York: John Wiley), pp. 210–11.

4.   For example, Hubel D. H. and Wiesel T. N. (1977) 'Functional architecture of Macaque monkey visual cortex'. Proceedings of the Royal Society London, Ser. B, 198: 1–59.

5.   Discussed by Richard Jung, 'Sensory research, historical perspective', chapter 1 of section 1 *The Nervous System* vol. III, ed. J. M. Brookhart, V. B. Mountcastle, *Handbook of Physiology* (American Physiological Society, 1984). See esp. p. 49.
     Since it is not possible for an observer to measure the intensity of the subject's sensations directly, Fechner introduced an indirect method of doing this, by measuring just noticeable differences. Let luminance of intensity L_2 be that which can be just distinguished as greater than luminance of intensity L_1; then, to a close approximation, L_2/L_1 is a constant. If it is assumed that all just noticeable differences are subjectively equivalent, i.e. represent a unitary difference in sensation, then the intensity of sensation must in-

crease as the logarithm of the physical stimulus magnitude, since, if L_2/L_1 is constant, so is $\log L_2 - \log L_1$.

Subsequently, using subjects' direct estimates of the intensity of stimuli (initially sounds), it was found that more complex power laws seemed to apply and they varied with the type of sensation. A succinct account of the history of psychophysics is given by D. R. J. Laming in *The Oxford Companion to the Mind*, ed. R. L. Gregory (Oxford University Press, 1987), pp. 655–7.

6. E. D. Adrian, *The Basis of Sensation: The Action of the Sense Organs* (London: Christophers, 1928).

7. Paul Churchland, *Matter and Consciousness*, revised edn (Cambridge, Mass.: MIT Press, 1988), p. 149.

8. M. H. Pirenne, 'Absolute thresholds and quantum effects', In: *The Eye. Visual Processes*, ed. H. Davson (New York: Academic Press, 1962), vol. 2, pp. 123–40.

9. Summarised in Laming, op. cit.

10. Max Born, *Einstein's Theory of Relativity* (New York: Dover Publications, 1965), p. 2.

11. Richard Dawkins, *The Blind Watchmaker* (Harmondsworth: Penguin, 1986), p. 36. Dawkins's 'explanation' is a spectacular example of 'top down' thinking (see chapter 4 and 'the return of the repressed'): experiences are different because the nervous system models them differently. Idealism with a vengeance: consciousness is bespectacled and the spectacles worn by consciousness are not the end organs, or even the more central structures; rather they are constituted out of the *structuring activity* of the nervous system! At least this view is more honest than that of most physiologists who get round the problem of the discrepancy between the monotonous nervous system (in which one impulse is much like another) by appealing to 'codes' and 'patterns'. (See later in this chapter). Dawkins, perhaps inadvertently, reveals the circular or tautologous nature of the logic beneath the CTP.

12. It is possible to imagine how the idea of a perceptual flow is generated:

$$\to E_o-1 \to E_o\ (t_1) \longrightarrow E_p \to E_p+1 \to$$
$$\searrow$$
$$P\ (t_1)$$

$$\to E_o-1 \to E_o\ (t_2) \longrightarrow E_p \to E_p+1 \to$$
$$\searrow$$
$$P\ (t_2)$$

$$\to E_o-1 \to E_o\ (t_3) \longrightarrow E_p \to E_p+1 \to$$
$$\searrow$$
$$P\ (t_3)$$

13. This point is made in Ernest Nagel (1961) *The Structure of Science* (New York: Harcourt Brace and World).

14. See, for example, the essays collected in C. V. Borst (ed.) *The Mind/ Brain Identity Theory* (London: Macmillan, 1970).

15. John Searle, *Intentionality* (Cambridge University Press, 1983), pp. 265–70.

    He presents very similar arguments in a more recent publication ('Minds and Brains without Programmes', in: *Mindwaves*, 1987, op.cit.). Indeed, he makes the suggestion that an event may causally interact with itself even more explicitly:

    > It is tempting to think that whenever A causes B there must be two discrete events, one identified as cause, the other as effect . . . (p. 223)

    And he then reiterates his belief that events at the macro level are caused by behaviour of events at a micro level – as if the existence of two levels were as good for establishing causal relations as the existence of two events. The higher (macro) levels are both caused by and realised in the lower (micro) levels: 'The intrinsically *mental* features of the universe are just higher level *physical* features of brains'. *Mindwaves* (p. 225).

16. Patricia Churchland, *Neurophilosophy* (Cambridge, Mass.: MIT Press, 1986) p. 326.

17. See, for example, U. T. Place, 'Is Consciousness a Brain Process?', J. J. C. Smart, 'Sensations and Brain Processes' and other papers in C. V. Borst, *The Mind/Brain Identity Theory* (London: Macmillan, 1970).

18. Saul Kripke, 'Naming and Necessity', in G. Harman and D. Davidson, eds, *Semantics of Natural Languages* (Dordrecht: Reidel, 1972). Kripke's argument against physicalist accounts of sensations has evoked several responses, including, for example, that by Colin McGinn, *Mental Content* (Oxford: Blackwell, 1989) pp. 32–5; but it remains valid.

19. Thomas Nagel, 'What is it like to be a bat?', *Philosophical Review*, 1974, 435–50.

20. The notion that objects are collections of perceptual experiences is, of course, particularly associated with Berkeley and Berkeleian phenomenalism is not completely dead, as a recent collection of largely sympathetic essays indicates (John Foster and Howard Robinson, *Berkeley* (Oxford University Press, 1985)). A. J. Ayer's attempts to make phenomenalism scientifically respectable and hard-headed, by analysing objects as logical constructs out of perceptual experiences and reducing object-talk to percept-talk (effectively linguistic phenomenalism), failed to account for the origin of perceptions or to produce rules accounting for the way in which perceptions aggregate around one object rather than another.

    The whole problem of understanding how it is that stable, unitary, public objects can be constructed out of perishable, multiple, private sense perceptions is exacerbated if we take the CTP literally and think of perception as the result of energy transferred from objects or events to our bodies. This energy is not of course part of the objects or events themselves; rather it is a kind of *sign* of them. If it is a sign, then it would seem to be a very unreliable, unstable sign; for the quantity and type of energy transferred from the object to the nervous system has many other determinants than the intrinsic properties of the object/event. How does it reliably signify the object? Or (to change the way in which the question is posed) why should the energy signify a constant object/event, or a recognisable (i.e. re-cognisable) object/event? Or (to give the question the right neurophysiological flavour) why should the nervous system extract characteristic features out of objects, types of objects, etc., when the energy through which they are signified has only a tenuous (and highly variable) relation to their intrinsic properties? Wherein lies the repeatability? To ask this is to pose the problem of object (and event) constancy at the deepest level, a level far beneath that at which neurophysiology and the CTP operates.

21. I owe this way of putting it to Stephen Harrison's unpublished *Artificial Intelligence: A Castle Built on Sand*.

Derek Parfit, *Reasons and Persons* (Oxford University Press, 1984) has made a notable attempt to provide a reductionist or impersonal account of the unity of consciousness. Nathan Oaklander ('Parfit, circularity, and the unity of consciousness', *Mind*, 1987, 525–9), however, has demonstrated that it is not possible to find a non-circular criterion for distinguishing 'my' memories from other events. In short, one cannot give an impersonal (non-circular) description of the basis of the unity of 'my' consciousness. What all my memories have in common, what gives them their collective unity, is that they are all mine. This is what entitles them to be considered as part of the same set. Their belonging all to the same set cannot without circularity therefore be what entitles them to count as being 'mine'.

This emphasises the *sui generis* nature of this unity and underlines how that unity would not be amenable to analysis in terms of the 'objective coherence' of, say, nerve impulses, even if it *were* possible to analyse that coherence in neurophysiological terms.

22. Charles Sherrington, *The Integrative Action of the Nervous System* (Oxford University Press, rev. edn, 1947).

Some believe that observations on so-called split-brain subjects (patients whose cerebral hemispheres are partially disconnected from one another by section of the corpus callosum) prove the role of the integrative activity of the nervous system in creating and sustaining unity of consciousness. I disagree. The fact that such patients appear to have, 'two independent streams of conscious awareness, each of which is cut off from and out of contact with the mental experiences of the other', (R. W. Sperry, 'Hemisphere de-connexion and unity in conscious awareness', *American Psychologist*, 1968; 23:723–33) does not prove that unity of consciousness is brought about by the kind of neurophysiological unity that could in a literal sense be divided by a surgeon's knife. At best it may suggest that the unified action of the nervous system (whatever that may be) is a necessary, but not a sufficient, condition of unity of consciousness. It does *not* suggest that the unified action of the nervous system accounts for, in the sense of bringing about, unity of consciousness.

Besides, too much a significance has, in my opinion, been attached to the effects of 'split-brain' operations. The experiences of the patients are not as different from those of ordinary people as has often been assumed. Thomas Nagel, ('Brain bisection and the unity of consciousness', in: *Mortal Questions*, Cambridge University Press, 1979), has emphasised 'the thoroughly integrated way in which patients behave under normal non-contrived conditions'. Brain-splitting lacerates rather than bisects or transects consciousness. Moreover, split-brain experiments do not demonstrate consciousness to be any more profoundly split than do epileptic fits, dream-filled sleep, sleep-walking or the time-gap experiences (see Chapter 7) that characterise most of everyday waking life. The objective discontinuities in the consciousness of the man who shows automatic behaviour during a partial complex seizure and can afterwards remember neither his behaviour nor his reasons for it does not override the moment-to-moment unity of consciousness he experiences during the episode or the unity that is reasserted (with resumption of a familiar world and its responsibilities) across the gap. Split-brain experiments reveal minor surface divides but do not impugn – or point the direction in which we should seek the basis of – the deep unity which characterises my consciousness.

The metaphysically interesting unity is the way in which the world is gathered at any given time into a wholeness around me; in which it is synthesised while retaining its extraordinarily rich multiplicity; and in which it is synthesised across moments. However multiple I seem to be, it is indisputable that:

  (i)   I have a unified sensory field;
  (ii) my successive moments cohere to a greater or lesser degree;
  (iii) my memories are attributable to me;
  (iv) I feel, and am held responsible for, events that have happened in the past and that I am required to bring about in the future; I have long- and short-term projects and long- and short-term responsibilities.

The problem of the unity of consciousness is not that of trying to explain a mythical Cartesian subject that has absolute and total unity but of trying to account for the degree of unity that we ordinarily experience in ourselves and observe in others and take for granted in our thought and talk about ourselves and others. Observations on split-brain subjects get no purchase on this fundamental level of unity of consciousness.

The literal-mindedness of those who would correlate brain-split states with mind-split states is really rather extraordinary, especially in view of the fact that:

    (i)   there is no connectedness between all the fibres that are supposed to subserve the mental phenomena that are co-conscious within and across modalities of perception, within and across moments of experience;

    (ii) connectedness itself explains nothing:

        (a) it produces only movement of inputs from one place to another in the brain;

        (b) convergence of impulses leads only to loss of information, not a guarantee of awareness of the co-present but distinct elements of experience.

23. Ludwig Wittgenstein, *On Certainty*. Trans. Denis Paul and G. E. M. Anscombe (Oxford: Blackwell, 1974).

24. The other way of emphasising intentionality, of making it visible, is to consider cases where the subject thinks of an object that isn't there, or constructs a mental image of something that isn't present.

25. This relationship is especially clear in David Papineau's *Reality and Representation* (Oxford: Blackwell, 1987). Papineau asserts that the essence of his book 'boils down to a simple formula: realism requires that beliefs should be caused by the facts they are about' so that beliefs should 'represent their truth conditions; (xi) (cf. perceptions should have their truth conditions as their content). This is connected with 'the biological purpose of belief', which was 'to occur in the presence of certain states of affairs, which states of affairs therefore counted as their truth conditions (p. xvi).

26. See note 6.

27. P. W. Nathan 'The gate control theory of pain: a critical review'. *Brain* (1976) vol. 99: 123–58.

28. P. N. Johnson-Laird, *The Computer and the Mind* (London: Fontana Press 1988), p. 61.

29. Ludwig Wittgenstein, *Philosophical Investigations*. Trans. G. E. M. Anscombe (Oxford: Blackwell, 1963), p. 115.

30. Peter Hacker, 'Languages, Minds and Brains', in: Colin Blakemore and Susan Greenfield (eds) *Mindwaves* (Oxford: Blackwell, 1987). The present book was well under way before I came across this article and I discovered that I was not unique in my critical attitude towards the language of neuromythology. Hacker's excellent piece, which makes many of the points covered in this Appendix is strongly recommended. It should be compulsory reading for anyone – neurobiologist, cognitive psychologist or philosopher – proposing to mix neurology and metaphysics. D. W. Hamlyn's critique of Dretske's *Knowledge and the Flow of Information*, and, in particular of Dretske's habit of conflating the engineering and ordinary senses of 'information', also touches on some of the points made here. See *In and Out of the Black Box* (Oxford: Blackwell, 1990), pp. 24–9.

31. This passage and the quotation from Shannon below are cited by Hacker, op. cit. They come from Shannon and Weaver's classic text, *The Mathematical Theory of Communication*, (Urbana: University of Illinois Press, 1949).

32. W. E. Hick, 'On the rate of gain of information', *Quarterly Journal of Experimental Psychology*, 1952; 4:11–26.
33. Patricia Churchland, op. cit., p. 36.
34. Johnson-Laird, op. cit., p. 14.
35. Richard Dawkins, *The Blind Watchmaker* (Harmondsworth: Penguin, 1988).
36. Colin Cherry, *On Human Communication* (Cambridge, Mass.: MIT Press, 2nd edn, 1966), p. 215.
37. Paul Churchland, op. cit., p. 174.
38. Even the most amorphous event or object can be analysed as if it were highly ordered. Fourier analysis presupposes that any time series can be analysed as the sum of (rhythmic) sinusoids of different frequencies. And the more amorphous it is, the more complex its analysis and, consequently, the more elaborate its apparent order. Even more pertinent is Hilary Putnam's proof (*Representation and Reality*, Cambridge, Mass.: Bradford Books, 1988, pp. 121–5) that 'every ordinary open system is realisation of every abstract finite automaton'. You can read any abstract structure into any concrete entity.
39. As I have already suggested, the tendency to fuse (structural) order and (functional) information is related to the tendency to fuse structural and occurrent memory. In a computer, and at a micro-anatomical level, it is not possible to make this distinction – which is why the use of memory with respect to computers and bits of brain is invalid. But in real life the distinction is all-important: it is the difference between implicit and explicit past, implicit and explicit being there.
40. Digital physics is summarised in Stephen Wolfram, 'Computer Software in Science and Mathematics', *Scientific American*, 1984 (251) September: 188.

CHAPTER 4: COMPUTERISING CONSCIOUSNESS

1. Christopher Longuet-Higgins, 'Mental Processes', *London Review of Books*, 4 August 1988, pp. 13–14.
2. In what follows, I shall discuss computational theories as if they were theories of consciousness. It has been suggested to me that computational theories are concerned not with consciousness – in the sense of subjective experiences, qualia, conscious thoughts, reflective self-awareness – but with mind. Mind, it is further suggested, has a wider meaning than consciousness; it refers to consciousness plus the unconscious processes in which it is rooted or upon which it depends. Computational theories are concerned primarily with these unconscious processes and it is these that are the real subject of such theories.
   These claims – or disclaimers – do not really bear on my criticism of computational theories of consciousness. Firstly, a computational theory of mind that deals only with unconscious processes is gravely deficient. Although mind without consciousness (or mind short of consciousness) may conceivably be plausibly modelled in

computational terms (unconscious algorithms modelling unconscious processes), this hardly addresses the really interesting feature of minds – namely that they are conscious. Secondly, many computational theorists actually do believe that they are modelling, or have something to say about the nature of, consciousness in the sense defined above.

Among the philosophers and philosophical psychologists who appear to subscribe to computational theories of consciousness are Boden, Dennett, Stich, Putnam, functionalists such as Armstrong and Shoemaker and Johnson-Laird himself. (No straw men – or women – these). Boden, for example, argues in *Artificial Intelligence and Natural Man* (Brighton: Harvester, 1977) that a programmed computer may be thought of as a subjective system, with subjectivity, purpose, freedom, choice, using its inner representations (subject to illusion and error like us) in interpreting and changing its world. In fact, she argues, this idea is so respectable, it makes it scientifically acceptable to describe *people* in 'radically' subjective terms. She is, however, inconsistent on this. For example, in a later piece (Animal perception from an AI viewpoint, In: *Minds, Machines and Evolution*, edited by Christopher Hookway (Cambridge University Press, 1984), she says that, although behavioural or biological evidence of a creature's ability or inability to perform certain computations could count as theoretical grounds for ascribing or denying experiences of a certain type to it, 'this is not to identify computation with consciousness. We know from the example of "blindsight" that "visual" computations can occur without any visual phenomenology' (Hookway, p. 172).

Fodor concedes that the problem of the qualitative content of consciousness is a serious threat to computational theories (in particular to functionalist versions) but believes that such theories can cope with the intentional content of mental states. (This is expressed particularly clearly in his popular account of functionalism, 'The Mind-Body Problem', *Scientific American*, 1981, January, 114–23). The basis for his belief that computational theories can cope with the intentionality of consciousness is that the relation between the mental content (or the computational event) and its intentional object is essentially representational and that representation can be reduced to causal relations. In other words, his computational theory of mind is half-way to being a computational theory of consciousness, with a little bit of unease about the missing small detail of qualitative content, or actual subjective experience.

The views of Dennett, Stich and Johnson-Laird will be discussed separately. It is perhaps worth noting Johnson-Laird's position on the question of the scope of computational theories of mind as he deals explicitly with 'conscious mind'. 'The conscious mind' he claims (Johnson-Laird, p. 360, see note 3 below) 'is the result of a special mode of processing that creates the subjective experience of awareness. Once an operating system had evolved, it could take on such a function, and this mode of processing, I believe, is our capacity for *self-awareness* . . . Self-reflection is similar to self-awareness . . . [and] . . . depends on the same mode of processing'. According to Johnson-Laird, self-reflection requires access to a particular mental representation – a representation that enables a processing system to understand itself. This self-understanding – a startling achievement, one might think, for an automaton – can be modelled by a Turing machine which, when presented with a blank tape, prints out a description of itself in binary notation. Such a 'self-describing' Turing machine will print out its own 'print' instructions. This involves a special procedure which 'when given a binary numeral prints out the description of a machine that would produce that numeral'. The vulnerability of such an account of self-awareness and self-reflection is all too obvious. For whom, one might ask, would one printout count as a description of another printout? And what would be the basis for discriminating between printouts and descriptions of printouts? The idea opens up a vista of receding homunculi extending for ever but getting no nearer to genuine awareness.

Like Boden, Johnson-Laird is not consistent on the question of whether consciousness could be computational in the sense of being based on brain computations. For example, in his contribution to *Mindwaves* (ed. Colin Blakemore and Susan Greenfield, Oxford: Blackwell), 'Consciousness from Brain Computations', he suggests that the computational architecture of the brain 'consists of a parallel hierarchy of finite state devices that compute asynchronously' (p. 257). At the highest level, 'there is an operating system that has access to a partial model of its own capacities'. He then adds that though these conditions appear to be necessary for consciousness, 'it remains an open question whether they are sufficient'. He believes that 'consciousness is the property of a class of parallel algorithms, but not of the functions that they compute, which could always be computed by a serial algorithm'.

Many neuroscientists subscribe to the view that mind in the widest sense is computational. Llinas, for example, ('Mindness as a State of the Brain', in: *Mindwaves*, op. cit.): 'I for one, as a monist, consider "mindness" to be but one of several global physiological computational states that the brain can generate'. Mindness for Llinas is 'high level awareness, including self-awareness' (p. 339).

In summary, either the computational theory of mind is a theory of mind in the larger sense (i.e. consciousness plus its unconscious basis), in which case it fails because, as I shall show in this chapter, it does not account for consciousness; or it is a theory solely about the unconscious processes underlying mind, in which case it is simply uninteresting from the point of view of someone trying to understand what is really interesting – and, I submit, distinctive – about mind, namely consciousness. There are certainly enough prominent, mainstream thinkers who believe that there are computational accounts of consciousness to make such accounts not merely a legitimate but also an important theme to address.

Robert van Gulick's 'Self Understanding Machines', in: A. Marcel and E. Bisiach (eds) *Consciousness in Contemporary Science*, (Oxford: Clarendon Press, 1988) – is a useful clarification of the scope of the claims of computational theorists of consciousness. In particular, he addresses the question of whether the claim that certain systems have intentional states, in the narrow sense of states that mediate the system's interactions with its environment, implies that they actually have intrinsic mentality; and the related question whether it is legitimate to attribute intentionality to systems that do not have a capacity for conscious subjective experience.

The embarrassment consciousness causes for computational theorists is explored in Keith Oatley's thoughtful contribution to the same collection ('On Changing One's Mind'), where he makes the observation that 'the more we understand mental processes in computational terms, the less need there seems to be for consciousness'.

3. P. N. Johnson-Laird, *The Computer and the Mind. An Introduction to Cognitive Science* (London: Fontana, 1988). I take this opportunity to underline my indebtedness to this brilliant synthesis of current thinking in cognitive science.

4. The same ambiguity marks Stephen Stich's 'Syntactic Theory of the Mind', in: *From Folk Psychology to Cognitive Science: The Case Against Belief* (Cambridge, Mass.: MIT Press, 1983). It is difficult to know whether the STM *is* a theory of mind or a theory of what should concern the scientist studying mind, of the proper scope of an autonomous cognitive psychology.

5. Patricia Churchland, *Neurophilosophy* (Cambridge, Mass.: MIT Press, 1986).

6. Paul Churchland, *Matter and Consciousness*, rev. edn (Cambridge, Mass.: MIT Press, 1988).

7. Longuet-Higgins, op. cit., p. 13.

8. Johnson-Laird, op. cit., p. 11.

9. John Searle, 'Minds, Brains and Programs', *The Behavioural and Brain Sciences*, 3, 1980, pp. 417–57.

It is in this paper that he develops his celebrated 'Chinese room' argument in which he shows how it is possible that an individual could convincingly simulate understanding without actually possessing or experiencing understanding. He envisages an individual ignorant of Chinese provided with a set of Chinese symbols and a set of rules for using them. Such an individual could respond to an input of Chinese symbols with an appropriate output despite knowing nothing of the meaning of either input or output.

The thought experiment precisely pinpoints what is missing in syntactic theories of consciousness and theories of mind that are based on an analogy with symbol-processing computers handling symbols producing appropriate outputs in response to inputs. Searle's paper, which comes complete with a series of replies to objections, demolishes a whole style of thinking about mind which began with the imitation game. Although the responses of the individual in the Chinese room are so slick and accurate that his behaviour is indistinguishable from that of a native Chinese speaker, he does not understand Chinese. Understanding Chinese – or understanding anything else, or being conscious of anything – is not just a matter of producing the right outputs in response to the relevant inputs, or of instantiating a certain formal program linking outputs with inputs.

Colin McGinn ('Could a machine be conscious?' In *Mindwaves*, op. cit., pp. 279–92) has suggested that the semantic content of the symbols manipulated by the cerebral computer is provided by their causal origin, so that Searle's claim that the cerebral computer would be a syntactic machine without semantics is invalid. 'Internal manipulations don't determine reference, but causal relations to the environment might.' This line of argument – also adopted by Fred Dretske in *Knowledge and the Flow of Information* (Oxford: Blackwell, 1983) – is deeply misconceived, for reasons that touch on the intuitions at the heart of this book about the underivability of explicitness, and of meaningful or meaning-bearing consciousness, from physical causal relations, in short from matter. (See, in particular, the discussion of stimulus theories of meaning and of language in Chapter 7.)

Interestingly, for Dennett, the causal relations of brain states make the brain a *syntactic*, not a semantic, engine. (Three kinds of intentional psychology, In: *Reduction, Time and Reality*, ed. R. Healey (Cambridge University Press, 1981) pp. 37–61.) The brain passes from state to state as a function of the causal properties of antecedent states, not as a function of what the states are 'about' or whether they represent something true about the world. According to this view, the causal relations themselves cut no semantic ice; and it is certainly true that they carry no intentionality, or do not, of themselves, create the basis for the intentional distance between consciousness and that which it is conscious of – for explicitness.

Searle's own positive doctrine – that consciousness and intentionality are inescapably biological – is less convincing and the supporting arguments uncharacteristically unclear:

> Whatever else intentionality is, it is a biological phenomenon, and it is likely to be as causally dependent on the specific biochemistry of its origins as lactation, photosynthesis, or any other biological phenomenon. No-one would suppose that we could produce milk or sugar by running a computer simulation of the formal sequences in lactation and photosynthesis, but where mind is concerned many people are willing to believe in such a miracle because of a deep and abiding dualism: the mind they suppose is a matter of formal processes and is independent of quite specific material causes in the way that milk and sugar are not.

It would seem that, for Searle, thought, and consciousness, are secretions or products of the brain, actual stuff in their own right.

Elsewhere (Minds and Brains Without Programmes, in: *Mindwaves*, op. cit., p. 226), he argues for the biological status of subjectivity as follows:

> My present state of consciousness is a feature of my brain and in consequence is accessible to me in a way that it is not accessible to you, and your present state of consciousness is a feature of your brain and is accessible to you in a way that it is not accessible to me. Thus the existence of subjectivity is an objective physical fact of biology.

To this one is entitled to reply: But what *biological* feature is it that makes a state of consciousness, and, moreover, *my* state of consciousness? On what basis does it belong in this way? It can hardly be because it is 'a feature of my brain', because the question then arises, what is it that makes a brain *my* brain? In the objective world of science there is no basis for 'my' or 'your', or even 'his'. So subjectivity, although it is undeniably an objective fact, cannot be explained within the framework of an objective biological world picture. For in such a picture there can be no viewpoints to establish 'my', 'yours', 'his', etc. (On this, see also Chapter 3, note 21).

10. As suggested by Paul Churchland, op. cit., pp. 146–55.
11. D. K. Lewis, 'General Semantics', in D. Davidson and G. Harman, eds, *Semantics of Natural Language*. (Dordrecht: Reidel, 1972).
12. K. Popper, 'Indeterminism in Quantum Physics and Classical Physics'. *British Journal of the Philosophy of Science*, 1 (2) 1950, 117–33. Of course calculations alone do not produce even truth. See Chapter 7.

The idea that pocket calculators calculate in the sense that humans calculate is but one of a whole class of similar anthropomorphic fallacies. For example, Gregory ('In Defence of Artificial Intelligence – A Reply to John Searle', in: *Mindwaves*, op. cit., pp. 235–47), suggests that the chess computer and the auto-pilot act for themselves without human intervention or interpretation. This is, of course, nonsense: in the absence of the consciously-conceived goals of the humans who devised and used them, the events that occur in these machines count as neither chess playing or auto-piloting. (How easily those of a physicalist persuasion forget the egalitarian attitude to all forms of matter that is their starting point.)

13. Equations seem to be doubly abstract, and so placed at a double distance from consciousness: they have form but no content; and they have no temporal directionality – the right hand side does not occur after the left hand side, except to a reader who happens to read it from left to right. More precisely, only the tokens occur in time and have time relations. But the time occurrences of the tokens are as irrelevant to their essence as their spatial location. An equation is only a representation of the general form of the possibility of events; it is not an actual happening. Equations are not even *about* actual, singular events: they are about the possible forms of events

as captured under a certain notational system. To be truly about, or to represent, or to be identical with, consciousness, equations would need somehow to be temporalised and to operate on a substrate that could not evaporate into mathematics. (See also note 23, below.) Consciousness-as-calculation seems to defer consciousness – to an even greater degree than consciousness-as-representation.

The notion that the entirety of mental life consists of symbols points to another profound flaw in the computational theory of mind: it overlooks how consciousness is being-here-now. Consciousness is not postponed or eternally displaced elsewhere. The image of a consciousness as being in a permanent state of suspension, verging on the edge of meaning, but forever lacking interpretation except in terms of other formulae, other symbols, is reminiscent of certain post-Saussurean versions of consciousness. (See Raymond Tallis, *Not Saussure*, London: Macmillan, 1988, especially chapter 6 on Derrida's accounts of consciousness).

14. Searle, op. cit., p. 368.
15. Ibid., p. 369.
16. Daniel C. Dennett, 'Three Kinds of Intentional Psychology', in *Reduction, Time and Reality*, ed. R. Healey (Cambridge University Press, 1981), pp. 37–61.
17. One of the attractions of the Causal Theory of Perception as discussed in Chapter 3 was that it seemed simultaneously to guarantee both the truth and the 'aboutness' of perception by making the object of perception the cause of its content. The phenomenal content of perception was determined by the object the content was about. This guarantee was empty (being circular); nevertheless, it seemed to show that a causal theory of mind need not be syntactic, that it need not sever mind from the world it is apparently about. In the causal theory of perception, so it seemed, representational truth and causation could converge, so that the brain proceeding from state to state, each of which is a function of the causal properties of the antecedent states, need not imply a brain functioning without reference to what the states are 'about' or whether or not they represent something true about the world.

There is, however, a deeper reason why the appropriate causal pedigree is insufficient to guarantee truth; or, more precisely, to make one event true of another; or, more precisely yet, to explain how it is that one event is able to be true of another. It is that such a causal pedigree does not explain how it is that the causally downstream event should be *of* the causally upstream event at all. How the causally downstream perceptions make the causally upstream perceived events *explicit*. This fundamental point (which lies behind the previous chapter's critique of the causal theory) will be developed more fully in the final chapter of this work.

18. Stephen P. Stich, *From Folk Psychology to Cognitive Science: The Case Against Belief*. (Cambridge, Mass.: MIT Press, 1983). See especially the chapter entitled 'The Syntactic Theory of Mind'.

19. Here, and elsewhere in the discussion of Stich, I am greatly indebted to the lucid and penetrating critical article on Stich's book by Flint Schier, 'The Withering Away of the Cognitive State', collectied in *Mind, Causation and Action*, eds Leslie Stevenson, Roger Squires and John Haldane (Oxford: Blackwell, 1986), pp. 152–73.

20. Simon Blackburn, 'Finding Psychology', in Stevenson, Squires and Haldane, op. cit., pp. 11–12.

21. The eviscerated, denuded, contentless cognitive state of the computational mind is the opposite of the embedded mind of philosophers such as Merleau-Ponty for whom sense perception and motor skills are inseparable and for whom 'we cannot react to the world without treating it as a more or less meaningful system of situations, contexts and relations' (See the discussion of Merleau-Ponty in Jenny Teichman, *Philosophy and the Mind* (Oxford: Blackwell, 1988) chapter 6). Nothing could be further than this assertion of 'the holism of the mental' from the cognitive orthodoxy that what matters is the programmes rather than the physical structure.

22. Fodor, who is particularly associated with the notion that the mind-brain is a device for performing logical operations on sentences, believes that the mind's sentences are cast in 'mentalese' and that there are devices (assemblers and compilers presumably) for translating sentences from the brain's machine code into higher-level languages. He believes, furthermore, that the semantic properties of the words and sentences we utter are inherited from the semantic properties of the mental states that language expresses, the 'mental symbols' he postulates. (See J. A. Fodor, *The Language of Thought* (Brighton: Harvester Press, 1975). Fodor's own fast-moving energetic, productive mind keeps him in sufficiently quick motion to conceal the fact that many of his ideas are reminiscent of those of the scholars Gulliver encountered in his travels.

23. Johnson-Laird, op. cit., p. 114.

24. Quoted in R. L. Gregory (ed.) *The Oxford Companion to the Mind* (Oxford University Press, 1987) p. 666. Einstein's famous statement comes to mind in this context: 'The creative principle resides in mathematics. In a certain sense, therefore, I hold it true that pure thought can grasp reality as the ancients dreamed'. Pure mathematical thought, however, leaves out the actual, the here-and-now, that which achieves singularity through its (deictic) relationship to a conscious individual whose consciousness and needs make of his body the absolute centre of a world in which all else is relativised. There are many ways of illustrating this; one way would be to underline the point made in note 13 that equations do not have a place in time (or indeed in space). They do not *occur*; even less are they the sum of all occurrences. They are a kind of nothing.

25. As will be discussed later in this chapter and in Chapter 7, the consequences of approaching perception (which is primarily of absolute particulars here-and-now) from the starting point of generalities makes recognition of singulars one of the most commonplace achievements of consciousness – at any given moment we are

ensleeved in a world of singulars – into an interminable process of approximation via classes more and more narrowly defined by increasingly complex constraints. Also, see Chapter 5 for more on the emptying of consciousness.

26. Sometimes, instead of information processing, we hear of 'computation over representations'. But the use of 'representations' in this context is inadmissible for the reasons given in the previous section.

27. Alan Turing, 'Computing machinery and intelligence'. *Mind* (1950) 59:433–60.

28. The argument about simulation and the examples used to illustrate the different kinds of simulation are derived from Teichman, op. cit., pp. 36–8.

29. This process whereby the criteria for intelligent or conscious machines are made tougher as machines become more sophisticated has been noted by others, for example Gregory (*Mindwaves*, op. cit., p. 236): 'It is a curious fact that with each advance, accepted criteria for "intelligence" tend to move back, so machines that would have been unbelievably intelligent a few years ago may now be regarded as inadequate for demonstrating mind in matter'. And then adds, with a touch of exasperation: 'Just what problems do engineers and computer programmers have to solve to demonstrate intelligence in a man-made machine?'

Of course, this tendency to move the goal posts is not accidental; and the idea of an 'intelligent' or conscious machine *systematically* eludes realisation in any actual machine. The acquisition by the computer of a certain function previously associated with the deployment of conscious intelligence merely shows that this function can be carried out, by a device set to act on our behalf, in the absence of conscious intelligence. (If we *were* to consider a chess-playing machine intelligent, in the sense of possessing conscious intelligence, we might run into difficulties, especially if – as is usually the case – the machine were not dedicated solely to this function but were an all-purpose device and the chess-playing facility were located on a floppy disk which could be loaded as required. Where would we locate the conscious intelligence? In the floppy disk; or in the machine; or in the interaction between them?)

The systematic elusiveness of the intelligent or conscious machine may prompt the response that there is something wrong with our intuitions about what is and what is not intelligent or conscious. The ascribing of consciousness is one of the privileges of folk psychology. According to Paul Churchland (*Matter and Consciousness*, pp. 71–2), folk psychology 'ascribes consciousness to other beings because this is the best hypothesis to account for their behaviour'. It is difficult to see how, on the grounds of behaviour alone, we should feel obliged to ascribe consciousness to anything. As pointed out in Chapter 2, the most complex operation in the world, the building of an embryonic brain, can be successfully completed without the involvement of consciousness. No form of behaviour, however apparently sophisticated or complex, can guarantee that the behaving entity is conscious or that we shall be obliged, or inclined, to attribute consciousness to it. Our failure to be metaphysically impressed by the most spectacular computer simulations confirms this. Observation of behaviour adds nothing to the probability that others are conscious – unless their behaviour is observed within the framework that they are 'like me', i.e . conscious. Which touches on a fatal weakness in the critique of folk psychology: only a conscious being would be likely to ascribe consciousness to another being – and then on the grounds that 'this creature is like me'. The ascription of consciousness to others presupposes the possession of consciousness oneself. The folk psychology that does such ascribing bears within itself the grounds of its own truth.

In this context, the following observations by Colin McGinn (based upon an argument of Thomas Nagel), regarding the need for *the right kind of explanation* of consciousness are worth citing:

> [It may be objected] that not just *any* kind of computation is sufficient for consciousness – consciousness requires a special *sort* of computational complexity or structure . . . But . . . these sophistications do not evade the fundamental problem, namely that such properties could be instantiated in the absence of consciousness . . . The difference here is one of principle: we have no understanding of how consciousness could emerge from an aggregation of nonconscious elements such as computational devices; so the properties of these devices cannot *explain* how consciousness comes about or what it is. It may indeed be true that, as a matter of fact, organisms get to be conscious just when their brains reach a certain level of computational complexity, as it is true that consciousness seems to require a certain degree of physiological complexity; but this observation does nothing to *explain* how consciousness depends on computational complexity, as a like observation about physiological complexity does not. A proper theory of consciousness in terms of the properties of the brain should make it *intelligible* that the brain is the basis of consciousness, but the computational properties of the brain do not furnish such a theory: it remains a mystery how cerebral computations could give rise to consciousness, as much a mystery as how mere matter could form itself into the organ of consciousness. (*Mindwaves*, p. 287)

The last sentence encapsulates the intuition behind McGinn's recent 'proof' of the insolubility of the mind/body problem. (Colin McGinn, 'Can we solve the mind/body problem?', *Mind* (1989) 98:350–66.

30. I am here particularly indebted to Johnson-Laird's characteristically lucid (and honest) account of the matter. I have also found W. A. Phillips's account of PDP ('Brainy Minds', *Quarterly Journal of Experimental Psychology*, 1988, 40A (2), 389–405) very helpful. Finally, I am indebted to Andy Clarke's critical evaluation of the possibilities and limitations of PDP computers, 'Connectionism: the Structure

Beneath the Symbols', in: Howard Robinson and Raymond Tallis (eds) *The Pursuit of Mind* (Manchester: Carcanet, 1991).

31. Phillips (see previous note).
32. Johnson-Laird, op. cit., pp. 192–3.
33. Ibid., pp. 189–90.
34. The detection of error, and the feeding back of that error to alter the weighting determining the subsequent input–output relations of the units, depends on someone or something outside of the system detecting the error. At any rate, there has to be an input into the system from outside to fix the way in which the weightings are re-set by a wrong answer. For consciousness, the brain, there is no outside to fix and correct the output weightings.
35. I first encountered this argument in Stephen Harrison's unpublished manuscript *Artificial Intelligence: A Castle Built on Sand*. The original source is Sir James Lighthill, *Artificial Intelligence, a General Survey* (London: Science Research Council Report, 1972).
36. The double exponential characterises the number of possible simple logical functions which can be formed from n binary two-state variables.

    The exploding explosion problem arises, ultimately, from trying to reduce the sensed world (or, indeed, consciousness) to 'information' that can be counted out in bits. If the experienced world is misrepresented in this way (so that perception is made up of, for example, an enormous number of forced choices, decisions, etc.), then an ordinary scene will become a giga-giga-giga . . . byte mass of information. In other words, to computerise experience, to see it as composed of discrete bits of information, is to render it non-computable – or not, at least, by any finite machine. Such computerisation is deeply misconceived: scenes, perceptions, experience, are not composed of discrete, countable elements, they are continua. And, in so far as elements can be discerned in them, these elements are not solely general, things assigned to a finite number of categories (though they may be that as well), but singulars, that transcend description, or to which endlessly extended descriptions would only approximate as to an asymptote.
37. Many writers appeal to creativity and innovation as evidence that minds are not comparable to computers. Computers merely carry out low-grade, non-innovative activity and could never match the genius of Shakespeare, Einstein, Gauss, etc. Such arguments are extremely weak. For a start, without a clear account of what constitutes genuine creativity, it is not possible to rule out in advance that a computer will one day be built that does exhibit creativity. But the argument is weak for another, much more fundamental, reason. Trying to demonstrate that human minds or brains can *occasionally* do things that computers cannot do *does not begin far enough back*. One has to look at ordinary consciousness – and not merely special sorts of consciousness – and see whether this can be reduced to computational functions or not.
38. Absolute identity cannot be intuited on the basis of qualitative

similarity (even less when, as in a computer, qualities are 'encoded' quantitatively). One can proceed from similarity to individual identity only via the underivable intuition of singularity, of the actual existence of the object. This intuition is not just of 'an x' but 'this x'; or 'x' and 'this'.; of an *haecceitas* that goes beyond a general '*quidditas*'. If we are presented on successive occasions with two cups that are identical in every respect, so that we cannot distinguish between them, we are at once aware of each presentation as being that of an individual, even though we cannot tell whether we have had two presentations of the same individual or one presentation each of two individuals.

39.   In *The Character of Mind* (Oxford University Press, 1981), See Chapter 3, pp. 38–40. In *Mental Content* (Oxford: Blackwell, 1989) he makes a related point: 'perceptual seemings are not necessarily as fine-grained as the reality that causes them'. McGinn's views in this latter work are more complex and tentative; but the fundamental misconception seems to me to remain. For example, he discusses whether 'the causal link between world and experience is *individuating* of experience' – as if the singularity of the object of experience had to be established on the basis of some feature of the content of experience. Singularity (which is inseparable from the intuition of actuality – 'that this thing really exists') could not, of course, be *derived*; it is a presupposition, not a conclusion. Like the real existence of the outside world, it can only be assumed, never proved. Anyway, McGinn's suggested basis for individuation of experience – the causal link between the experience and that which it is an experience of – seems unsatisfactory because presumably that link would not be available to experience; or not directly, or primitively.

40.   Ludwig Wittgenstein, *Philosophical Investigations* (Oxford: Blackwell, 1953), p. 177.

41.   It has been suggested (James Russell, 'Cognisance and cognitive science. Part One: The generality constraint', *Philosophical Psychology*, 1988; 1 (2): 235–58) that computers may be regarded as intelligent or cognitive systems, though not 'cognisant'. We can imagine, he says, 'a system which is prodigiously skilled, but which is not an experiencer of a physical world'. This system could outperform many humans but would not itself be cognisant. A cognisant system would possess self-world dualism; it would be characterised by 'the possession of *knowledge* on whose possession we are, in principle, capable of reflecting – Kant's "The 'I think' which must be capable of accompanying all my presentations"'.

The distinction between a cognitive and a cognisant system is an interesting one. However, it concedes too much when it leads to the suggestion that there can be non-cognisant intelligent systems and that computers could be such systems. For the reasons given in this chapter I do not accept that we can speak of a computer being skilled, or carrying out tasks. Even less can we think of it as being 'intelligent' and yet unaware of what it is doing – indeed not experiencing a physical world. Computers (taken in isolation) are no more 'prodigiously skilled' or 'intelligent' than they do arithmetic.

CHAPTER 5: EMPTYING CONSCIOUSNESS: FUNCTIONALISM

1. The idea that functionalism is, in fact, a form of eliminative
    materialism, has been developed in Howard Robinson's illumin-
    ating *Matter and Sense* (Cambridge University Press, 1982)
    pp. 29–34. The symbols in a computer – or rather the states of the
    computer – stand in need of interpretation. This must imply,
    ultimately, expression through the publicly visible and meaningful
    behaviour of peripherals. In short, behaviour.
2. Hilary Putnam, *Minds and Machines*. In *Philosophical Papers*, vol. II,
    Mind, Language and Reality, 1975; 362–85 (Cambridge University
    Press 1982.) As Fodor ('The Mind-Body Problem', *Scientific Amer-
    ican*, January 1981, pp. 114–23) points out, there seems to be 'a level
    of abstraction at which the generalisations of psychology are most
    naturally pitched. This level of abstraction cuts across differences in
    the physical composition of the systems to which psychological
    generalisations apply'. Fodor sees functionalism as providing a
    solution to the problems of both logical behaviourism and central-
    state materialism. Logical behaviourism – in which mental terms are
    synonymous with dispositions to (observable) behaviour – dissolves
    mental states into things a scientist can get a grip on while still
    seeming to retain the mentality of such states in the way that
    Watsonian behaviourism does not. Unfortunately dispositional ex-
    planations are rooted in individual events and dispositional causa-
    tion in event–event causation. Moreover, event–event causation is
    common in the realm of the mental and there is no dispositional
    account of this. The logical behaviourist, Fodor concludes, believes
    deep down that mental causes do not exist. The alternative material-
    ist theory of mind, central state materialism, which identifies mental
    events with neurophysiological events in the brain, allows for the
    possibility that mental events may interact causally without giving
    rise to a behavioural effect: a lot can go on centrally without
    external, behavioural manifestation. The trouble with this account is
    that it does not seem to have the right kind of abstraction or
    generality that would cut across differences in the physical composi-
    tion of the systems to which psychological generalisations apply.
    The unsatisfactoriness of these theories calls for a theory that
    exploits the positive features of both while not encountering the
    problems associated with either. This need is met, Fodor assures us,
    by a relational account of mental properties that abstracts them from
    the physical structure of their bearers. Enter functionalism.
        Putnam no longer believes in the version of functionalism most
    associated with his name and has recently published an attack on
    his former philosophical psychology (*Representation and Reality*,
    Cambridge, Mass.: MIT Press, 1988). His main argument against his
    former identification of mental states with computational ones is
    that intentional relations reach beyond the scope of machine-logic;
    beliefs, for example, cannot be identified with the logic of Turing
    machine states because they are situated in an holistic nexus of

other beliefs. Intentionality is an implicature. The human computer has to know an awful lot of world in order to know anything about the world and to entertain even simple beliefs about it.

3.   There seems to be an irreducible ambiguity about the notion of function as used by functionalists, as has been pointed out by Jenny Teichman, *Philosophy and the Mind* (Oxford: Blackwell, 1988), pp. 29–31. One interpretation of function, she points out, is mathematical, in which function is defined as 'a variable quantity regarded in relation to one or more other variables in terms of which it may be expressed, or on the value of which its own value depends'. And this is an interpretation applicable to certain explicitly computational forms of functionalism, in which the mind is thought of as a Turing machine. Other functionalists, such as David Lewis, however, repudiate the mathematical intepretation of function and think of functions as 'roles'. As Teichman points out, it is by no means clear that mathematical and non-mathematical uses of the word 'function' can be kept clearly separate. As I shall argue later in this chapter, the mathematical version leaves a doubly-emptied consciousness; for not only are mental contents 'referred elsewhere' to their causal ancestors and descendents; but they have the status only of variables, of possibilities, of the general form of what is, or might be, the case.

There are narrower – and seemingly less harmful – versions, or definitions, of functionalism. For Pylyshyn (Z. W. Pylyshyn, *Computation and Cognition*, Cambridge, Mass.: Bradford Books, MIT Press, 1986, p. 24), a functional description or a functionalist theory is 'a theory that does not refer to the physical properties of the particular system in question, only the way it operates'. There is nothing wrong with such descriptions; what *is* wrong is functionalism that (a) reduces consciousness to a system, and (b) reduces the system to its way of operating. A functionalism that, for example, reduces perception to a system (the system of the brain) and reduces the system of the brain to the way it operates.

4.   Robinson, *Matter and Sense*, p. 31. It may be worth noting at this juncture that logical behaviourism (to which functionalism is, in a sense, a successor) is for a similar reason little different from radical, crude behaviourism (as Putnam now concedes; *Minds and Machines*, 125) For, unless we allow that dispositions to act are mental states, entities in their own right, they dissolve without remainder into patterns of behaviour or their (notional) probabilities. Dispositions, in logical behaviourist terms, are statistical constructs derived from observations of stimulus-response relations. As Fodor ('The Mind-Body Problem') observes, according to logical behaviourism, 'it is a necessary truth that any system that has our stimulus-response contingencies also has our headaches'.

5.   Teichman (*Philosophy and the Mind*, p. 34) questions whether 'expressions like "cause of . . . ' ever by themselves capture the intrinsic nature of real items in the real world . . . Can the intrinsic nature of Bill Sykes be captured entirely via a collection of predicates

like "whoever caused the disappearance of the family silver"?' Her objection seems valid, though the example is not perhaps entirely appropriate. For Bill Sykes is the cause of innumerable events and the effect of many others. The causal account of him would therefore be endless. It does, however, draw attention to the fact that the apparent plausibility of the causal theory must depend at least in part upon the assumption that the causal relations of mental events can be clearly delineated and delimited; that, in other words, a given mental event can be regarded as having, intrinsically, a finite number of causal ancestors and causal descendents. Even if the length of the causal stream that is regarded as relevant to its definition cannot be delimited, the stream should not be too wide.

Teichman also points out that defining mental contents in terms of their causal relations ('that which, or whatever is, the cause of . . . ') makes them into *theoretical* entities and that this hardly captures the reality of pains, pleasures, sensations or colours, which seem furthest from being theoretical entities. Moreover, a description such as 'the cause of X', is not a rigid designator, and is often a holding term used to describe something whose nature and identity has not yet been established (for example 'the cause of AIDS', prior to the discovery of HIV). In other words, it has a generic, as well as a theoretical, status. Again, pains, etc. are utterly and indisputably particular, whatever their intentional reference.

6.   Paul Churchland, *Matter and Consciousness* (Cambridge: MIT Press, 1988 (pp. 40–1. A less defensive approach to the problem posed by qualia for physicalism is exemplified in Daniel Dennett's recent comprehensive attack on the qualia ('Quining qualia', in: A. Marcel and E. Bisiach (eds), *Consciousness in Contemporary Science* (Oxford University Press, 1988). He argues that there is no intrinsic property to experiences above and beyond their various dispositional, reaction-provoking properties. In support of this Rylean position he considers various cases where it is not possible for the subject on his own to say what qualia he has had or to pronounce with authority on what has happened to his qualia, as a result of brain injury, time-related changes in his perceptions, etc. In other words, the individual may not have the last word on the classification of his qualia. This argument is not decisive. Unless one adopts a behaviourist position (which is precisely the position those who invoke qualia are specifically trying to avoid), one must distinguish an individual's inclination to say one thing rather than another about his qualia from the qualia themselves. Dennett seems to think that those who believe in qualia must also believe that the subject must be an infallible authority on them. This is not necessarily the case. The subject may not be a final authority on the classification of his qualia but this does not impugn his uniquely immediate access to them or mean that the qualia themselves are given over to the public domain and the community of language speakers.

7.   Ned Block, 'Troubles with Functionalism', in *Readings in the*

Philosophy of Psychology, ed. Ned Block (Cambridge, Mass.: Harvard University Press, 1980).

8. Paul and Patricia Churchland, 'Functionalism, qualia and intentionality', *Philosophical Topics*, vol. 12, no. 1 (1981).

9. Thomas Nagel, 'What is it like to be a bat?' *Philosophical Review*, 1974, 83, 435–50.

10. Thomas Nagel, *The View from Nowhere* (Oxford University Press, 1986).

11. Frank Jackson, 'Epiphenomenal qualia', *Philosophical Quarterly*, 1982, 32:127–36.

12. Paul Churchland, op. cit., p. 34. McGinn, in his sceptical discussion of functionalism ('Could a Machine be Conscious?' in: *Mindwaves*, Colin Blakemore and Susan Greenfield (eds), Oxford: Blackwell, 1987), points out that its attractiveness lies in its seeming to raise mind above the *level* of physico-chemical states of the brain. The materials of which the brain are composed are of the same kind as are those found in non-conscious nature (including other bodily parts). They cannot, therefore, account for the unique property attributed to the brain, that of sustaining consciousness. Instead we have to look beyond the material of the brain to certain higher-order properties, namely the supposedly more abstract causal properties possessed by that material.

> The first-order physico-chemical properties are . . . of the wrong kind to constitute consciousness, but their causal roles will do better . . . Pain for example, is a higher-order property of physical states which consists in having a certain pattern of causes and effects . . .

In order to derive the mental from the physical, all one has to do is to redescribe the behaviour of the latter in more abstract terms; in terms not of physical events occurring in physical stuff but in terms of the 'pattern of causes and effects'. The abstraction created by redescription is then projected back into matter and becomes a suitable substrate for the mental! The objection to this procedure, as already discussed in Chapter 3, is that patterns, levels, abstractions, etc. require mind in order to come into existence; their existence is virtual or notional until minds (unexplained by patterns, levels, etc.) bring them into being.

13. Michael Tye, 'The Subjective Qualities of Experience', *Mind*, 1986, pp. 1–17. The arguments presented here are essentially those in Raymond Tallis, 'A Critique of Tye's The Subjective Qualities of Experience', *Philosophical Investigations*, 1989; 12 (3): 217–222.

14. Fodor, 'The Mind-Body Problem, p. 122.

15. Minds, Machines and Mathematics', in Colin Blakemore and Susan Greenfield (eds) *Mindwaves* (Oxford: Blackwell, 1987). He elaborates this argument in *The Emperor's New Mind* (Oxford University Press, 1989), where he points out that much of our consciousness (including even that which is involved in forming *mathematical* judgements)

influences truth-judgements in a non-algorithmic way. He also cites Godel's theorem and the evolutionary and biological basis of consciousness as arguments against understanding consciousness in algorithmic terms (see especially pp. 414–18).

16. Colin McGinn, op. cit.
17. K. S. Lashley, 'The Problem of Serial Order in Behaviour', in: L. P. Jeffress (ed.), *Cerebral Mechanisms in Behaviour: The Hixon Symposium*, 1951, pp. 112–36.
18. Paul Churchland, op. cit., p. 105.
19. Another example of the digitisation of consciousness is the appeal to 'vector spaces' in the discrimination of particulars. Churchland (ibid. p. 150), in his discussion of the recognition of faces, suggests that this is handled by a 'vector-coding strategy'. A particular face is coded by a unique combination of stimulations of different pathways, each of which encodes a particular feature. If we assume that a given pathway can discriminate five levels within each feature and that there are ten pathways, then we can credit humans with a 'facial space' of greater than 10 million discriminable positions. This, according to Churchland, explains our extraordinary ability to discriminate faces. Does, however, the realisation, or fulfilment or occupation of a position in a vector space correspond to recognition, to the sense of familiarity that accompanies encounter with someone whom one knows? I think not. Moreover, a system that has 10 million states may not be able to discriminate between those states in terms of its self-experience. After all, a pebble has an uncountable number of states.

CHAPTER 6: MAN, THE EXPLICIT ANIMAL

1. Gilbert Ryle, *The Concept of Mind* (Harmondsworth: Penguin, 1967), p. 310.
2. I owe this point (and this way of putting it) to Mary Midgley whose excellent *Beast and Man. The Roots of Human Nature* (London: Methuen, 1980) I read after the first draft of this chapter (which goes a long way back in my own thinking) had been completed. The present version has been enormously influenced by her passionate, witty, erudite, lucid and, above all, sane book. Reading Midgley saved me from some of the naiveties that beset philosophers when they find themselves – somewhat reluctantly in my own case – having to become armchair zoologists; and she has sharpened my appreciation of the mines with which the field of man–animal comparisons is sewn. *Beast and Man* has made me aware not only of my own prejudices about animals (her insights felt their way into the basement of my preconceptions) but also of the venerable historical tradition of which they are a part. In addition it has furnished me with many thought-provoking examples of animal behaviour analysed in such a way as to force me to modify, or at least to disambiguate, the fundamental point I was trying to make

and the use to which I was putting animals (or my concept of them). The numerous references to *Beast and Man* will give only an incomplete account of my debt to it.

3.   The apparent success in describing animals in machine terms is almost certainly due to our ignorance of what goes on in them – as Midgley has so eloquently argued.

4.   For a discussion of this, see E. R. Leach, *Levi-Strauss* (London: Fontana, 1970).

5.   This view is developed in *Madness and Civilisation*. The madman, too, provided rational, civilised man with an image of his opposite, to iterate his sense of being rational and civilised. The connection between madness and animality in Foucault's thought is well expressed by Alan Sheridan (*Michel Foucault: The Will to Truth*, London: Tavistock, 1980, p. 30):

> madness was perceived by the eighteenth century as a relapse into animality. In the first case, man had lost the use of reason and had sunk into the innocent, amoral condition of the animal; in the second, man had deliberately chosen to rid himself of the guidance of reason, of his very humanity. The 'furious' lunatic was seen and treated as a wild beast. Many accounts of madmen in confinement attest to their extraordinary resistance to extremes of hunger, heat, cold and pain. This was regarded as further proof of the animality of the mad.

6.   Midgley, op. cit.; see especially chapter 10, Speech and Other Excellences.

7.   Jane Goodall, *In the Shadow of Man* (Boston: Houghton Mifflin, 1971) pp. 250–1.

8.   They have been discussed extensively by writers such as Stephen Clarke. See, for example, 'Animal Consciousness', in: Howard Robinson and Raymond Tallis (eds) *The Pursuit of Mind* (Manchester: Carcanet, 1991).

9.   The relationship between reason and unreason in 'irrational' behaviour is rather analogous to that between consciousness and the unconscious in the enactment of neuroses. Just as the successful enactment of neuroses in irrational behaviour requires the full resources of rational daylit consciousness, so the pursuit of irrational ends (ends that seem against the best interests of the agent or at cross-purposes to his real goals) requires unremitting rationality.

Consider this example, drawn from my own experience, of a patient who exhibited neurotic behaviour (a situation in which the unconscious and its manifestation in irrationality should be at its most dominant). The case will demonstrate how, while the basis of the neurotic's behaviour is unconscious and irrational, the behaviour itself is fully conscious and pervaded with rationality. Or, rather, how unconsciously driven, irrational behaviour has to be enacted through a medium of consciously chosen, rational acts.

The patient in question was a woman in her late twenties who developed a neurotic anxiety about breast cancer. She repeatedly found, or thought she had found, lumps in her breast. Whenever she detected such a lump, she could not prevent herself rushing off at once to her general practitioner to be examined. After examination, she would be reassured for a few days; but she would soon find another lump and would request another emergency appointment with her doctor. The anxiety about breast cancer was, of course, a symptom of a deeper anxiety – traceable to the death of her father, by suicide, when she was aged twelve and the conscious motivation of her behaviour was quite different from its real, unconscious, motivation. While it was apparently motivated by a rational fear of breast cancer triggered off rationally by the observation of a breast lump, it was really driven by a need for security, fatally undermined by the sudden death of her father, and for a father love denied by her father's decision to remove himself from her life. She needed the kindly father-substitute general practitioner to palpate her breasts, literally and metaphorically to soothe her bosom, and tell her that she was all right, that all was well and that she was loved and cared for.

A clear example, then, of an apparently rational action driven by motivations of which the actor is apparently unconscious. Even so, the complex behaviour is still conscious even where it is most obviously driven by unconscious forces. In examining herself, in ringing up for an appointment to see the doctor, in planning to catch a particular bus to take her to the surgery, in waiting her turn, in going into the consulting room when her name is called, in telling her story to the doctor, she is fully conscious and deploying a good deal of extremely complex reason. (Try programming a computer to do a thousandth of what the patient achieves in getting to see the doctor). In short, the unconsciously driven act is still a conscious act – or a complex suite of conscious acts – and the patient's engagement in it is not an intermission in consciousness or reason.

Consciousness of a high order and rationally-driven activity are essential for the unconscious to be enacted in apparently irrational behaviour. Moreover, that consciousness, unlike coma or dream, has the openness of ordinary consciousness; it is still able to take account of and respond to, data that are quite irrelevant to the enactment of the neurosis. Even neurotics have to eat, and plan supper for the kids and remember to get mother-in-law's books from the library and to ring up the department store to complain about the problems with the vacuum cleaner. On her way to the doctor's, the patient is still able to recognise and to greet and to converse with her next door neighbour whom she happens to encounter; she is still able to take note of the weather, to avoid the unexpected car bearing down on her as she crosses the road, to note that the price of potatoes is lower in the greengrocer's than it was last week and act on that knowledge when, on the way back from the doctor's, she decides to buy her potatoes there rather than in the supermarket.

The neurotic patient is thus neither unconscious nor is she

somnambulating, even in that small proportion of her daily life when she is acting out her neurosis, in the hours when she is in the grip of behaviour that is clearly driven by unconscious needs rather than the conscious agenda it thinks it is enacting. Consciousness, and even rationality, still dominate in this paradigm of unconsciousness-driven, irrational, behaviour. This is manifest not only in the patient's ability to continue ordinary life and make ordinary observations and take ordinary steps to bring things about and in her continuing responsiveness to the accidental, contingent details of the outside world through which she has to act out her neuroses; but also in the present anguish she feels. The domination of the present external world by the internal one of the past is only partial; and where she is possessed by the past, the experience is still a present conscious experience. The present, conscious experience of the feelings and motivations, howsoever they are interwoven with self-deception, are the reason the neurosis matters and so desperately needs treatment.

In order to enact our dreams, as opposed to dreaming that we enact them, we have to be fully conscious: to be manifestly possessed by the night, we have to be daylit. The unconscious does not operate like epilepsy or blot out the conscious like a coma. And it operates through reason: it is through the unremitting use of reason that neurotics reinforce the validity of their fears. Phobias and other manifestations of the unconscious and the irrational do not prove that either consciousness or reason is any sense marginal. Just as false consciousness is still consciousness, so even the patient, even in those moments when she is most clearly in the grip of irrationality forces, is unremitting in her reasoning.

10.   Karl Marx and Frederick Engels, *The German Ideology*, edited and introduced by C. J. Arthur (London: Lawrence & Wishart, 1974) p. 42.

11.   According to some authorities, the transition from hunter-gathering to farming may not have been beneficial. It is as if the advance towards explicitness has a momentum of its own that is not only not driven by evolutionary benefit but may be at cross-purposes to it.

12.   Jean-Paul Sartre, *Critique of Dialectical Reason*, translated by Alan Sheridan (London: Verso, 1982) p. 260. Sartre's enormously long discussion of the extraordinary capacity of human beings to generalise themselves, to see themselves as terms in series and equivalent to other terms in the series, is intermittently illuminating.

13.   'The value of a commodity is expressed in its price before it goes into circulation, and is therefore a precedent condition of its circulation, not its result', Karl Marx, *Capital*, vol. 1, translated by Samuel Moore and Edward Aveling (London: Lawrence & Wishart, 1970).

14.   Richard Swinburne, *The Evolution of the Soul* (Oxford University Press, 1986) p. 2.

15.   John Maynard Smith, *The Theory of Evolution*, 3rd edn (Harmondsworth: Penguin, 1975) p. 311.

16.   Levi-Strauss's views are accessibly summarised in Leach, op. cit. An

interesting and entertaining critique of Levi-Strauss is by his erst-while pupil J. G. Merquior in *From Prague to Paris: A Critique of Structuralist and Post-Structuralist Thought* (London: Verso, 1986).

17. Maynard Smith, op. cit., p. 313.

18. Man the weapon-maker is a rather too obtrusive sub-division of man the toolmaker.

19. Attributing classifying behaviour to primitive organisms on the basis of their discriminant behaviour is a particularly obvious example of misplaced explicitness. Less obvious, but much more widespread, is the tendency to attribute propositional attitudes to non-human organisms. A belief, say, is inferred from an animal's behaviour. Well and good. But that belief is then cast in propositional form in the language of the observer. Not so good. To suggest that a dog believes that his master is kind is not as absurd as attributing a belief to a thermostat. But it implies that the dog has the concepts 'master', 'kind', etc. and also that it operates with subject–predicate relations. This fallacy – which combines inappropriate proposition-alisation with misplaced explicitness – is very widespread indeed and accounts in good part for the extraordinary extent to which the difference between man and animals has been overlooked. It is more dangerous than anthropomorphism because it is more subtle.

20. This has caused much impatience amongst certain cognitive psycho-logists, for whom belief in man's uniqueness seems to represent an unwarranted mysticism and a barrier to serious investigation. For example, Christopher Longuet-Higgins in a review article in *London Review of Books*: 'Why are theoretical linguists so infernally sensitive about the linguistic uniqueness of *homo sapiens*?' ('Mental Processes', 14 August, 1988, pp. 13–14).

21. George Steiner, *Real Presences* (London: Faber, 1989), pp. 53–4.

22. George Steiner, *After Babel* (Oxford University Press, 1975).

23. See Gabriel Marcel, *A Metaphysical Diary* (available in *Being and Having*, London: Fontana, 1965), pp. 47–63.

24. This is explored further in the next chapter.

25. Raymond Tallis, *Not Saussure* (London: Macmillan, 1988).
    One point perhaps worth making here is that animal calls are neither 'merely general' (as some writers would claim), referring to general concepts or categories such as 'danger'; nor are they explicitly particular, referring to particulars, such as a particular danger (or 'that predator over there'). They are intrinsically neither general nor particular. That is why under our linguistic descriptions they can be glossed as either. The co-emergence of the explicitly particular and the explicitly general is one of the many features peculiar to human language.

26. Midgley (*Beast and Man*, p. 249) suggests that the great leap forward may have been a mutation that enabled better control of the larynx but that this alone is insufficient:

    To compel a general change as strenuous as learning to use conventional instead of natural signs, it is not enough for an exceptional individual or two to be born capable of starting the game. All must take the trouble to join in . . . What we need to make the origin of speech intelligible, in fact, is a line of hominids which does not just have a lucky mutation, but has in general the right temperament – is exceptionally cooperative, persistent, and thorough in using what it gets. They must not just be lucky opportunists; they must be stayers . . . sheer stout-hearted persistance could be the crucial distinctive factor that led the species to out-distance and eventually put out of business all its near relatives and competitors, thereby leaving itself in that strange isolation which has made it so deeply confused about its status (pp. 250–1).

This is thought-provoking; but I do not think it cuts down far enough: it fails to recognise the depth of the problem. Persistence would not solve anything if the animal did not have the vision – the conception, at any rate – of what it was persisting at. The opportunity to become civilised would not present itself to an animal that was not on the lookout for civilisation. Even together, laryngeal mutation and a certain dogged determination towards self-betterment could not explain the transition to an infinitely expandable discursive self-awareness.

27.   A. N. Whitehead, *Science and the Modern World*, (New York: New American Library, 1925). See in particular the opening chapter on the origins of modern science:

In the first place, there can be no living science unless there is a widespread instinctive conviction in the existence of an *Order of Things*, and, in particular, of an *Order of Nature* . . . [The] scientific mentality instinctively holds that all things great and small are conceivable as exemplifications of general principles which reign throughout the natural order . . . the faith in the possibility of science, generated antecedently to the development of modern scientific theory, is an unconscious derivative from medieval theology. (pp. 4, 5 and 10)

The entirety of this chapter by Whitehead could be seen as a brilliant meditation on the theme of 'man, the sense-making animal'. Whitehead, however, is concerned with the extent to which man woke up from his earlier self, rather than the much greater and even more mysterious distance of human from animal consciousness.

28.   It might be worth noting at this juncture a minor symptom of the sense-making animal, namely is that he is the laughing animal. According to Hazlitt, 'Man is the only creature that laughs and weeps; for he is the only animal that is struck with the difference between what things are, and what they ought to be' (*Lectures on the English Comic Writers*). How true this observation is, I should not like to say. Midgley (p. 228) suggests that non-human primates also laugh.

29. Midgley, op. cit., p. 248.
30. See the next chapter and chapters 4 and 7 of *Not Saussure* (op. cit.) for further discussion of this point.
31. The work of the philosopher consists in assembling reminders for a particular purpose', Ludwig Wittgenstein, *Philosophical Investigations*, translated by G. E. M. Anscombe, (Oxford: Blackwell, 1953), p. 50e.
32. Curiously, this is recognised even by that hardline machinist Skinner: 'Only humans can not only see things, like rats, but also see that they are seeing them. That is, humans become aware or conscious of their own behaviour, in a way that is true of no other animal species' (B. F. Skinner, 'The operational analysis of psychological terms', *Behavioural and Brain Sciences*, 1984; 7:547–81). It is difficult to know how Skinner can be so sure of the lack of self-consciousness in rats but it is extraordinary to encounter him acknowledging the existence of second-order consciousness in humans.
33. The tendency to read humanity into animal behaviour is part of a larger tendency to import explicitness and self-consciousness into descriptions of places where it simply does not exist. This sometimes results from equating perceptual experience with information and regarding the latter as equivalent to the words that encapsulate it. See, for example, Daniel Dennett, 'When Frogs and Others Make Mistakes' in: *The Intentional Stance* (Cambridge, Mass.: Bradford Books, 1987) and, in particular, the discussion beginning p. 112 with the remarkable statement that 'the frog is bathed in sensation but we are bathed in information'. Most of the difficulties Dennett addresses so engagingly in that chapter arise from a misplaced explicitness that fails to distinguish between tacit and explicit beliefs. For example, contradictory tacit beliefs can exist side by side without the person being fairly described as irrational (or not wilfully so, anyway). Only when beliefs are uttered can you start looking at their entailments, their consistency with other beliefs, etc. *Any* attribution of a belief to an animal couched in human language runs the risk of being over-explicit; and the further we go down the evolutionary scale, the more absurd that over-explicitness becomes.
34. F. Nietzsche, 'Truth and Lie in the Extra-Moral Sense'. This is available widely in numerous translations; for example, Geoffrey Clive (ed.), *The Philosophy of Nietzsche* (New York: Mentor, 1965), pp. 503–15.

CHAPTER 7: RECOVERING CONSCIOUSNESS

1. See, for example, Howard Robinson, *Matter and Sense* (Cambridge University Press, 1982).
   I have, of course, no quarrel with computers. As one whose academic life has been transformed by the acquisition of a word

processor, I am enormously grateful to them. Nor do I underestimate the impact they have made on the world at large or the
genius of the accumulated insights that have gone into the making
of the humblest pocket calculator. I dissent only from the claim that
human consciousness is computational or that a computer could be
a stand-alone mind.

2. We could add a further line to Johnson-Laird's syllogism:
   Cognitive psychologists are human beings
   Therefore: Cognitive psychologists are machines.

3. See G. F. Reed's excellent article on 'Time-Gap Experience', in: R. L.
   Gregory (ed.) *The Oxford Companion to the Mind* (Oxford University
   Press, 1987).

4. See, for example the chapter on Derrida in my *Not Saussure*
   (London: Macmillan, 1988), especially pp. 215–19 and 233–4.

5. For a useful discussion of this see 'Intentional Action, Sometimes a
   Matter of Luck', Charlotte Katzoff, *Philosophical Investigations*, 1989;
   12(3):234–42.

6. See L. R. Squire. 'Mechanisms of memory'. *Science*, 1986; 232:1612–
   19; and W. G. Phillips and G. D. Carr, 'Cognition and the basal
   ganglia: a possible substrate for procedural knowledge', *Canadian
   Journal of Neurological Sciences*, 1987; 14:381–5.

7. Some psychologists have further subdivided declarative memory, or
   non-procedural memory – memory for experiences – into memory
   for items of general knowledge, such as the meanings of words, and
   memory for specific autobiographical experiences. This further
   distinction has considerable intuitive appeal: it draws particular
   attention to that vast sub-group of memories which are infused by a
   sense of 'I was there', to true first-person, particular memories that
   form the basis of the sense of self – of 'I am' and 'I am this';
   memories that mark the individual's self-rootedness, his irreplace-
   able deictic here-and-now reality.

8. P. N. Johnson-Laird, *The Computer and the Mind* (London: Fontana,
   1988) p. 172.

9. According to W. A. Phillips ('Brainy minds: A critical notice of
   "Parallel Distributed Processing"', *Quarterly Journal of Experimental
   Psychology*, 40A, 389–406, 1988) PDP showed how 'our ability to
   recognise objects and retrieve information on the basis of unpredictable, partial, and noisy data can arise from the dynamics of neural
   nets'. This confident claim is based on an assimilation of recognition
   to discriminant responsiveness. However, such responsiveness is
   nothing like true recognition: absolute identification of a particular,
   accompanied by the sense of familiarity, by the feeling that *I* have
   encountered this individual before. The greater power of discrimination of the PDP circuits does not bring the circuits any nearer
   recognition or their overall activity any nearer consciousness.
   Excitation of a particular 'word unit', for example, does not amount
   to recognition of the word, even less the sense of its meaning or its
   being meant.

10. Or used to be. Since the structuralists and post-structuralists have

arrived on the scene, a rather excessive affirmative action on behalf
of language has been evident and its role in structuring the
perceived and social worlds has been somewhat exaggerated. See
my *Not Saussure*, op. cit.

11. Jean-Paul Sartre, *Being and Nothingness*, trans. Hazel Barnes (London: Methuen, 1957).
12. *A Treatise of Human Nature*, book I, part III, sec. XIV. Husserl, too, emphasised the inseparability of the perception and the perceived object; of the consciousness from its intentional objects.
13. Aristotle, *De Anima*, Book 2, 424 (a), 18–24.
14. Kohler, W. and Wallach, H., Proceedings of the American Philosophical Society, 1944; 88: 269–357.
15. Hermann Helmholtz, 'Concerning the Perceptions in General', in: R. M. Warren and R. P. Warren (eds) *Helmholtz on Perception* (New York: John Wiley, 1968) p. 188.
16. The reader might wish to compare this with statements about the 'world' and 'the general form of propositions' in sections 1 and 4.5 of Wittgenstein's *Tractatus*.
17. The limitation of what can be said about consciousness itself does not mean that the accounts given of the essence of consciousness have all been brief. On the contrary, as the literature bears out, the descriptive phenomenology of consciousness may be extremely lengthy indeed. The massive published oeuvre of Husserl is supplemented, so we are told, by some 45 000 pages of unpublished manuscript, largely devoted to elucidating the essence of consciousness. And the collected edition of the works of Husserl's pupil Heidegger has now reached its 65th volume. Sartre, too, is not famous for brevity. The incidental insights afforded by these writers – on being-there, on time consciousness, on the fundamental human project – are often illuminating, in spite of the turbid material in which they are buried. Sometimes one has the sense that the continental phenomenologists endlessly circle round, rather than penetrate to, the root-mystery of consciousness. Nevertheless, I have learnt enormously from them and owe to Sartre and Heidegger some of the few metaphysical moments that have been triggered by reading. This book, and my attitude to human consciousness, is in part a late response to the experience of reading the continental phenomenologists at a time when I was being trained in medicine and taught conventional neurophysiology.
18. Daniel Dennett, 'Cognitive Wheels: The Frame Problem of AI', in: Christopher Hookway (ed.) *Minds, Machines and Evolution* (Cambridge University Press, 1984).
19. I have discussed the emergence of truth in, 'Facts, Statements and the Correspondence Theory of Truth', Chapter 7 of Raymond Tallis, *Not Saussure* (London: Macmillan), 1988.
20. Of course, I discover who I am in the sense of discovering what my capabilities are, who, or what, I am *like*, my type or kind, what position in the world suits me best, etc. I have, as it were, to learn the various genres to which I belong. But what I learn is not what

particular I am but what kind(s) I belong to. We must not, in other words, confuse self-consciousness as self-judgement with self-consciousness as the fundamental tack of consciousness: I am *this*.

21. To know what it is like to be something, it is not sufficient to be that thing. Contrary to Michael Lockwood's Russellian (and Schopen-hauerian) suggestion in his *Mind, Brain and Consciousness* (Oxford: Blackwell, 1989; see chapter 10, 'Berkeley, Russell and the Inscruta-bility of Matter', esp. 156–60), being something is not a sufficient condition of knowing it. We do not get past the veil of phenomena to the noumenal reality behind it through, and in, the objects or events that we ourselves are. It is not legitimate to equate, as Lockwood does, 'knowing certain brain events by virtue of their belonging to one's own conscious biography' with 'knowing them . . . *as they are in themselves* – knowing them "from the inside"'. 'Living' brain events, 'self-reflectively *being* them' is neither an explanation of, nor explained by, knowing them from the inside. *That I am these things* (so that I then have access to them from within) is precisely what needs to be explained. Nerve impulses, for example, do not explain the emergence of consciousness if this explanation depends upon taking for granted the emergence of a 'what it is like to be' from those impulses and the iteration by them that they *are* this collection of events.

22. Parfit's attempt to give a reductionist account of personal identity – an impersonal description of the unity of a person's life based on a continuity of quasi-memory (Derek Parfit, *Reasons and Persons*, Oxford University Press, 1984) – has been shown to run into circularity problems. L. N. Oaklander (Parfit, 'Circularity, and the unity of consciousness', *Mind*, 1987, 525–9), has demonstrated that it is not possible to define 'my' memories (or even 'my' quasi-memories) without referring to an already established self that will provide a criterion for identifying memories as mine. It is as if there is deictic tautology – these are my memories because they are had by me – presupposed in occurrent memory.

23. Colin McGinn, *The Subjective View* (Oxford; Clarendon Press 1982). See especially chapter 2.

24. Of course, we can make *any* signs – linguistic or non-linguistic, conventional or natural – carry higher-order, complex conscious-ness. For example, the fact that I am wearing new shoes may, in a first-order way, indicate that I am trying hard to please and/or impress. Or I may use this fact to give the impression that I am trying hard to please or impress. Or I may use this rather obvious sign that I am trying hard to please/impress as a way of signifying my naivety in order to disarm someone. Or I may use this sign of my trying to disarm that person ironically as a way of signifying my sophistication. And so on. It is not so much the means or medium that distinguishes the operations of explicitness but what is done with it. That is why Mary Midgley's reference to the fact that human language is rooted in para-linguistic phenomena such as gestures as

an argument in favour of a closer relationship between human and animal language is misconceived. (See *Beast and Man*, chapter 10, especially pp. 239 *et seq.*). It is not the material that we use for our communications but the kinds of uses we make of it that distinguishes us from animals.

25.   See for example, H. P. Grice, 'Meaning', *Philosophical Review*, 1987, 66:377–88. His views have been developed by others, notably Jonathan Bennett, 'Stimulus, Response, Meaning', *American Philosophical Quarterly*, 1975, 9: 55–88.

Fred Dretske (*Explaining Behaviour: Reasons in a World of Causes*, Cambridge, Mass., MIT, 1988) has argued, against Grice, that natural signs *do* intrinsically carry information and that they indicate even in the absence of a consciousness to indicate to: 'there is something *in* nature (not merely in the mind that struggles to comprehend nature) some objective observer-independent fact or set of facts, that forms the basis of one thing meaning another or indicating something about another.', p. 58). He claims that denying that natural signs indicate in the absence of consciousness is 'merely a specialised version of the more general and even more implausible idea that nothing is true unless it is true for someone.' (p. 55). I would turn Dretske on his head by saying that the belief that natural signs signify in the absence of any consciousness to signify to is merely a specialised version of the more general superstition that meaning, reference and truth can inhabit material objects, a superstition that is more compatible with panpsychism than materialism and which I deal with in the pages to come. The belief that truth inheres in material things is also criticised in my *Not Saussure* (London: Macmillan, 1988).

If Dretske's belief that natural objects and events could signify in the absence of consciousness were true, the problem would arise as to determining which sub-group of objects would count as signs, which as significates and which neither; presumably all objects and events would have equal claim to the status of signs. All cats would be iconic signs of all other cats; every object would be an iconic sign of every object like itself. Every effect would indexically signify its causes and every cause its effects. *Und so weiter*. Dretske's natural world would be a place of total self-indication, an horrendous unbounded endlessly iterative pandiculation.

26.   Ludwig Wittgenstein, *On Certainty* (Oxford: Blackwell, 1969), para. 676.

27.   From *Pollen*, available in *Hymns to the Night and other selected writings*, trans. Charles Passage (New York: Liberal Arts Press, 1960).

28.   A similar view has been advanced by John Searle:

> Since sentences – the sounds that come out of one's mouth or the marks that one makes on paper – are, considered in one way, just objects in the world like any other objects, their capacity to represent is not intrinsic but is derived from the intentionality of the mind. The intentionality of mental states, on the other hand,

is not derived from some more prior forms of intentionality but is intrinsic to the states themselves.

(*Intentionality*, Cambridge University Press, 1983) p. vii).

29. Jonathan Bennett, 'Stimulus, Response, Meaning'. *American Philosophical Quarterly*, 1975, 9:55–88.
30. Skinner's views are summarised in B. F. Skinner, 'The operational analysis of psychological terms', *Behavioural and Brain Sciences*, 1984; 7:547–81. This is a revision and reprint of his classic 1945 paper, usefully combined with twenty or so responses from experts and Skinner's own response to these responses.
31. The relationship between the theories of language and theories of perception – and between the mystery of language and the mystery of perception – is well expressed by Searle (*Intentionality*, op. cit.). See, for example, this passage:

> A basic assumption behind my approach to the problems of language is that the philosophy of language is a branch of the philosophy of mind. The capacity of speech acts to represent objects and states of affairs in the world is an extension of the more biologically fundamental capacities of the mind (or brain) to relate the organism to the world by way of such mental states as belief and desire, especially through action and perception. (p. vii)

32. Colin McGinn, 'Could a Machine be Conscious?', in: Colin Blakemore and Susan Greenfield (eds) *Mindwaves* (Oxford: Blackwell, 1987) p. 284. In this essay, McGinn expresses considerable pessimism about the possibility of solving the mind–body problem. This pessimism has been fully developed in a recent paper ('Can we solve the mind–body problem?', *Mind*, 1989 vol. xcviii, no.391, July, pp. 349–66) in which he argues that the problem is essentially insoluble. He begins with the Nagel-like point that we have two modes of access to phenomena: either directly, via introspection; or indirectly, via our external senses. The former will give us access to one term of the mind–brain relation, namely mind; and the latter will give us access to the other term of the relation, namely brain processes. Neither will give us access to the relation, P, between the two terms, and so enable us to see how they are linked. The mind–body problem will remain forever insoluble. This marvellous piece of philosophical nihilism is spoilt only by the reasons he gives for our being unable to solve the mind–body problem: a cognitive closure which he relates to the fact that 'minds are biological products like bodies' and they 'are more or less suited to certain cognitive tasks' – a relapse into a dogmatic naturalism that sits ill with the sophisticated agnosticism of the rest of his paper.
33. The image of a consciousness in a permanent state of suspension, verging on the edge of meaning, but forever lacking interpretation except in terms of other formulae, other symbols is reminiscent of certain post-Saussurean versions of consciousness. See *Not Saussure* op. cit., especially chapter 6, on Derrida.

34. Roger Penrose, 'Minds, Machines and Mathematics', in: *Mindwaves*, op. cit.

35. Penrose has presented a greatly expanded version of his ideas about the nature of mind in *The Emperor's New Mind* (Oxford University Press, 1989). Apart from a thorough attack on the idea that consciousness is computational, this book does not advance the quantum theory of mind that is hinted at throughout and apparently justifies the massive, and often fascinating, digressions into modern mathematical physics. In particular, the final chapter, enticingly entitled 'Where lies the physics of the mind?', is disappointing and tempts the reader to answer: 'Not in this book'. The substantive, if obscure, thesis that mind may operate with quantum computers is introduced only to be (with commendable honesty) criticised.

36. Sir John Eccles, 'Brain and Mind: Two or One?' in: *Mindwaves*, op. cit.

37. Henry Margenau, quoted in Eccles, op. cit., p. 301.

38. Ibid.

39. P. C. W. Davies and J. R. Brown, *The Ghost in the Atom*, quoted in Eccles, op. cit., p. 301 (Cambridge University Press, 1986) summarises recent trends very accessibly.

40. I do not know the original provenance of this passage. It is cited by Stephen Harrison in his remarkable unpublished manuscript *Emanational Physics*.

41. Michael Lockwood, *Mind, Brain and Quantum: the Compound 'I'* (Oxford: Blackwell, 1989).

42, Howard Robinson, *Matter and Sense* (Cambridge University Press, 1982) contains a powerful statement of the difficulties inherent in the concept of matter. See chapter 7, 'Matter: Turning the Tables'.

43. As Robinson puts it, 'the production of mentality can never be expressed as an aspect of physical potentiality'. Ibid., p. 120.

44. Stuart Hampshire, *Spinoza* (Harmondsworth: Penguin Books, 1951).

45. For an excellent brief account of this, see D. F. Pears, 'Russell's Philosophy of Mind: Neutral Monism', in: R. L. Gregory (ed.) *The Oxford Companion to the Mind* (Oxford University Press, 1987) pp. 690–1.

46. Helmholtz seems to operate inside this tautology when he talks of 'presentabilia'. The observer, he says, is at any time 'bound to a certain range of presentabilia, from which he can choose any one he wishes through execution of the appropriate movement' ('The Facts of Perception', in: R. M. Warren and R. P. Warren, *Helmholtz on Perception: Its Physiology and Development*, p. 215).

47. Hilary Putnam, *Representation and Reality* (Cambridge, Mass.: Bradford Books, 1988).

Index